access to history

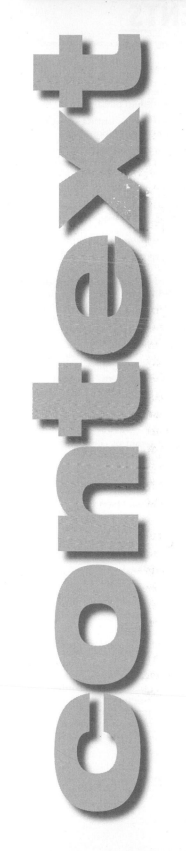
context

D0243712

An Introduction to

STUART
BRITAIN
1603–1714

Angela Anderson

Hodder Murray
A MEMBER OF THE HODDER HEADLINE GROUP

ACKNOWLEDGEMENTS

The front cover shows Mountjoy Blount, Earl of Newport and George, Lord Goring by A. Van Dyck reproduced courtesy of Roy Fox/National Trust Photo Library.

The publishers would like to thank the following individuals, institutions and companies for permission to reproduce copyright illustrations in this book:

The Bridgeman Art Library pp. 13, 36 (bottom); The Bridgeman Art Library © Weston Park Foundation p. 45; The British Library p. 127; The British Museum pp. 87, 192; The Fotomas Index (U.K) pp. 73, 117, 148, 152, 159, 228, 231; Hulton Getty p. 122; The National Gallery p. 80; National Maritime Museum, London p. 67; The National Portrait Gallery, London pp. 3 (both), 21, 36 (top), 38, 61, 80, 111, 171, 175; © NPG London p. 156; The Royal Collection © 1999 Her Majesty The Queen p. 23; Private Collection on loan to SNPG p. 133.

The publishers would also like to thank the following for permission to reproduce material in this book:

The Historical Association for the extracts from *The Local Community and the Great Rebellion* by A. Everitt, 1969; International Thomson Publishing Services Ltd for the extract from *The Causes of the English Revolution, 1529-1642* by Lawrence Stone, Routledge, 1972; Orion House for the extracts from *Autobiography* by R. Baxter (ed.) J.N.H. Keeble, 1974 and *Memoirs of the Life of Colonel John Hutchinson* by L. Hutchinson, (ed.) J. Hutchinson, 1968; Extracts from *History of the Rebellion* by Clarendon are reproduced by permission of Oxford University Press; Extracts from 'The Search for Religious Liberty' by M. Goldie and 'Britain and the World under the Stuarts' by J. Reeve in *The Oxford Illustrated History of Tudor and Stuart Britain* (ed.) J. Morril, 1996 are reproduced by permission of Oxford University Press; Extracts from 'The Baptists – Found of all Heresy' by J.F. McGregor in *Radical Religion in the English Revolution*, 1984 are reproduced by permission of Oxford University Press; Extracts from *Crime and Punishment in England* by J. Briggs, UCL Press, 1996 are reproduced with permission from Taylor & Francis.

Every effort has been made to trace and acknowledge ownership of copyright. The publishers will be glad to make suitable arrangements with any copyright holders whom it has not been possible to contact.

Orders: please contact Bookpoint Ltd, 130 Milton Park, Abingdon, Oxon OX14 4SB Telephone: (44) 01235 827720, Fax: (44) 01235 400454. Lines are open from 9.00 – 6.00, Monday to Saturday, with a 24 hour message answering service. You can also order from our website: www.hoddereducation.co.uk

British Library Cataloguing in Publication Data
A catalogue record for this title is available from The British Library

ISBN-10: 0 340 73744 1
ISBN-13: 978 0 340 73744 6

First published 1999
Impression number   10   9   8   7   6   5
Year   2005

Typeset by Wearset, Boldon, Tyne & Wear.
Printed in Great Britain for Hodder Murray, an imprint of Hodder Education, a member of the Hodder Headline Group, 338 Euston Road, London NW1 3BH by Arrowsmith, Bristol.

CONTENTS

List of Figures

List of Profiles

List of Tables

PREFACE

Access to History Context

Structure

In some ways *Access to History: Context* volumes are similar to most textbooks. They are divided into chapters, each of which is focused on a specific topic. In turn, chapters are divided into sections which have self-explanatory headings. As is the case with most textbooks, *Context* authors have organised the chapters in a logical sequence so that, if you start at the beginning of the book and work your way through to the end, everything will make sense. However, because many readers 'dip' into textbooks rather than reading them from beginning to end, care has been taken to make sure that whichever chapter you start with you should not find yourself feeling lost.

Special Features in the Main Text

Points to Consider – at the start of each chapter this shaded box provides you with vital information about how the chapter is organised and how the various issues covered relate to each other.

Issues boxes are a standard feature of each chapter and, like Points to Consider boxes, are designed to help you extract the maximum benefit from the work you do. They appear in the margin immediately following most numbered section headings. The question(s) contained in each issues box will tell you which historical issue(s) the section is primarily going to cover. If the section you intend to start with has no issues box, turn back page by page until you find one. This will contain the questions the author is considering from that point onwards, including the section you are about to read.

Boxed sections appear in both the margin and the main column of text. In each of the boxes you will find a self-explanatory heading which will make it clear what the contents of the box are about. Very often, the contents of boxes are explanations of words or phrases, or descriptions of events or situations. When you are reading a chapter for the first time you might make a conscious decision to pay little attention to boxed entries so that you can concentrate your attention on the author's main message.

Q-boxes appear in the margin and contain one or more questions about the item they appear alongside. These questions are intended to stimulate you to think about some aspect of the material the box is linked to. The most useful answers to these questions will often emerge during discussions with other students.

Activities boxes – as a general rule, the contents of activities boxes are more complex than the questions in Q-boxes, and often require you to undertake a significant amount of work, either on your own or with others. One reason for completing the task(s) is to consolidate what you have already learned or to extend the range or depth of your understanding.

Profiles – most of these are about named individuals who are central to an understanding of the topic under consideration: some are about events of particular importance. Each Profile contains a similar range of material. The two aspects you are likely to find most useful are:

▼ the dated timeline down the side of the page; and
▼ the source extracts, which provide you with ideas on what made the subject of the Profile especially notable or highly controversial

Profiles also provide useful points of focus during the revision process.

End-of-chapter Sections

The final pages of each chapter contain different sections. It is always worthwhile looking at the **Summary Chart** or **Summary Diagram** first. As their names suggest, these are designed to provide you with a brief and carefully structured overview of the topic covered by the chapter. The important thing for you to do is to check that you understand the way it is structured and how the topics covered inter-relate with one another.

The **Working on. . .** section should be studied in detail once you have finished your first reading of the main text of the chapter. Assuming that you read the Points to Consider section when you began work on the chapter, and that you followed any advice given in it when you read the chapter for the first time, the Working on. . . section is designed to suggest what form any further work you do on the chapter should take.

The **Answering extended writing and essay questions on. . .** sections, taken as a whole throughout the book, form a coherent body of guidance on how to tackle these types of examination questions successfully.

The same is true of the **Answering source-based questions on. . .** sections which have been carefully planned bearing in mind the ways you need to build on the skills you have already developed in this area. You may find these sections particularly helpful during the time you are preparing for an exam.

The last part of each chapter contains a **Further Reading** section. These are of vital importance to you in chapters covering topics you are expected to know about in some detail. To do well in any History course it is essential to read more than one book. However, it is possible to find individual books which can act as your guide and companion throughout your studies, and this is one of them. One of the major ways in which it fulfils this function is by providing you with detailed guidance on the way you can make the most effective use of your limited time in reading more widely.

This book is an integral part of the *Access to History* series. One of its functions is to act as a link between the various topic books in the series on the period it covers, by drawing explicit attention in the Further Reading sections to where, within the series, other material exists which can be used to broaden and deepen your knowledge and understanding. Attention is also drawn to the non-*Access to History* publications which you are likely to find most useful. By using material which has been written based on the same aims and objectives, you are likely to find yourself consistently building up the key skills and abilities needed for success on your course.

Revision

Context books have been planned to be directly helpful to you during the revision period. One of the first things many students do when starting to revise a topic for an examination is to make a list of the 'facts' they need to know about. A safer way of doing this (because it covers the possibility that you missed something important when you originally worked on the topic) is to compile your lists from a book you can rely on. *Context* volumes aim to be reliable in this sense. If you work through the chapter which covers the topic you are about to revise and list the events contained in marginal 'events lists' and in boxed lists of events, you can be confident that you have identified every fact of real significance that you need to know about on the topic. However, you also need to make a list of the historical issues you might be asked to write about. You can do this most conveniently by working through the relevant chapter and noting down the contents of the 'issues boxes'.

For almost everybody, important parts of the revision process are the planning of answers to all the main types of structured and essay questions, and the answering of typical questions (both those requiring extended writing and those based on source material) under exam conditions. The best way to make full use of what this book has to offer in these respects is to work through the two relevant sets of end-of-chapter sections (Answering extended writing and essay questions on . . . and Answering source-based questions on . . .) in a methodical manner.
Keith Randell

Author's Note

Why Contexts?

An Introduction to Stuart Britain is not intended to be a general text-book for the seventeenth century, but to focus on key themes and issues and to consider them in a wider context. The central issue is the nature and significance of the so-called English Revolution of 1640–60. Both contemporaries and historians have debated why it happened and what it meant, raising questions about its causes, impact and longer-term significance. These questions have shaped the structure of the book.

The 'English Revolution' encompassed civil war, the execution of a reigning monarch and Britain's only period of republican government. To explain such momentous events it is necessary to study their root causes in the years between 1603 and 1640, and to examine in some detail how the crisis developed into war and revolution. Some of these causes, however, date from Tudor England, and the problems faced by the Stuarts cannot be understood without some awareness of this wider context. Chapter 1, therefore, considers the situation inherited by James I from his predecessors, and establishes the nature of government and society at the end of the sixteenth century. Chapters 2 to 4 then examine the causes of the Civil War and how far it was the result of long-term structural problems as opposed to the influence of individuals and personalities. Chapters 5 and 6 consider the impact of war, and offer an explanation of why it led to the abolition and then restoration of the monarchy.

However, some of the effects of the English Revolution need to be examined within a wider context. An account that ends with the Restoration of 1660 tends to emphasise the permanence of that restoration and to assume that the survival of the monarchy was inevitable, given the failure of the republican alternative. Nor does it allow full consideration of what was restored, and how far the monarchy had been changed by the crisis. To consider these issues, and what they reveal about the nature of the crisis, it is necessary to examine how government developed after 1660, and the factors that shaped its further development. This is discussed in Chapter 7.

The focus of these chapters is political, but because religion and the Church were key political issues in this period they also deal with religious divisions and the part they played in the political conflict. The traditional interaction of Church and State had been enormously strengthened by the sixteenth-century Reformation, in which the monarch assumed responsibility for the spiritual welfare as well as the physical safety of his subjects. The result was that politics and religion were intertwined to the point of being virtually impossible to separate. However, politics and government are also linked to economic and social developments. It is therefore important to consider the part played by wider economic, social and cultural factors in shaping political development, as well as the extent to which they are affected by it. The transformation of Britain in the seventeenth century included the creation of a single Anglo-Scottish kingdom, the expansion of trade and the acquisition of an overseas empire, as well as the development of scientific thought and religious toleration. The final chapter therefore traces these developments across the century. The purpose is to offer a wider context, in which the nature of change and the causes of development can be more thoroughly explored, to establish an understanding of the seventeenth century and its revolutionary impact.

How to Go About It

A further aim, however, is to introduce students to the range of historical concepts and skills that are required at AS and A level in particular. Explaining the past and its relationship to the present requires you to consider the concepts of cause and effect, and the nature and processes of change.

In addition, it is useful to establish a process of historical investigation. This has three main stages:

▼ collecting information, usually from secondary sources, to establish some initial ideas about what happened and why;

▼ raising new questions and carrying out further research to test and develop these ideas; this usually involves both secondary and primary sources, and requires evidence to be interpreted and carefully evaluated;

▼ presenting and supporting overall conclusions based on the evidence available.

This methodology is addressed in the activities and the end-of-chapter study guides. These are intended to be progressive, so that students can develop and build up the skills that they require, and gradually apply them to possible examination questions. The activities within the chapters introduce the techniques related to making notes and interpreting sources; the end-of-chapter sections add exercises using diagrams and flow charts as a means of recording information, and introduce essay planning. The first six chapters focus on the concept of causation, considering essay questions that relate to the role of different causal factors, their interaction and relative importance. The last two chapters deal with the concept of change, and how to approach essays that require explanation of the processes involved in change and development. In addition, these offer opportunities to apply the skills of source interpretation and evaluation to the kind of document questions that appear in some examination papers.

History and Key Skills

Historical investigation also involves a number of techniques that are useful and applicable to a variety of other situations, such as research techniques, problem-solving and methods of communication. However, what makes history unique is the nature of the evidence upon which research is based. By definition, it is incomplete, fragmentary, and influenced by the attitudes and perceptions of those who provide it. It requires interpretation and therefore enables students to practice and develop reasoning skills and to formulate judgements on this basis. As the methodology outlined below suggests, this involves a process of debate and hypothesis testing, that offers a basis for further development in both academic and vocational contexts.

HISTORICAL INVESTIGATION	KEY SKILLS
Collect information to . . .	Read, understand and record information, using notes, charts and diagrams.
Establish initial ideas	Synthesise and summarise.
Evaluate, and raise questions	Define problems and formulate a strategy for solving them. Plan an investigation, using a variety of resources (books and libraries, videos, computers).
Find and collect more information by . . .	
Interpreting and evaluating evidence from primary and secondary sources	Use inference and reasoning – analysis, inference, deduction, cross-reference, evaluation, synthesis.
Review and refine hypotheses	
Present and sustain conclusions	Use written, oral and visual forms of communication to set out conclusions and support them with evidence from the sources used.

Further Reading

The material in this book is intended to be sufficient to enable students to understand the main events and developments associated with the English Revolution and the changes that took place in Stuart Britain. For many students, however, it will not offer sufficient detail on some issues, and it certainly should not be the only book that you read. At the end of each chapter there is a list of further reading, relating specifically to issues dealt with in that chapter. There are, however, a number of books that cover several chapters, or the period as a whole. A list of these books is printed here so that students can look out for them. It is not an exhaustive bibliography, but a list of personal recommendations, of books that the author has found to be clear and helpful to anyone studying the Stuart century.

Books in the Access to History Series

The Access to History series contains a number of relevant volumes which are suitable as the next stage of reading. The volumes for the Stuart period are: *The Early Stuarts, 1603–1640* by Katherine Brice; *The Civil Wars, 1640–49* by Angela Anderson; *The Interregnum, 1649–60* by Michael Lynch; *Charles II and James II* by Nicholas Fellowes; and *Stuart Economy and Society* by Nigel Heard.

General

There are a number of good general textbooks covering the period. Barry Coward's recent volume in the Longman Advanced History series, *Stuart England 1603–1714* (Addison Wesley Longman 1997) is excellent for following up particular issues, and *The Years of Turmoil* (ed. R. Wilkinson, Hodder & Stoughton, 1999) offers a stronger narrative spine. Derek Hirst's *Authority and Conflict 1603–58* (Arnold 1987) is an excellent advanced textbook, which is easy to dip into and often provides clarification not offered elsewhere. It is best approached when you have enough knowledge to identify what you are looking for. J.R. Jones's *Country and Court: England 1658–1714* is the next volume in the same series (published by Edward Arnold 1986) and is also highly informative. The later years of the century are well covered by W.A. Speck, *Reluctant Revolutionaries* (OUP 1988). It is also worth looking at one or two older interpretations – Christopher Hill's *Century of Revolution* (Nelson 1980) remains a readable source of ideas and information, though his interpretation has been challenged.

There are also several thematic overviews. In particular, A.G.R. Smith, *The Emergence of a Nation State* (1984) has been described as an outstanding 'starter' textbook, while Professor G. Holmes has produced a helpful survey in *The Making of a Great Power: Late Stuart and Georgian Britain 1660–1722* (Addison Wesley Longman 1993). Conrad Russell's extended essay, *The Crisis of Parliaments: English History 1509–1660* (OUP 1971) is similarly useful. Barry Williams' *Elusive Settlement* (Nelson 1984) traces political developments with an emphasis on change and continuity as well as extensive use of primary sources.

One way of making extra reading more accessible is to work through personalities and use some of the many excellent biographies available. It is impossible to list them all here, but you could usefully read Roger Lockyer's study of James I, Charles Carlton's analysis of the personality of Charles I, or one of the many biographies of Oliver Cromwell. Christopher Hill's *God's Englishman* (1970) is highly readable, as is Barry Coward's *Oliver Cromwell* (Addison Wesley Longman 1991). A collection of essays edited by John Morrill and entitled *Oliver Cromwell and the English Revolution* (Addison Wesley Longman 1990) includes some fascinating insights into the formative influences that helped to shape Cromwell's character. Similar insights about Charles I are provided in a documentary collection edited by Christopher Daniels and John Morrill (*Charles I*, CUP 1988).

Another way of making extra reading manageable is to use some of the many good collections of essays that are available for the period, which allow you to focus on particular issues and also to acquaint yourself with the work of a variety of historians. Given that your time is limited, it would be difficult, for example, to read Kevin Sharpe's interesting but monumental study of Charles I, but the essay that he contributed to the Oxford *History* cited below does introduce you to his arguments and ideas. As your knowledge of the period and its historiography develops, you will be able to select issues and authors to study in greater depth. The largest and most wide-ranging has been published as *The Oxford Illustrated History of Tudor and Stuart Britain*, edited by John Morrill and published by OUP in 1996. More recently, for those interested in the war and how it was waged, *The Civil Wars: a military history 1638–60* consisting of essays, edited by John Kenyon and Jane Ohlmeyer has been issued from the OUP in 1998. There are also excellent collections of essays dealing with the *Causes of the English Civil War* by Conrad Russell (OUP 1990) and the *Origins of the Civil Wars* (ed. Conrad Russell) and *Reactions to the English Civil War* (ed. J. Morrill) published by Macmillan (1982) in the Problems in Focus series. Further essay collections by John Morrill have been published as *The Impact of the Civil Wars* (Collins 1991) which includes various contributors, and a collection of John Morrill's own essays published as *The Nature of the English Revolution* by Addison Wesley Longman in 1993.

The list above could be further extended with many useful and interesting titles, some of which are referred to in the end-of-chapter advice on further reading. If you come across other books and want to know how useful they might be, or want to find more possibilities, you need to use some of the collected bibliographies that are available in many libraries. There is an extensive bibliography contained in the *Oxford Illustrated History* mentioned above, while Barry Coward provides very helpful advice on further reading in his book on *Stuart England*. You would also find a great deal of help in R.C. Richardson's *Debate on the English Revolution Revisited* (Methuen 1988) which analyses the different schools of thought and approaches adopted in the ongoing debate on the Civil Wars and assesses the value of various contributions.

INTRODUCTION: THE CRISIS OF MONARCHY

POINTS TO CONSIDER

It will be clear from the brief comparison of James I and George I that there were significant changes in the nature of the monarchy across the century. Historians have spent much time and energy debating how and why they occurred, and what significance can be attributed to particular events within the process, especially the so-called English Revolution of 1640–60. While parliamentary monarchy in Britain finally took shape after the Glorious Revolution of 1688–9, some historians have argued that it was made virtually inevitable by the English Revolution and the underlying problems that caused it. Others disagree, and attribute much more importance to chance and the actions of individuals. You will be able to form your own ideas by studying the chapters that follow, but it will help if, to begin with, you can establish an overview of the period and the processes involved.

When Queen Elizabeth died in 1603, James travelled south from Scotland to take up his English inheritance. The new King was neither handsome nor impressive in his appearance, but he was an experienced monarch. He had governed the restless kingdom of Scotland with some success, and had displayed some skill in balancing the different factions among the Scottish nobility and the leaders of the Church. It is therefore surprising to find that difficulties between the King and Parliament in England emerged almost immediately, and continued intermittently for most of the reign. Disagreements over money, religion and the relationship between his three kingdoms led to tensions in Parliament, which increased in the reign of Charles I and led to a breakdown of government in 1642.

This sequence of events has caused some historians to suggest that the resulting Civil War had its roots in the problems that developed during James's reign and has encouraged the idea of an inevitable clash between a monarch with inflated ideas of his own power and status and an increasingly assertive Parliament. These historians interpreted the seventeenth century as a struggle between kings who believed in their divine right to govern and parliaments who believed in the liberties of the subject and the rule of law. The struggle involved a breakdown of government in the Civil War, a flawed Restoration in 1660, and a decisive Revolution in 1688, in which the rights of Parliament were finally secured and the foundations of parliamentary government were established. This process is outlined in Figure 1.

> **PROTESTANT**
> A number of separate Protestant churches were established in Europe in the sixteenth century following the religious Reformation started by Martin Luther. Varied in organisation and emphasis, they had in common their rejection of the authority of the Pope and the Roman Catholic Church. 'Anglican' and 'Presbyterian' describe different forms of Protestant belief. The state Church of England was Anglican, the Scottish Kirk (Church) Presbyterian.

Figure 1 The seventeenth century crisis in government.

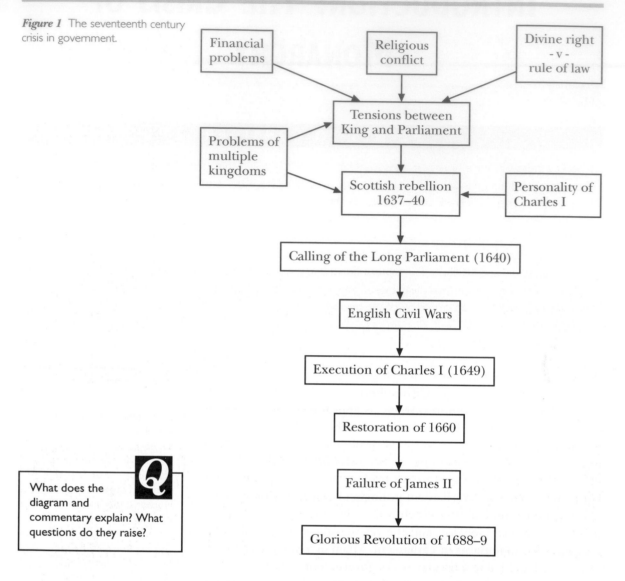

What does the diagram and commentary explain? What questions do they raise?

ACTIVITY

▼ Make a list of the main differences between James I and George I.
▼ Are there any similarities?
▼ Decide which king you consider to have been more powerful.

Like most interpretations that emphasise a single issue, this line of argument has been challenged at a number of levels. Those who defend James have argued that he inherited problems from Elizabeth, and that he handled a difficult situation with some skill. They say that in many areas, King and Parliament cooperated well, and

JAMES VI AND I, 1603–25 (b.1566)

-Profile-

Ruled over three separate kingdoms, England (with Wales), Ireland, and Scotland with separate Parliaments and legal codes. His subjects spoke three languages and believed in three different forms of the Christian religion (Catholic, Anglican and Presbyterian) but in each kingdom they were expected to attend the state Church chosen by the King.

James ruled by divine right and claimed to be appointed by God. He ruled as well as reigned – which means that he made most of the important decisions himself, or chose ministers to do so. He became King of England because he was the nearest relative of the previous ruler, Queen Elizabeth. The fact that he was a Protestant in religion, not a Catholic, was an advantage.

The kingdoms were small and poor compared to others in Europe. Even England was only a minor power situated on its western rim. France was larger and Spain had a huge colonial empire in the Americas. England possessed few overseas colonies, and world trade was dominated by the markets of Italy and the Low Countries (now the Netherlands and Belgium) and the naval power of the Dutch.

GEORGE I, 1714–27 (b.1660)

-Profile-

Ruled over one kingdom – Great Britain and Ireland. His subjects still spoke three languages, but English was the language of government. They still preferred different religions, but they were allowed to choose which. However, it was a big advantage to choose the Anglican form. George became king of Great Britain because Parliament chose him. He governed with Parliament, and his ministers had to have support in Parliament. He spoke very little English but that did not really matter, because he reigned, but did not really rule. He was not the nearest relative of the previous monarch, but he was the nearest Protestant relative – and by 1714, that was essential for a king of England.

By 1714, Britain was becoming a major world power. She had acquired a large overseas empire, especially in north America and India, and had overtaken the Dutch as a naval power. She had just defeated France, the greatest European power of the day, and gained useful new colonies. Her people were increasingly prosperous, enjoying good standards of living compared to Europe. Exports of food and many different goods paid for luxury imports like tea, coffee and tobacco.

ISSUE
How did these changes happen?

there was a considerable degree of harmony in the Church. They suggest that it was the personality of his son Charles that destroyed the relationship with Parliament. Others have disagreed about the relative importance of religion, or social changes, and recent research has emphasised the complications involved in governing three separate kingdoms. What emerges is a complex picture, in which any explanation of the changing relationship between King and Parliament can be challenged by competing interpretations.

The complexity of the issues arises partly from the fact that the process of change took place over a century of conflict, and did not occur through a simple chain of events, but through stages of development. It is clear that certain events – the outbreak of war, the execution of Charles I, the restoration of Charles II, and the 'abdication' of James II – defined key stages, and brought about new situations that require recognition in forming new questions. The process can therefore be viewed as a spiral of development, in which each level leads into the next. Each stage is defined by key events, and can be investigated using key questions as set out. The overall process can then be reconstructed by linking the separate stages to form an overview of development in Figure 2.

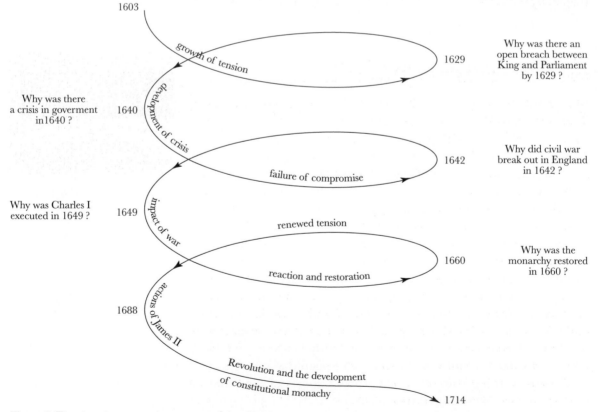

Figure 2 The changing monarchy – stages of development.

THE TUDOR LEGACY: BRITAIN IN 1603

CHAPTER 1

POINTS TO CONSIDER

The material in this chapter is essentially background material, chosen to enable you to familiarise yourself with the nature of politics and government in this period. The activities and exercises included in the main text and at the end of the chapter are designed to help you understand how government worked, in theory and in practice, and the key issues and problems that concerned people at the time. The better you understand what James I inherited from his Tudor predecessors, the more able you will be to assess how effectively he dealt with it. You can also begin to examine the nature of the problems that led to the English Revolution. Although this chapter will do little more than introduce the issues, it will provide you with the basis for examining how they developed, a question which is considered in later chapters.

KEY ISSUE
How secure was the monarchy that James inherited in 1603?

1 The British Kingdoms

ISSUE
What was the relationship between the different parts of Britain and the people who lived in them?

By 1603 the process of uniting the British kingdoms had already begun. Wales had been conquered before 1500, and was incorporated into the English kingdom by three Acts of Union passed during the reign of Henry VIII. These had introduced English law and the system of county government based on Justices of the Peace, so that Wales was governed as an integral part of England. Henry had also extended the traditional claim of English kings to be 'lord of Ireland' into a claim of kingship. While this proved difficult to enforce in practice, strategic needs made it essential. The Protestant Reformation had divided Europe, and after Henry rejected the authority of the Pope and seized control of the English Church in 1534, there was a serious danger of Catholic reprisal. Since the majority of native Irishmen and Old English settlers remained Catholic, Ireland offered a potentially convenient base for an invasion, and it was therefore necessary to assert English control there. English influence, which had been limited to the area around Dublin known as the Pale, gradually increased through the sixteenth century. Irish chieftains were persuaded to accept English titles of nobility. Successive rebellions provoked by the arrogance of some

English administrators provided the excuse for extending English military control. In the 1590s a major rebellion led by Hugh O'Neill, Earl of Tyrone was defeated by Elizabeth's generals, and after a period of uneasy peace, the Earls of Tyrone and Tyrconnel, the last great chieftains of Ulster, fled to Spain in 1605, leaving the English in control of the whole island.

There had been similar problems between England and Scotland ever since the failure of English attempts to conquer Scotland in the thirteenth and fourteenth centuries. By securing a marriage between his daughter Margaret and James IV of Scotland in 1502, Henry VII had hoped to bring the two kingdoms together, but the more aggressive policies of Henry VIII had ensured that traditional hostilities lingered, and had encouraged the Scots to maintain an alliance with France. The accession of James as ruler of both kingdoms in 1603 brought an end to national hostilities, but left the matter of the relationship between the English and Scottish peoples in doubt. While James and his heirs had a natural desire to create greater uniformity of government and perhaps even to unite the two kingdoms, there were deep-seated cultural differences both within Scotland itself (see the map on page 14) and between the Scots and English. There was also a bitter legacy of hostility and warfare. The English feared an invasion of Scots seeking wealth and opportunity, while the Scots feared the loss of independence and resented English arrogance. In these circumstances, the problem of ruling multiple kingdoms and of regulating relationships between them became one of the most significant issues facing the Stuart monarchy.

2　Religious Divisions

ISSUE
Why was this a period of religious conflict?

The problem of ruling separate kingdoms was made more difficult and complex by religious divisions that cut across national borders. The Protestant Reformation had shattered the religious unity of Europe, and resulted in reform taking its own course in different areas. While there is no need to discuss the Reformation in detail here, it is necessary to understand some of its main features and effects, because they influenced the political and cultural development of the British kingdoms in important ways.

a) The European Reformation

Christianity in Western Europe had developed under the control of the Catholic Church, centred in Rome and led by the Pope, who claimed to have inherited the power given by Christ himself to the disciple Peter. In different countries the Church was administered by bishops who were often chosen by the monarch, although they received their spiritual power from the Pope. The key features of Roman Catholic belief were:

▼ that Jesus Christ, the Son of God, had sacrificed himself on the Cross to atone for human sins;

▼ that humans could avoid the punishments of hell and reach heaven once they died by believing in Christ and following his word;

▼ that the knowledge of Christ's word and the power to help human souls had been passed to Peter, and from him to those whom the Church ordained as priests;

▼ that this power was exercised by the priests in the ceremonies and sacraments ordered by the Church. The most important of these were the Mass, which re-enacted the Last Supper of Christ and his disciples, and the confession, in which the priest could forgive the sins of those who truly regretted them;

▼ that it was the duty of the Church to enforce its rules and doctrines, so that souls were brought to God.

The implications of these beliefs were that Christians could only reach God through the Church, and that the clergy were a special order, separated from the laity (non-clergy), and superior to them. Over the years the Church had become increasingly wealthy and powerful and, like many powerful institutions, had lost some of the spiritual strength that had justified its position. By 1500, there were many complaints that religion had become mechanical, faith had degenerated into superstition, and the leaders of the Church had become embroiled in politics and luxurious self-indulgence.

This was the background to the protest mounted by Martin Luther, a German monk who challenged the authorities and demanded reforms. Unlike most reformers, Luther challenged the ideas as well as the practices of the Church. The core of his argument was:

▼ that salvation – in which the human soul gained a place in heaven with God – could not be guaranteed by the Church or by good works, but only by individual faith;

▼ that God offered salvation as a free gift to those who believed in Him and followed Christ;

▼ that belief came from private prayer and study of the Bible, the Word of God;

▼ that church ceremonies and sacraments only symbolised internal faith, and too many encouraged ignorance and superstition;

▼ that, in God's eyes, priests and laity were equal, meaning that priests had no special powers; while the Church remained important as a source of guidance, teaching and preaching, there was no justification for the wide-ranging authority claimed by the Catholic Church.

SACRAMENTS

Sacred acts or ceremonies. The key point about sacramental religion is that taking part in the ceremony is considered to be a sacred act in itself, regardless of the spirit or level or understanding of the laity who take part. This gave great power to the Church that organised the sacraments, and could encourage mechanical or superstitious acts by the congregation.

The Counter-Reformation

This process of internal reform, known as the Counter-Reformation, began with the Council of Trent in 1570. The authority of the Pope was reinforced, administration was improved, and many of the scandals that had provoked Luther's protests were eradicated. The resulting renewal of faith, and of papal authority, strengthened the loyalty of Catholics and the fears of Protestants, and led to war in Europe. It also contributed to Catholic plots against Queen Elizabeth and James I, and to the anti-Catholic paranoia that affected many English Protestants in the seventeenth century.

Figure 3 The religious map of Europe showing major wars and civil wars.

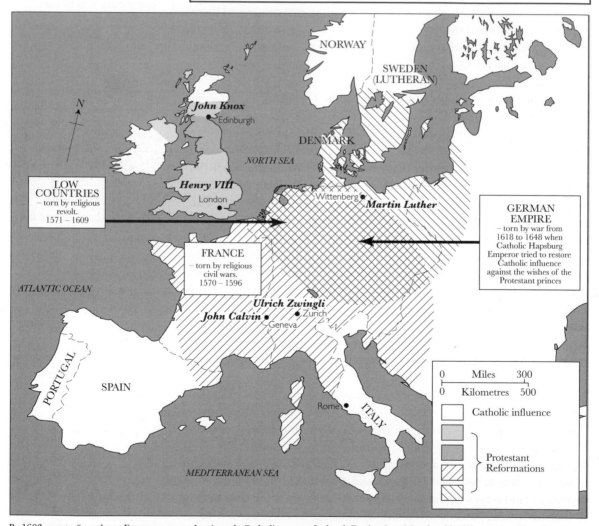

By 1603, most of southern Europe was predominantly Catholic, as was Ireland. England and Scotland had Protestant Churches. Northern Germany was mainly Lutheran, and Switzerland was dominated by Calvinist churches, which were also influential in parts of Germany and Holland. France was officially Catholic, but with an accepted Protestant minority known as Huguenots.

The Pope and the leaders of the Church responded by declaring Luther a **heretic** and driving him out of the Church. He was not the first reformer to suffer this, but the rulers of Saxony, where Luther lived, protected him from the Church and its allies. This allowed him to develop and publish his views. Those who took up his ideas became known as Protestants, and by 1550 there were Protestant churches in much of Germany and Scandinavia as well as the Netherlands and England. Thereafter, the Catholic Church began to reform itself internally in a Counter-Reformation, and to reassert the authority of Rome and the papacy.

In 1570 the Pope's decisions were declared to have the authority of God himself. The new spirit was represented by the establishment of the Society of Jesus, or Jesuits. Its founder was an ex-soldier, Ignatius Loyola, whose vision of a missionary order was based on the concept of soldiers of Christ. By the end of the sixteenth century Europe was divided between a militant Protestantism which rejected the authority of the past and looked for its rules and inspiration to the Bible, and a militant Catholicism determined to recover its control and destroy heresy.

> ### HERETIC
> The name given by the Roman Catholic Church to anyone who challenged its teachings or denied its beliefs. Heretics could be 'excommunicated' (expelled from the Church) or imprisoned. Ultimately, if they refused to give up their views they were handed over to the civil authorities to be burned alive.

b) Britain and the Effects of the Reformation

In England, the Reformation was carried out on the instructions and in the interests of Henry VIII. Henry was no Protestant, and his seizure of the Church and its property was motivated by a desire for power and wealth, as well as the need for a divorce in order to marry Anne Boleyn and, hopefully, to produce a male heir. Nevertheless, by rejecting the authority of the Pope he placed himself in the Protestant camp, and was forced to grant positions of influence in the Church to men with Protestant ideas. The result was a genuinely Protestant Reformation carried out during the short reign (1547–53) of his son, Edward, which his Catholic daughter Mary could not entirely reverse during her even shorter reign (1553–8). Her persecution of Protestants and her links with Spain (she married the heir to the Spanish crown) created a backlash against Catholicism. Perhaps equally important, her persecution drove some Protestants into exile in Europe, where they came into contact with other Protestant groups.

The development of Protestant ideas posed a number of problems for government. Luther argued that the rules for church government, as well as salvation, could be found in the Bible, and that the Christian monarch, or godly ruler, had the power and responsibility of interpreting and enforcing them. However, the Bible – part history, part mythology, part poetry – was often unclear and contradictory, and men and women who believed that their salvation

> **ISSUE**
> How did these issues create political conflict in Britain?

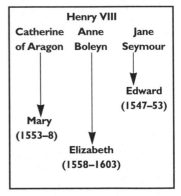

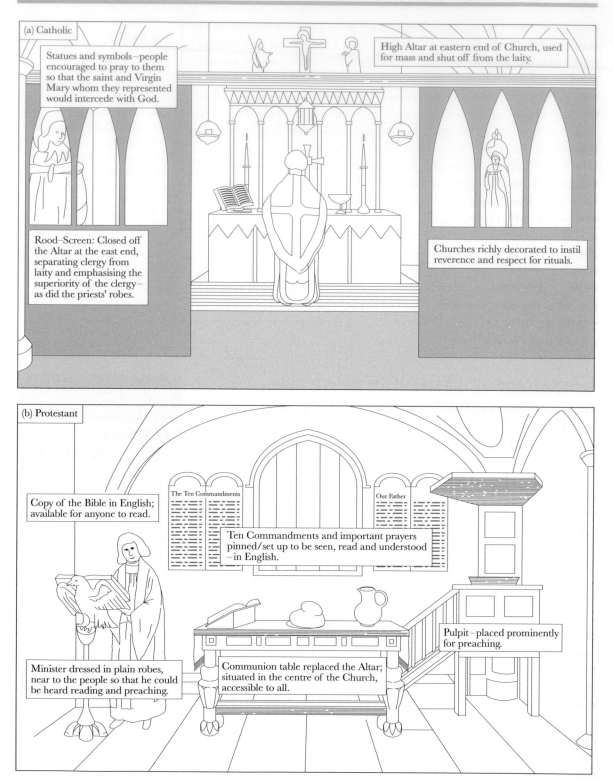

Figure 4 The key differences between Catholic and Protestant ideas.

depended on it were inclined to interpret it for themselves. The result was that Protestant ideas soon began to develop in different ways, and the varied and piecemeal nature of reform in different areas reinforced these differences. By the time of Mary's death, there was considerable variation of opinion on what constituted a 'true' church.

The model favoured by many was that established by the French reformer, John Calvin. Calvin had extended Luther's ideas about salvation to establish the doctrine that some people were predestined to be saved, because they were able to accept the gift of salvation and the disciplined Christianity that went with it. The sign of such **predestination** was the ability to live a godly life and accept the rules of a godly church. The idea that God would exclude some souls from a gift that He granted freely was in some ways illogical, and would be rejected by later religious leaders, but such assurance of salvation did encourage great dedication and commitment among Calvin's followers. The result was that many exiles returned after Mary's death, determined to reform the Church along Calvinist lines. This meant getting rid of all traces of Catholic ceremonies and rituals (see Figure 4) and allowing ministers to concentrate on preaching the Word of God and ensuring that their parishioners lived godly lives (whether or not they wanted to!). In Scotland the reformer John Knox was able to establish a Calvinist system known as Presbyterianism, but in England the reformers came up against a Queen who was more interested in political control and religious peace than in their cherished schemes of reform.

As the daughter of Anne Boleyn, whose marriage to Henry had never been recognised by the Catholic Church, Queen Elizabeth was bound to establish a broadly Protestant form of worship when she came to the throne in 1558. But as a skilful politician she recognised the need for healing and reconciliation in the religion of England. The result was the Elizabethan settlement, and the establishment of an Anglican Church which sought to provide a compromise, a 'middle way' between the Catholic and Protestant extremes. Undeniably Protestant in doctrine, it retained many of the familiar ceremonies and services inherited from the Catholic Church, as well as bishops, whom Elizabeth appointed and controlled and who therefore maintained her authority. It was able to satisfy the needs of most of her subjects but, like most compromises, it left dissatisfied minorities at both ends of the spectrum (see Figure 5).

A minority of English Catholics gave primary loyalty to the Pope; their treason in attempting to replace Elizabeth with the Catholic Mary, Queen of Scots and their links with Spain did much to create anti-Catholic feeling in England. More significantly, a Protestant minority was dissatisfied with a half-reformed Church, and sought to

PREDESTINATION
The Christian belief, expounded by Calvin and his followers, that God chooses beforehand those to whom He will grant salvation.

PURITANS
Those who believed that the Church of England fell short of the 'true' church, because of the remaining traces of Catholic ceremonial and the failure to establish and maintain effective discipline among members. The existence of leaders like Thomas Cartwright, a Cambridge scholar who put forward a model for further reform along Presbyterian lines in 1570, encouraged historians to think of Puritans as an identifiable movement within the Church. However, recent research has emphasised the variety of opinion among 'Puritans' and the extent to which they shaded into mainstream thinking.

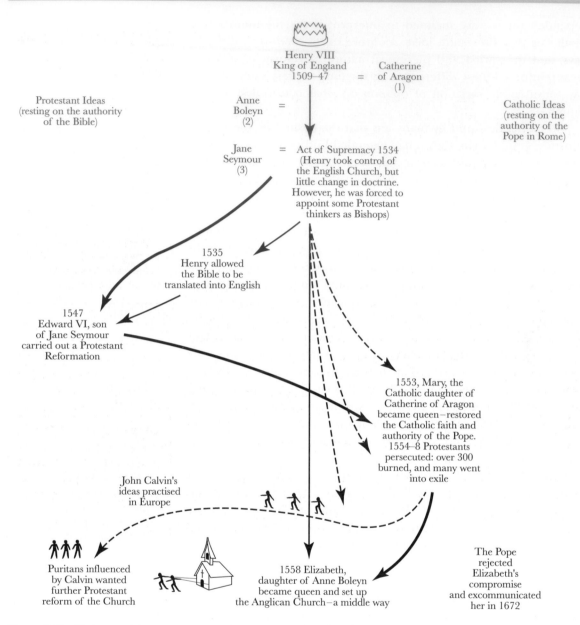

Henry VIII
King of England
1509–47   =   Catherine
of Aragon
(1)

Anne
Boleyn   =
(2)

Jane
Seymour   =   Act of Supremacy 1534
(3)   (Henry took control of
the English Church, but
little change in doctrine.
However, he was forced to
appoint some Protestant
thinkers as Bishops)

Protestant Ideas
(resting on the authority
of the Bible)

Catholic Ideas
(resting on the
authority of the
Pope in Rome)

1535
Henry allowed
the Bible to be
translated into English

1547
Edward VI, son
of Jane Seymour
carried out a Protestant
Reformation

1553, Mary, the
Catholic daughter of
Catherine of Aragon
became queen–restored
the Catholic faith and
authority of the Pope.
1554–8 Protestants
persecuted: over 300
burned, and many went
into exile

John Calvin's
ideas practised
in Europe

Puritans influenced
by Calvin wanted
further Protestant
reform of the Church

1558 Elizabeth,
daughter of Anne Boleyn
became queen and set up
the Anglican Church–a middle way

The Pope
rejected
Elizabeth's
compromise
and excommunicated
her in 1672

Figure 5 The Tudor pendulum.

persuade or pressurise the Queen into further change. Their desire for further purification of the Church led them to be nicknamed **'Puritans'**. In the 1570s attempts were made to introduce reforms through Parliament, prompting the angry Queen to forbid such discussions and raise political conflict over MPs' rights to free speech. Having lost this battle, Puritan preachers attempted to change the Church from within. Elizabeth, who was determined to maintain the system of bishops as the best method of ensuring her own, royal control, suppressed their meetings and silenced their protests.

The result was that James inherited a legacy of religious divisions across

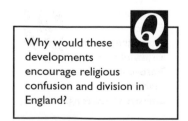

Why would these developments encourage religious confusion and division in England?

JOHN CALVIN (1509–64)

-*Profile*-

John Calvin was the most influential Protestant reformer after Luther. He established his own church in the city of Geneva. His doctrine became dominant among Protestants in France, Switzerland, Scotland and the Netherlands and to an extent within the early Church of England. It's core was the idea of predestination which claimed that God divided humanity into 'saints' who were predestined to follow the path of true religion and escape sin, and sinners, the 'unregenerate' who were condemned to hell. The sign of sainthood lay in a daily struggle to avoid sin and to carry out God's will in daily life, a struggle that required the discipline and support of a Calvinist Church. These gave great authority to the minister and certain senior members of the congregation (known as elders or presbyters) to control the behaviour and lives of their followers. Only those who were able to accept the restrictions entailed by this discipline could be sure of salvation.

The harshness of this doctrine led it to be first softened (by an implied expansion of the number of possible saints and reduction of the number of irretrievable sinners) and later challenged by other reformers. It also came to be abused by some known as Antinomians, who argued that since they were predestined to heaven by God, they need not fear to sin in their daily life. For most Calvinists, however, the belief that, as long as they genuinely sought a godly life, they could be sure of ultimate victory over sin, was a powerful inspiration. They could serve God in whatever capacity they had – as a merchant or labourer as well as a minister – and any success was evidence of God's approval, as well as enhancing the reputation of God's people. The task was not easy, and it was important that the church to which they had access should support them with good preaching and instruction, and not hinder them by unnecessary and possibly corrupting ceremonies and sacraments. Hence Calvinist enthusiasts required the correct forms and organisation within their church, to reflect doctrine in practice as well as in words.

three kingdoms. In Scotland the Presbyterian Church dominated the lowland areas, but a sizeable Catholic minority remained in the Gaelic highlands. In Ireland the majority of the population remained Catholic, and the loss of traditional chieftains encouraged the people to look to Catholic priests as leaders in the community. English control, however, led to the imposition of an Anglican Church as the official Church of Ireland, while Protestant settlers, especially those from Scotland, who settled in Ulster, brought an extreme Protestant or Presbyterian tradition. In England the established Church was Anglican, based on Elizabeth's 'middle way', with a small Catholic minority who remained loyal to the Pope. Within the Church, however, there was a significant movement seeking to achieve further reform.

Define the meaning of Calvinist, Puritan, Presbyterian and Anglican. Explain the main points of difference between them.

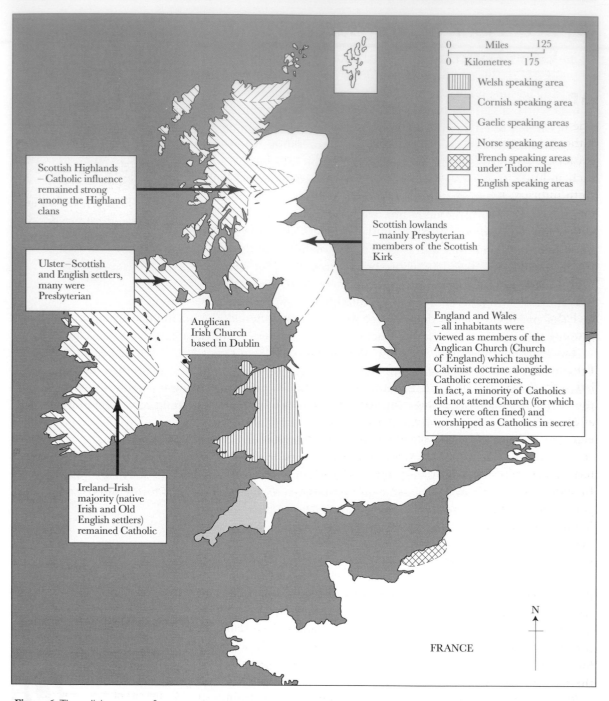

Figure 6 The religious map of Britain.

The map legend:

0 Miles 125	
0 Kilometres 175	
Welsh speaking area	
Cornish speaking area	
Gaelic speaking areas	
Norse speaking areas	
French speaking areas under Tudor rule	
English speaking areas	

Scottish Highlands – Catholic influence remained strong among the Highland clans

Ulster – Scottish and English settlers, many were Presbyterian

Anglican Irish Church based in Dublin

Ireland – Irish majority (native Irish and Old English settlers) remained Catholic

Scottish lowlands – mainly Presbyterian members of the Scottish Kirk

England and Wales – all inhabitants were viewed as members of the Anglican Church (Church of England) which taught Calvinist doctrine alongside Catholic ceremonies. In fact, a minority of Catholics did not attend Church (for which they were often fined) and worshipped as Catholics in secret

FRANCE

N

Why it was so difficult for different churches to coexist peacefully at this time, especially in Britain.

3 Economy, Society and Government

a) Population and Economy

The economy of Stuart England depended above all on agriculture. Although some primary industries, such as coal, tin and lead-mining existed, the vast majority of the population relied on farming, and such industry as existed was small-scale and craft-based. Even the cloth industry, the source of England's main export, was organised on a domestic basis, with clothiers delivering the raw fleeces to cottage workers and collecting the finished product at a later date. Most cloth workers were therefore also agricultural labourers or cottagers. Outside London there were few towns of any significant size; with the exception of ports like Bristol and Hull, most were market towns populated by craft workers organised in guilds, and many included sizeable areas devoted to gardens and plots suitable for growing food.

The main factor shaping economic development in early modern Britain was population and, in particular, the long-term rise in population from about 1500 to the mid seventeenth century. Thereafter the rate of increase slackened and there was probably a slight fall after 1660, followed by a more gradual rise which lasted into the eighteenth century. Population statistics are notoriously difficult to compile for this period, since the records available from parish registers and social commentators are invariably partial and inaccurate. In addition, the detailed studies that have been carried out in particular parishes or regions reveal wide variations, so that overall figures, even when thought to be relatively accurate, can be misleading for any given area. It is therefore not possible to do more than establish general trends and suggest their likely effects over time.

The graphs in Figure 7 illustrate these general patterns and show the likely effect of population change on wages and living standards. After the Black Death of 1349 and the recurrent plagues that followed it, the fall in the population led to a labour shortage and a time of relative prosperity for many ordinary people. High wages and low rents allowed some to purchase their own land and establish themselves as independent **yeomen**.

The sixteenth century saw population recovery turn to rapid rise, bringing price inflation and lower wage levels. For those on fixed or limited incomes there was hardship and poverty. Wage labourers and cottagers suffered most severely, but the great landlords and aristocracy were also affected. Traditionally they leased out land for rent, often on long leases, rather than involving themselves directly in

ISSUES
What were the main features of the Stuart economy? How did population changes affect society and government?

YEOMEN
A class of independent farmers that emerged in the later Middle Ages between the gentry and the mass of peasants and labourers. Some were able to buy land freehold, that is free of rent, while others rented land from landowners. If they rented 'copyhold' – with a copy of their lease in writing – they were usually secure and able to hold down their rents as long as the lease lasted. Where agreements were unwritten and based on customary rights, their prosperity depended on the attitude of their landlord. These variations explain why some yeomen were able to prosper still further in the sixteenth century, while others faced hardship.

Figure 7 Population patterns and the effects on wages and prices.

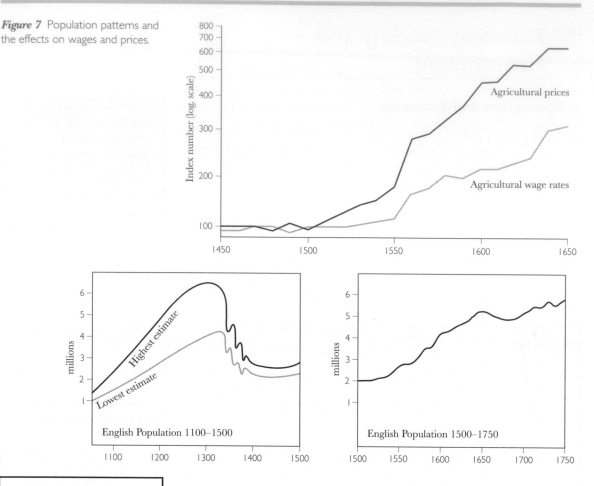

POOR LAWS

A series of laws had been passed to punish vagrants and make provision for the needy within their own parishes, and had been drawn together in the Great Poor Law of 1601. Nevertheless, governments remained concerned about social tensions and popular unrest, especially at times of shortage and bad harvests. In addition, unemployment continued to encourage some population mobility, and helped to swell the population, criminal and otherwise, of that magnet for migrants, the city of London.

agricultural management, and they were dependent on the fixed rents that resulted. For those who owned their land freehold, or were able to limit their costs, however, population and price rises presented an opportunity. Food production and profits increased, new land was taken into cultivation, and the growing wool trade encouraged the development of sheep farming as a highly profitable enterprise. Yeomen and merchants were able to grow rich enough to purchase landed estates and move into the ranks of the minor gentry, while the minor gentry, who also managed their estates themselves rather than renting out their lands, were able to increase their wealth and status within the governing class. At the same time, some of the independent peasantry slipped into the class of wage labourers, while unemployment reduced a growing section of the labour force to the status of paupers. Ultimately, the rise in population produced a growing gap between rich and poor, and associated problems of vagrancy and popular unrest. By 1603, when James became king, the worst problems of vagrancy and unemployment had been brought under control by the Poor Laws.

b) Society and Government

i) The King and his Powers

The inheritance that James took up in 1603 was therefore a complex arrangement of partly unified kingdoms, each with its distinctive culture, religious structure and government institutions. His original kingdom, Scotland, had its Parliament in Edinburgh, a Church Assembly, and a Scottish **Privy Council** which advised the King and supervised government in his absence. The Scottish legal system was, and remained, different from that of England. Ireland was ruled as conquered territory, with a Lord Deputy to govern in the King's name and its own Parliament meeting in Dublin. As the largest and wealthiest of the kingdoms, England provided the dominant political culture. It was a personal monarchy, governed by a King with the help of a Privy Council, a system of law courts, and occasional meetings of the governing class in Parliament. Sources A and B describe his powers

> **PRIVY COUNCIL**
> The King's private council of advisers, who met regularly to discuss decisions and supervise how they were carried out. As a private council, it was entirely dependent on the King for its membership and the source of its power.

ACTIVITY

The king distributes his authority and power in the fashion of five things: in the making of laws and ordinances; in the making of battle and peace with foreign nations; in providing of money for the maintenance of himself and defence against his enemies; in choosing and election of the chief officers and magistrates; and fifthly, in the administration of justice. The first and third are done by the prince [king] in Parliament. The second and fourth by the prince [king] himself. The fifth is by the great assize [law courts].

Source A From *De Republica Anglorum*, Sir Thomas Smith 1583.

The King's power is double, ordinary and absolute... That of the ordinary is for... particular subjects, for the execution of civil justice, and this is exercised by equity and justice in ordinary courts, and is known as common law, and these laws cannot be changed without Parliament. The absolute power of the king is...that which is applied to the general benefit of the people, and this power is most properly named policy and government. This absolute power varies according to the wisdom of the king for the common good; and these being general...all things done within these rules are lawful.

Source B From *The Judgement of Chief Baron Fleming in Bates' Case*, 1606.

Questions on Sources A and B

1. What powers did the King exercise according to Source A?
2. What limits were placed on the King's 'ordinary' power?
3. In what circumstances did the King's 'absolute' power apply?
4. Who would you expect to decide when circumstances were appropriate for the King's 'absolute' power to apply?

ELITE

Describes a group of people with particularly high status. It can refer to social class, political power, or particular skills and talents such as an intellectual elite. Seventeenth-century England was governed by a ruling elite whose status was based on both social position (normally as substantial landowners) and their role in government.

PREROGATIVE

The King's personal power, as opposed to power dependent on law. It allowed him to take action and make decisions without reference to written laws or Parliaments, and could only be exercised by the King himself or anyone who was deputising for him, such as a privy councillor.

How did the structure of government outlined in Figure 8 concentrate power into the hands of the King?

ii) The Structure of Government

The Privy Council contained the King's closest advisers, the heads of major government departments, representatives of the greater nobility, and the monarch's personal favourites. As well as advising the King, its functions included the supervision of central administration and local government. Local government was carried out by Justices of the Peace who were appointed by the King and Council with the help of a county Lord Lieutenant who usually came from one of the leading county families. JPs were appointed from the ranks of gentry in the county, and from wealthy citizens or a merchant **elite** in towns and boroughs. Thus the system of local government represented a social as well as a political elite; their offices were unpaid, but carried considerable prestige and influence in the community, and were therefore highly prized. These arrangements are outlined in Figure 8.

Central administration consisted of major government departments such as the Treasury, but also of central Law Courts. The Court of King's Bench dealt with criminal cases, while the Court of Common Pleas covered civil law. Both drew on the common law, a mixture of custom and precedent, royal proclamations, and statute law made in Parliament. Judges were appointed and dismissed at the King's discretion, giving him considerable control over their interpretation of law. In addition, previous monarchs had developed a number of **prerogative** law courts, whose authority came directly from the King himself. Staffed by privy councillors acting directly in the King's name, they were widely respected for their rapid decisions which were not influenced by local interests and pressures. They did, however, favour the King's interests, and could cause resentment as a result.

Control was also exercised through the institution of the Church, of which the monarch was head. Bishops were appointed by the King, and could be relied upon to support his wishes in the House of Lords as well as in the administration of the Church. Most importantly, announcements and instructions from the pulpit reached into every town and village in a way that no other form of communication could achieve. Its teaching of deference, obedience to authority and loyalty to the monarch reinforced royal power and protected the social and political hierarchy on which it depended – in modern terms it provided a controlled media and an unrivalled propaganda machine.

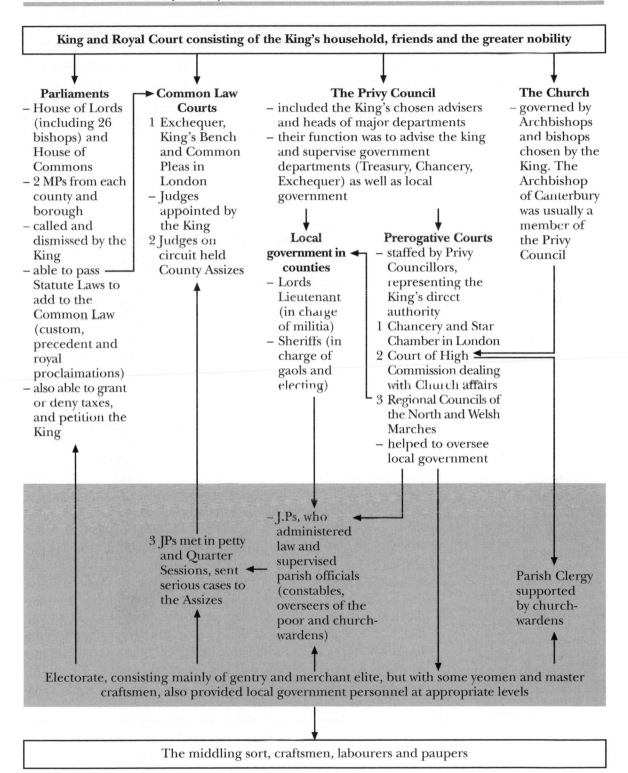

King and Royal Court consisting of the King's household, friends and the greater nobility

Parliaments
– House of Lords (including 26 bishops) and House of Commons
– 2 MPs from each county and borough
– called and dismissed by the King
– able to pass Statute Laws to add to the Common Law (custom, precedent and royal proclaimations)
– also able to grant or deny taxes, and petition the King

Common Law Courts
1 Exchequer, King's Bench and Common Pleas in London
– Judges appointed by the King
2 Judges on circuit held County Assizes

The Privy Council
– included the King's chosen advisers and heads of major departments
– their function was to advise the king and supervise government departments (Treasury, Chancery, Exchequer) as well as local government

The Church
– governed by Archbishops and bishops chosen by the King. The Archbishop of Canterbury was usually a member of the Privy Council

Local government in counties
– Lords Lieutenant (in charge of militia)
– Sheriffs (in charge of gaols and electing)

Prerogative Courts
– staffed by Privy Councillors, representing the King's direct authority
1 Chancery and Star Chamber in London
2 Court of High Commission dealing with Church affairs
3 Regional Councils of the North and Welsh Marches
– helped to oversee local government

3 JPs met in petty and Quarter Sessions, sent serious cases to the Assizes

– J.Ps, who administered law and supervised parish officials (constables, overseers of the poor and church-wardens)

Parish Clergy supported by church-wardens

Electorate, consisting mainly of gentry and merchant elite, but with some yeomen and master craftsmen, also provided local government personnel at appropriate levels

The middling sort, craftsmen, labourers and paupers

Figure 8 The structure of government and the governing class.

ACTIVITY

Almighty God hath created and appointed all things in heaven, earth, and waters in a most excellent and perfect order . . . . Every degree of people in their vocation, calling and office hath appointed to them their duty and order; some are in high degree, some in low, some kings and princes, some inferiors and subjects, priests and laymen, masters and servants, fathers and children, husbands and wives, rich and poor: and everyone hath need of other: so in all things is to be lauded and praised the goodly order of God.

Source C From an Elizabethan Homily; read in churches and widely taught to children.

Question on Source C

1. How would the ideas in Source C help to reinforce royal authority?

PATRONAGE

A system of influence in which a patron uses a position of power and influence to help and encourage individuals in an inferior position in return for their respect or support.

FACTIONS

The seventeenth century equivalent of political parties, but much smaller, and based on personal relationships more than on political beliefs. They gathered around influential figures at Court and created a rivalry for power that was linked to personalities and personal ambitions and only by chance to attitudes and beliefs. A skilful political figure could greatly increase his influence by working with, or manipulating other factions, while a skilful monarch could use his control of patronage to balance factions for his own purposes.

iii) The Importance of Patronage

Government worked through a system of **patronage** that emanated from the King and operated through the royal Court. The Court encompassed both government offices and the King's personal household. It was therefore both the pinnacle of the social hierarchy and the centre of political influence. The key to power, position and wealth was access to the King, and this could come through a position in the royal household, such as Gentleman of the Bedchamber, or through an administrative post such as Lord Treasurer or Secretary of State. Most offices were unpaid, but provided opportunities for profit and for royal gifts and grants. By virtue of their birth and social position, the greater nobility expected to hold such posts and exercise power, but kings also appointed talented advisers of humbler birth, and granted them lands and titles to raise them to the appropriate status. The nobility acted as a vital link between central government and the local communities. They expected to be leading figures in their county communities, and ambitious men could apply to them for an introduction or a position at Court. If they could grant it, their own status was enhanced, and in return they expected support from their clients in Parliament, in county affairs and in Court politics. The result was the formation of Court **factions**, which were also linked to regional and local interests through the power and prestige of the nobility within them. The regional power base of factional leaders served to enhance their position with the King, while their ability to persuade the King to offer posts and positions to their clients strengthened their local connections. The system operated to oil the machinery of government, and if skilfully manipulated by the monarch, enhanced his or her control over the social and political hierarchy.

THE ESSEX REBELLION: A FAILURE OF PATRONAGE

-Profile-

Robert Devereux, Earl of Essex (1566–1601), painted by Marcus Gheeraerts

The importance of manipulating patronage effectively was shown towards the end of Elizabeth's reign in the rebellion led by the Earl of Essex in 1601. Essex had come to the Court as the stepson of Elizabeth's friend and favourite, the Earl of Leicester, and when Leicester died he became the leader of those who favoured extending the war against Spain to include a land campaign. He was opposed by the Cecils – Elizabeth's chief adviser, William Cecil, Lord Burleigh, and his son Robert – mainly on financial grounds. Elizabeth agreed with the Cecils, and although she favoured Essex in the courtly games at which such a handsome young man excelled, she denied him any real power.

Essex was unable to gain seats on the Privy Council for his allies, or positions for his clients. Instead, the Cecils gained a stranglehold on appointments, and blocked the progress of even such talented members of the Essex faction as Francis Bacon, later Lord Chancellor. Bacon, among others, deserted his patron, and Essex displayed such petulance towards the Queen that she boxed his ears. In reply he went for his sword, and had to be forcibly restrained. While many of his problems were the result of his own arrogance, Essex drew some support from those who resented the power of the Cecils.

In 1599 Elizabeth gave him a chance to show his talents and to reward his friends by appointing him to command her armies in Ireland. Essex squandered the opportunity, and when he returned to Court, Elizabeth refused to see him. In February 1601 he attempted to seize London, failed, and was executed for treason. Nevertheless, the revolt reflected widespread discontent among the nobility, although the Earls of Rutland, Southampton, Bedford and Sussex, as well as Lords Mountjoy, Sandys and Cromwell were implicated with Essex, none was brought to trial. This weakness reflected Elizabeth's political isolation and failure to distribute patronage with the sure touch that she had previously displayed.

iv) The Function and Powers of Parliament

While the Church, Privy Council and prerogative courts represented royal power, the functions of Parliament were more complex. It was controlled by the monarch, who called and dissolved parliaments when he chose and who exercised considerable direct influence over the Lords in the Upper House. The functions of Parliament were to advise the King, grant taxation, and to turn royal decisions into legal statutes, the highest form of law. Edward I had first called representatives of the knights and 'commons' to join the nobility in the 'parlement' (meeting) of his Great Council in 1297, in order to gain their support for royal taxation. Over the centuries the regular meeting, procedures and composition of parliament had gradually

ISSUE
What part did parliaments play in government?

taken shape according to the needs of the monarchy. Its primary function was therefore to support and enhance royal power. At the same time, however, MPs represented the communities who elected them, and stood for the **rule of law** and the liberties of the subject. They provided an opportunity for the expression of public opinion and symbolised the legal limits of royal power, but they were neither permanent, nor a necessary part of daily government.

MPs represented the county elites described above, being elected mainly by the gentry and merchants with some of the better 'middling sort' of yeomanry and master craftsmen. Most were amateurs, called occasionally, and for short periods only, to represent the views of their friends and neighbours, although a few might well be office-holders favoured by the Privy Council. As such, they had neither the ability nor the desire to take positive measures or formulate policies, and attempts by any minority to use Parliament in this way, such as the Puritan reformers of Elizabeth's reign, were both ineffective and short-lived. Their powers were largely negative, in refusing to formalise or finance the King's decisions, but they could, and sometimes did, limit or restrain his exercise of power. In addition, it was assumed that the King should govern within the law, and that law at its highest was made in and with Parliament. Just as efficient administration depended on a partnership of the monarchy and governing class through the medium of patronage, its legal and financial framework required that partnership to work in Parliament.

A number of historians have argued that the power and independence of Parliament, and of the House of Commons in particular, had increased during the sixteenth century. This was the result of growing wealth and of the Reformation of the 1530s, in which Henry VIII seized control of the Church and its very extensive assets (including about one-third of the country's farming land) using parliamentary legislation to ensure that the changes were legally enforceable. Not only had this process encouraged the development of parliamentary procedures and experience, it had also allowed Parliament to legislate concerning religion, the succession to the throne and the monarch's powers. Above all, it ensured that future changes would also have to be made through Parliament, significantly increasing its importance.

The Reformation also brought Protestant ideas to England, with religious, social and political consequences. Protestant ideas emphasised the importance of Bible-reading, and therefore literacy. Combined with the increasing reliance on educated laymen to fill government posts once held by priests, this resulted in a larger, more powerful, more confident and articulate gentry, who dominated the House of Commons. Some of them held strong religious views, which they were determined to express. Religious quarrels also

RULE OF LAW

The idea that law made by the King in Parliament is supreme and must be accepted by Kings as well as subjects. It therefore guaranteed subjects rights as well as regal authority. While it was accepted that Kings made the law and could change it, the rule of law meant that they could not simply ignore it at their convenience.

ISSUE

Were parliaments becoming more powerful and assertive in this period?

Figure 9 Henry VIII opening Parliament in 1519, The size of the figures is intended to reflect their relative importance; hence the King, Councillors and Archbishops are shown as larger than the other Lords, whilst the Commons are standing as small figures in the top corner.

became important in defining political factions among the nobility, and the existence of Parliament encouraged such factions to play out their rivalries there as well as, more traditionally, at Court. The Catholic Counter-Reformation and the influence of Catholic Spain created intense religious fears, and Queen Elizabeth's refusal to eradicate all traces of Catholicism from the new Church of England led some MPs to try to bring in reform through Parliament. The Queen forbade such discussions, raising issues related to MPs' right to free speech, as the following extract from a statement read in the House of Commons by Lord Keeper Puckering indicates:

> For liberty of speech her Majesty commandeth me to tell you that <u>to say yea or no to bills, God forbid that any man should be restrained or afraid to answer according to his best liking</u>, with some short declaration of his reason therein, and therein to have a free voice, which is the very true liberty of the House; not, as some suppose, to <u>speak there of all causes as him listeth</u>, and to frame a form of religion or a state of government as to their idle brains shall seem meetest. She saith no king fit for his state will suffer such absurdities, and . . . <u>she hopeth no man here longeth so much for his ruin as that he mindeth to make such a peril to his own safety</u>.

ACTIVITY

The extract above was from a statement read in the House of Commons by Lord Keeper Puckering in 1593. MPs had been discussing a Bill for reform of the Church, and when forbidden to do so, had claimed a traditional right to free speech.

1. Explain in your own words what Elizabeth meant by the phrases that are underlined.
2. What kind of free speech does it seem she was prepared to allow?
3. How did this differ from what MPs were trying to do?

MONOPOLY RIGHTS

Monopoly rights refer to the practice of granting a royal charter declaring that a particular group of merchants had the sole right to produce or import a particular commodity. This was sometimes justified to protect new trades or industries but, more often, they were simply ways of gaining money for the Crown, since the merchants usually paid handsomely for their privilege. Monopolies were highly unpopular, since they usually caused a rise in prices and a decline in quality.

Parliament's influence was also increased by the Crown's financial problems. These increased the need for additional taxation which only Parliament could grant. To some extent the financial problems were the result of a rising population and inflation across Europe, but they were made worse by the frequency and expense of warfare. Elizabeth attempted to control expenditure by avoiding war, but Spanish interference eventually made this impossible. Nevertheless, the political pressures made her reluctant to increase taxation even by updating assessments in line with inflation. Instead, she sold Crown lands worth £800,000, underpaid her officials and resorted to financial expedients such as the sale of **monopoly rights** – passing on to James an outdated tax system, a debt of £100,000, and a good deal of parliamentary irritation on the subject of finance.

Recent historical research has led to a number of these arguments being challenged. Historians have pointed out that Elizabeth successfully resisted attempts to reform the Church through Parliament, and imprisoned the MPs who abused their right to free speech. Since she called only thirteen parliaments in her reign, she was clearly able to govern effectively without them, despite her financial problems. Nevertheless, her attempts to do so added to the financial problems faced by her successors, and the later years of her reign provide evidence of considerable annoyance among MPs regarding both finance and the Church. It could perhaps be argued that Elizabeth controlled any tendency for Parliament to overstep its traditional bounds because she knew how to operate the governing partnership with a combination of firmness and tact. In her old age, when her political skills were weakening, there were signs of the friction that could develop if the partnership came to be handled less effectively. The situation could be illustrated by the monopolies incident of 1601. The Queen had been granting monopoly patents on a considerable

Figure 10 The Tudor legacy.

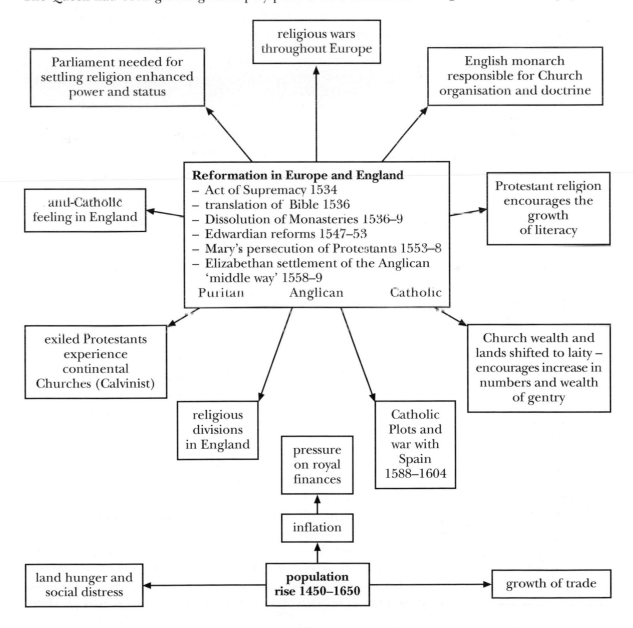

religious wars throughout Europe

Parliament needed for settling religion enhanced power and status

English monarch responsible for Church organisation and doctrine

anti-Catholic feeling in England

Protestant religion encourages the growth of literacy

Reformation in Europe and England
− Act of Supremacy 1534
− translation of Bible 1536
− Dissolution of Monasteries 1536–9
− Edwardian reforms 1547–53
− Mary's persecution of Protestants 1553–8
− Elizabethan settlement of the Anglican 'middle way' 1558–9

Puritan   Anglican   Catholic

exiled Protestants experience continental Churches (Calvinist)

Church wealth and lands shifted to laity – encourages increase in numbers and wealth of gentry

religious divisions in England

Catholic Plots and war with Spain 1588–1604

pressure on royal finances

inflation

land hunger and social distress

population rise 1450–1650

growth of trade

scale, and by 1601 complaints were mounting. Angry MPs threatened to refuse a grant of taxes unless the Queen agreed to withdraw many patents. Making a virtue of necessity, she came to Parliament and promised compliance with such grace and generosity that the crisis became a triumph. Under pressure, she was still able to exhibit the political skill required to make the Tudor system work.

The Tudor legacy to James was therefore mixed. On the one hand, he inherited a strong monarchy, a stable society and a fund of political and religious loyalty. At the same time, he inherited an expensive war, financial problems and political and religious tensions. The evolution of British government would depend on how these problems were dealt with by James and his successors.

▼ Working on the Tudor Legacy

You do not need to remember the events described in this chapter in detail, but it will help you later on if you clearly understand the concepts and ideas that are explained here. The exercises below are intended to help you think about some of them. The primary purpose of this introduction is to give you a working knowledge of how Britain was governed in 1603, so that you can begin to examine how it changed in the years that followed. This might be approached by using four key questions to draw together and synthesise your ideas about the issues defined alongside the text above:

1. Who held the power to govern?
2. What skills were needed to make this power effective?
3. Why were religious issues so important and so divisive?
4. What problems would the system pose for a new king in 1603?

Before trying to answer these questions, you need to find some ways of organising the information contained in the chapter so that you can select what you need from it. One approach is to make notes; making notes helps you to remember what you have read and gives you a record of key points that you can use later for revision. In this case, however, you are primarily concerned with concepts and their practical implications, so some approaches that focus on exploring ideas may be useful.

One way is to use sources. The chapter text includes certain source extracts, which illustrate particular issues and ideas. The questions included alongside them should have helped you to analyse the key features of government that they referred to. However, by considering them together, cross-referencing between them, and interpreting them in the context of the wider awareness that you have gained from reading the chapter, you can clarify your understanding of the problems and resources that James inherited.

▼ EXERCISE 1: QUESTIONS ON SOURCES

1. Read Sources A and B on page 17.
   (a) In what ways do they differ in describing royal power?
   (b) Do they disagree about anything?
   (c) Can the apparent disagreements be explained?
   (d) Can you see any potential problems arising from them?
   (e) Using both sources, explain the nature and extent of royal power.
2. Read Source C and the source on page 24.
   (a) Sources A and B do not specifically describe the monarch's powers in religion. How would Elizabeth justify her claim that she, not Parliament, controlled the organisation and doctrine of the Church?
   (b) Using Source C and the source on page 24 together, explain her attitude towards the attempts by MPs to debate religion and reform the Church.
   (c) Using these sources supported by your wider knowledge, explain why religion was such an important political issue in this period.
   (d) Using all the sources interpreted in the context of your wider knowledge, explain what problems the nature of government in 1603 might create for a new monarch.

▼ EXERCISE 2: USING DIAGRAMS

Another approach is to use diagrams, as you have already been asked to do on page 18. Diagrams are particularly helpful in showing how different aspects of a situation affect one another, and in illustrating causal or sequential relationships. Diagrams can include timelines, flow charts and spider diagrams, for example. One approach is to summarise what you have read in diagrammatic form (the chapter includes some examples for you to consider). Equally useful is the reverse process – to interpret and explain a diagram in words. These techniques can be used to address question 4 above.

(a) Using the Tudor Legacy diagram in Figure 10 and the information included in this chapter, describe the problems facing the monarchy in Britain in 1603. You may find it helpful to arrange your answer in four sections, headed:

▼ Religious Divisions;
▼ Monarchy and Parliament;
▼ Finance and Administration;
▼ Governing Three Kingdoms.

(b) Construct a similar diagram to show how religious divisions affected and/or led to the other problems facing the new King.

(c) James I was a foreigner when he came to England in 1603. If you were a member of his English Privy Council, what actions would you advise him to take in order to deal with these problems effectively?

Finally, you can summarise and record your knowledge of Britain in 1603 by writing out brief answers to questions 1–4.

Further Reading

Books in the Access to History Series

There are a number of volumes in the Access to History Series that you could use to extend your knowledge of the sixteenth century, although you do not need to know about the century in great detail. Of particular use would be:

Elizabeth I: Religion and Foreign Affairs, by John Warren;
Elizabeth and the Government of England, by Keith Randell;
Tudor Economy and Society, by Nigel Heard.

General

There are also some thematic accounts that cover both the sixteenth and seventeenth centuries together, which would give you the kind of overview that you need. Two of the best examples are: A.G.R. Smith, *The Emergence of a Nation State, 1529–1660* (1984) which is an excellent starting point, and Conrad Russell, *The Crisis of Parliaments: English History, 1509–1660*, (OUP 1971) which is a long, interpretative essay. Either of these will help you to establish an overview of the period, and both would be worth rereading at a later point, when you have more knowledge of what happened after 1603.

You could also refer to the *Oxford Illustrated History of Tudor and Stuart Britain* (see page xiv) for information on particular issues.

THE ORIGINS OF CONFLICT, 1603–29

CHAPTER 2

POINTS TO CONSIDER

If we accept that James inherited a reasonably effective system of government, then the causes of the tension that had clearly developed by 1629 have to be sought in the actions and events of his reign and that of Charles I. This does not deny the pre-existence of problems, but assumes that they were not insoluble and forces us to focus on how they were handled by the first two Stuarts. Although James died in 1625, the issues and tensions that existed at that point already involved Charles, and the new reign should be seen as demonstrating continuity in relations with Parliament rather than change. It is therefore more logical to continue the investigation in this chapter to 1629, when the dissolution of Charles's third Parliament marked an open breach between the King and Parliament.

1 James VI and I – the Scottish Connection

ISSUE
How did James's background influence the early years of his reign?

a) Religious Issues

The accession of James I was greeted with relief by most of Elizabeth's subjects – a male Protestant king with several children offered the prospect of security and a stable succession. There were many who expected his accession to be to their advantage. Catholics hoped that respect for his dead mother, Mary, Queen of Scots, would encourage the King to ease the persecution that they suffered, while Puritans hoped that his upbringing in the Presbyterian Church of Scotland would lead him to favour their plans for reform. In the event, both were disappointed. James did suspend the collection of fines for **recusancy**, but when faced with complaints in Parliament, and perhaps regretting the loss of income, he reimposed them. This encouraged an extremist minority to look for help from Spain, and led to the Gunpowder Plot of 1605, in which Catholic conspirators attempted to blow up Parliament while the King was present.

The initial hopes of the Puritans, expressed in the Millenary Petition (supposedly signed by 1000 ministers) were also short-lived. James agreed to meet them at a conference, held at Hampton Court

ISSUE
How did James handle religious problems?

RECUSANCY
A refusal to attend Anglican services on a regular basis, which had been made compulsory in the reign of Elizabeth. Absentees (usually Catholics) were required to pay a fine. The fines provided a useful source of revenue for the Crown.

IMPROPRIATION

The practice of taking over the collection of tithes (a 10 per cent tax on all households in a parish levied as income for the parish priest). This allowed the impropriator to play a part in choosing the minister. Many parishes had come under the control of the local gentry in this way. Another way of controlling the choice of minister was to buy up the advowson for the parish, which gave the holder the right to nominate a particular minister. Many advowsons were held by the King and the bishops, but a significant number were acquired by the gentry and by borough corporations.

in 1604. But at the meeting he rejected their ideas and warned them that if they would not conform to the rules laid down in the Prayer Book he would 'harry them out of the Kingdom'. Like Elizabeth, James saw the Church primarily in political terms (as an institution that upheld royal power) and was determined to maintain his control through bishops appointed by, and dependent on, him. He followed up his uncompromising stand by appointing the authoritarian Richard Bancroft as the new Archbishop of Canterbury. Bancroft enforced rules on the use of ceremonies and ceremonial dress, and some ministers lost their livings (jobs) because of their refusal to conform.

Within a few years, however, James had softened his stance considerably. Having asserted his authority, he was wise enough to see that political harmony could best be achieved by avoiding unnecessary provocation. Although recusancy fines continued to be levied, the policy was intermittently applied, and discreet Catholics could often worship undisturbed for long periods. Similarly, Puritan ministers who conformed to the Prayer Book occasionally in recognition of the King's authority could often ignore unpalatable rules and ceremonies for much of the time. In 1611, when Bancroft died, he was replaced by the sympathetic George Abbot, who treated Puritan sensitivities with tact. Puritan ministers were expected to demonstrate their obedience to the King by occasional use of signs and ceremonies that they disliked. In return, they were left undisturbed for much of the time.

In addition, James did recognise the need to improve the numbers and quality of the clergy, and shared the Puritan enthusiasm for good preaching. He had no objection to the widespread practice of lay **impropriation**, which enabled gentry with Puritan sympathies to ensure that Puritan preachers were appointed to many parish livings. Supporters also endowed weekday lectures, often to be held in market towns, which enabled Puritan ministers to preach for a living without undertaking the ceremonial duties required of a parish minister. While the arrangements may have lacked neat logic, they did provide a measure of peace in the English Church, and allowed Puritan reformers to coexist with others as one faction within it.

Meanwhile, in Scotland, James took cautious steps to bring Presbyterian practice into line with English arrangements. By 1621 he had persuaded the Scots to accept bishops, albeit with limited powers. An attempt to establish a Prayer Book similar to that used in England aroused great opposition, and James withdrew it until a more favourable opportunity arose. By such cautious and tactful measures he hoped gradually to bring the two Churches together and to create uniformity across the two kingdoms. The success of James's approach to the religious problem can be seen from the relatively few complaints voiced in Parliament. These were mainly limited to grumbles that recusancy fines were not levied rigorously enough, or that the King's foreign policy was insufficiently 'Protestant'. Shortly after his accession he brought Elizabeth's long, expensive war with Spain to an end. While some of the 'hotter sort' of Protestants and Puritans might have reservations about this, the peace was wise and financially necessary. In general terms, religion was not a major cause of tension in Parliament, until the outbreak of the Thirty Years' War in 1618 created new conflicts across Europe.

b) Constitutional Issues

Nevertheless, in the first few years of his reign, the political atmosphere soured, with both King and Parliament showing signs of irritation. In 1604 there was a disputed election in Buckinghamshire and a clumsy attempt by the government to reverse the result in favour of the Court candidate, Sir John Fortescue. The House of Commons was already sensitive on the matter of its rights and privileges, after its difficulties with Elizabeth. MPs may also have been concerned about the King's extravagant claims to divine power and status. James had always regarded himself as something of a political philosopher. In 1598 he had published a learned work entitled *The True Law of Free Monarchies*, in which he had claimed that 'Kings are justly called gods for that they exercise a manner or resemblance of divine power on earth' and that 'they make and unmake their subjects, they have power of raising and casting down, of life and death'. Whatever the reason, the House reacted sharply in asserting the right of the Commons to determine their own membership. James reminded MPs that their privileges had been granted by monarchs, and, by implication, suggested that they might be removed in the same way. In practice, however, he applied his theories with a measure of tact. Faced with a Commons' *Apology,* which set out and asserted Parliamentary rights, James defused the crisis by suspending the parliamentary session, and quietly allowing the Buckingham issue to be dropped.

When Parliament reassembled in 1605–6, a mood of Protestant unity created by the Gunpowder Plot led to reconciliation and a parliamentary grant to settle the King's debts. However, problems arose over his desire for Anglo-Scottish union. Wales and Ireland were effectively conquered territories, and could be treated as subordinate to England, but Scotland was an independent kingdom. Either James must continue to rule it separately, or a new relationship with England must be established. James desired a 'perfect' union, which would amalgamate the best Scottish and English

ISSUE
How did constitutional difficulties arise?

KEY DATES: KING AND PARLIAMENT

1603 James becomes King;
1604 peace with Spain; disputed election leads to quarrel in Parliament and Commons 'Apology'
1605 debates over union with
–7 Scotland lead to tension and failure of James's plan.

ACTIVITY

Use the headings and questions in Section 1 to make brief notes on the early years of James 1. You will find it useful to set these notes out clearly using a main heading, sub-headings and sub-points. For example, the material that you have read so far would fit neatly as follows:

Main heading: JAMES I and VI: THE SCOTTISH CONNECTION
Use numbered points to briefly outline his Scottish background and characteristics.
Sub-heading: (A)   Personality and Experience:
　　　　　　　　　1.
　　　　　　　　　2. etc.
Sub-heading: (B)   Religious Policies:
Use numbered points to outline the actions taken by James to deal with religious issues
　　　　　　　　　1.
　　　　　　　　　2. etc.
Sub-heading: (C)   Constitutional Issues:
　　　　　　　1. The Divine Right of Kings:
　　　　　　　　　(a) Theoretical claims
　　　　　　　　　(b) Behaviour in practice
　　　　　　　　　(c) Effects on Parliament
　　　　　　　2. Anglo-Scottish Union:
Use sub-points as in C1 to outline the problems over this issue.

If you use and practise this kind of organisation of your notes, it will help you to think about what you have been reading and ensure that you understand it. It will also provide you with factual information and ideas that are recorded in a clear and easily memorised form for later revision. Making notes in this way tends to be slow at first, but you will get faster with practice and it is worth the effort in the long run. To begin with, look for headings in the book to help you structure your notes, but as you become more confident, you will devise your own headings and incorporate more of your own ideas alongside the facts that you collect. For example, complete this exercise with a conclusion that explains how far you think that James's Scottish background was a help or a hindrance in governing England.

institutions, seeing the possibility for reform and improvement of the governing system in both kingdoms. However, many Englishmen were deeply anti-Scottish – a legacy of past hostilities that had been aggravated by the new King's numerous gifts of titles and pensions to his Scottish friends and courtiers. MPs refused to countenance the idea that English institutions could be improved by importing any Scottish ideas. Sir Edwin Sandys suggested that the 'perfect' union could be achieved by abolishing Scottish law and replacing it with the law of England, but even this was unacceptable to some MPs, who saw the Scots as penniless adventurers. 'If one man owns two pastures', declared one MP, 'with one hedge to divide them; the one pasture bare, the other fertile and good; a wise owner will not pull down the hedge, but make gates to let them in and out, otherwise the cattle will rush in and not want to return.' This attitude was deeply insulting to the King, but it was further aggravated by James's generosity to his Scottish companions; and complaints about the King's finances were already mounting. It was this issue of finance that was to cause the most serious damage to the relationship between King and Parliament.

2 Financial Problems

a) Revenue and Resources

> **ISSUE**
> **Why did the King face financial problems?**

Income and Revenue, 1603

▼ Crown lands, Feudal rights and Prerogative – the 'Ordinary Revenue'.
Crown lands – leased out for rent, but often on long leases that did not keep up with inflation. Income had also declined because of sales of land by Elizabeth.
Wardship – the King's right to act as guardian to the children of tenants who died before the child was old enough to inherit. Profits could be made from administering the estate and from profitable marriages and dowries.
Marriage – the King's right to arrange marriages for the female heirs of tenants or the remarriage of widows.
Livery – the King's right to receive a gift of money (set by him) from those who inherited land held from him in feudal tenancy.
Purveyance – the King's right to buy food and supplies for the Court at reduced prices.
Monopolies – the King's right to grant exclusive rights to make and sell goods of particular kinds
Justice – fines, court fees, etc.

▼ Customs Duties.
Tunnage and Poundage – customs duties on wine and wool, normally granted to the King for life by his first Parliament.
New impositions – new import duties which the King was entitled to raise to protect English trade and industry.

▼ Occasional Sources.
Benevolences/Forced loans (gifts and loans from individuals).
Loans on credit, Sales of assets.

▼ Direct Taxes – granted by Parliament.
Tenths and Fifteenths – a tax on movable goods (except personal clothing) paid by all.
Subsidies – a tax on income for landowners, office-holders and wage-earners, or movable property for merchants, craftsmen and tenant-farmers. It was not levied on the poor.
Poll Tax – a tax paid by individuals (rare).
Ship Money – a tax levied in wartime from coastal areas for building ships.

The financial problems of the Crown arose from two factors. The first was that years of rising prices had left royal income increasingly inadequate for the expenses of government. The second was that James's handling of money and some aspects of his lifestyle amounted to financial irresponsibility, and made a difficult problem far worse. The box on page 33 shows the nature and sources of royal revenue. According to the political conventions of the time, the King was expected to 'live of his own' in peacetime, that is, to finance government and maintain his household out of ordinary revenue and the customs duties that he was granted at the beginning of his reign.

By 1603, that had become impossible, for a number of reasons:

▼ Before 1600, a combination of price inflation and Elizabeth's sales of Crown land to finance the war with Spain had made ordinary revenue inadequate. James inherited a debt of approximately £100,000.

▼ As a family man, James's expenses were bound to be greater than those of Elizabeth – he had to maintain a wife and children, including a separate establishment for the heir to the throne, the Prince of Wales.

▼ In addition, Elizabeth had failed to update tax assessments in line with inflation. Combined with an inefficient system of collection, this meant that even when Parliament did grant extra taxes, the King received much less than was intended.

b) Strategies for Reform

Faced with these difficulties, his chief financial adviser, Robert Cecil (created Earl of Salisbury in 1605) tried a variety of strategies. In 1606 a legal ruling that the King had the right to impose new customs duties was used to issue a new Book of Rates in 1608, which imposed new duties on some goods and increased the rate of payment on others. These 'impositions' were deeply resented, and complaints were raised in Parliament in 1610, and again in 1614. There was further indignation among MPs when the sale of monopolies was renewed (they had been abandoned by Elizabeth amidst great public rejoicing). While the complaints were significant in themselves, they also contributed to the failure of Cecil's more fundamental reform, the Great Contract. This was a plan whereby the King would give up some of the more irritating feudal dues that he could still levy from his subjects and tenants, in return for a regular parliamentary income of £200,000 a year. Had it been successful, the plan would have placed royal finances on a sound basis. As it was, both sides had reservations which caused them to withdraw. While the King was aware that he would lose a useful means of controlling his more powerful subjects, the House of Commons were wary of providing an income that might give the King financial independ-

ISSUE
How well did James and his advisers handle these problems?

KEY DATES: FINANCE

1606 Bates Case – judges approve the 'imposition' of new duties;

1608 new Book of Rates published;

1610 complaints in Parliament about 'impositions'; failure of the Great Contract;

1612 death of Robert Cecil;

1614 impositions help to cause chaos in the 'Addled Parliament'.

ence. As the lawyer James Whitelocke pointed out 'Considering the greatest use they make of assembling Parliaments, which is the supply of money', there was reason to believe that Parliament would be giving up their most valuable weapon in obtaining redress of any grievances.

c) The King and his Court

While most of these difficulties were unavoidable, and caused as much by the reluctance of MPs to face reality as by government errors, they were compounded by the behaviour of James himself. He significantly overestimated the wealth of his new kingdom, and was consistently overgenerous towards his friends and favourites, to the extent of being financially irresponsible. Complaints that he exclusively favoured his Scottish cronies were not entirely fair. James was careful to distribute patronage and presents across all factions, although he was particularly generous to some of his Scottish friends. In 1606, when Parliament granted three subsidies to settle his debts, James promptly gave £44,000 to three Scottish friends. In 1611 he gave away £90,688, with £67,498 of it going to eleven Scotsmen.

Parliamentary resentment of this extravagance was increased by the King's lifestyle and the behaviour of many of his courtiers. The nature of these is illustrated by the examples portrayed in the Profile on the Court of King James. James's love of hunting, his preference for the company of handsome young men, and his excessive eating and drinking set a tone which degenerated into corruption and scandal. Even efficient ministers like Cecil (Earl of Salisbury) lined their own pockets from the proceeds of government, and the behaviour of the Howards after Cecil's death in 1612 amounted to embezzlement. James's homosexual relationships and the Overbury scandal of 1616 showed a Court guilty of sexual licence and murder – and the political nation found it doubly insulting when the King asked them to pay for it. Historians' judgements of James and his financial management have varied from total condemnation to the argument that his extravagances were relatively insignificant compared to the underlying financial problems. His behaviour and habits undoubtedly added to the problem and increased its political effects, but there were fundamental difficulties that went beyond individual responsibility.

d) The Difficulties of Reform

The basic problem lay in the system of patronage by which the King was expected to reward those who served him. Most offices in government were unpaid, and it was normal for ministers and

ISSUE
What structural problems stood in the way of reform?

THE COURT OF KING JAMES: CORRUPTION AND SCANDAL

The more self-respecting of the Lords preferred the retirement of their mansions. . .to Court masques [plays] in which ladies were too drunk to perform their parts, divorce cases and adulteries, and the whisper, scarcely hushed, of scandals yet more vile.

According to the historian G.M. Trevelyan, in England under the Stuarts, 1904

There were numerous complaints about the general tone of James's Court, and the drunkenness and gluttony practised by the King and many courtiers. The King was addicted to hunting and this gave him the occasion to enjoy young male company, of which he was equally fond. His open affection towards certain favourites raised questions as to whether he was actively homosexual. Despite a marriage and large family, he clearly had homosexual tendencies, although it is less clear that he indulged them physically. The more established nobility particularly resented the power and wealth given to the favourites, who were placed above them in influence and status.

The first of these favourites was Robert Carr, a young Scot whom James created Earl of Somerset. In 1613 Carr fell in love with Frances Howard, then Countess of Essex, and a divorce was hastily arranged on the grounds that the Earl of Essex was impotent. This was probably untrue, but the Howards were anxious to secure a marriage with the King's favourite. The marriage led to a huge scandal in 1616, when Carr and his wife were found guilty of involvement in the murder of his secretary, Sir Thomas Overbury, and imprisoned in the Tower. They were later pardoned by James, but were banished from Court.

Carr was replaced in James's affections by the young George Villiers (later to become the Duke of Buckingham), who had been introduced to the Court by a rival faction in 1613. By 1618 he had taken control of royal patronage. The Howards therefore introduced a handsome rival, William Monson to the King's circle, provoking Buckingham to destroy them. With plentiful evidence collected by his protégé, Lionel Cranfield, he brought charges of corruption against the Earls of Nottingham and Suffolk, securing their dismissal from office and Suffolk's trial in 1619. Buckingham was and remained supreme.

Portrait of Frances Howard, painted by William Larkin (National Portrait Gallery, London).

Portrait of Charles Howard, painted by Daniel Mytens, 1620 (National Maritime Museum, Greenwich).

advisers to be rewarded by the grant of pensions or, for example, the right to collect fines and payments related to particular government courts and departments. Hence there was little distinction between a valid payment for work carried out, and a simple gift to a friend or favourite. The system also encouraged courtiers to take gifts and bribes for providing access to the King or pleading an individual's case – and there was a fine distinction between such customary practices and outright corruption. While Cecil grew rich by staying just on the right side of it, Lord Chancellor Bacon threw away an equally promising career by straying over it. In 1621 he was impeached (see pages 41–3) by the Commons for taking bribes, and although pardoned by the King, he was dismissed from office, fined £40,000, and banned from sitting in Parliament.

The nature of these problems can be demonstrated by considering the attempts to reform the King's finances undertaken by Lionel Cranfield. In 1618 he became Master of the Court of Wards, and later Lord Treasurer and Chancellor of the Exchequer. He established a series of interlocking commissions to examine royal finances, and by 1620 he had reduced the King's household expenses by over 50 per cent. By 1621 it seemed that King, courtiers and MPs were at last cooperating to deal with the government's problems. However, this was an illusion. Cranfield did make some difference, but he had risen to power through the influence of Buckingham, the King's personal favourite and a product of the very factional rivalry and corruption that lay at the heart of the problems. At least part of Buckingham's enthusiasm for reform lay in the fact that he could use it to bring about the downfall of his rivals, the Howards. By 1620 he had taken control of the whole system of royal patronage, relieving James of the burden of making appointments, and using it to reinforce his own power as well as to line the pockets of his large and needy family. While he encouraged Cranfield's efforts, he never allowed the new financial restraints to extend to himself, and the prosecution of Bacon in 1621 was partly managed by Buckingham to deflect attacks on his own power. Even worse, Cranfield himself proved to be no different. In 1624, now Earl of Middlesex, he tried to extend his own influence at Buckingham's expense by introducing the King to his handsome nephew. Buckingham arranged his fall by encouraging members of Parliament and resentful courtiers to impeach him for bribery. Cranfield had certainly taken bribes as Master of the Wards, and he now paid the price.

Cranfield's failure illustrates the complexity of the Crown's financial problems, and the difficulty of reforming the system from within. It also indicates that the difficulties faced by James were more deep-seated than personal extravagance. It was not only that income was inadequate, it was also badly managed. Essentially, the English

KEY DATES: FAILURE OF FINANCIAL REFORM

1618 Lionel Cranfield becomes Master of the Court of Wards and begins to reorganise royal finances;

1620 expenses reduced by 50 per cent;

1621 impeachment of monopolists and of Lord Chancellor (Francis Bacon) for bribery;

1624 fall of Cranfield; Parliament passes an act to restrict the sale of monopolies.

GEORGE VILLIERS, DUKE OF BUCKINGHAM (1592–1628)

-Profile-

George Villiers, Duke of Buckingham, was born in 1592, and educated at Billesdon School, Leicestershire. His father, Sir George Villiers, was a member of the minor gentry of the county, but the family fortunes were transformed by his son's charm and good looks. He was introduced to the King in 1613, in an attempt to undermine the influence of Robert Carr and the Howards. In 1614 he was appointed Cup-bearer to the King, and knighted and made a Gentleman of the Bedchamber in 1615. There is little doubt that his relationship with the King had homosexual elements, the full extent of which are impossible to gauge. Buckingham undoubtedly exploited the King's sexual preferences but private letters written to James by his 'Steenie' reveal genuine affection. Certainly, Buckingham was charming and affable, no more ambitious and somewhat less vicious than other royal favourites.

From 1615 his rise in status was rapid. He became Viscount Villiers in 1616, Earl of Buckingham in 1617, Marquess in 1618 and Duke of Buckingham in 1623. His rapid rise and the manner of his influence incensed the more established nobility, and his control of offices, selling of titles and creation of monopolies caused bitter resentment. Attempts to undermine him, however, were unsuccessful, as Cranfield discovered. He was skilled in the factional politics of the court, and although he relieved the King of some of the burdens of government, he personified much that was wrong with the political system. Essentially, he was able to manipulate royal patronage in the interests of himself and a large number of needy relatives.

Nevertheless, his influence on affairs of state was limited, and James remained in control of key policies. It was not until he became chief adviser to Charles I that his political influence proved disastrous. Initially disliked by the reserved and pious Charles, he was able to win his friendship during the visit to Madrid in 1623, and thereafter his political influence and significance increased. With a young and uncertain monarch, Buckingham was able to indulge his own pride and ambition, and embark on an aggressive foreign policy that England could ill afford. While he was capable, and even gifted, in controlling and manipulating Court rivalries and factions, he lacked statesmanship and had no political vision to pursue. The wars against Spain and France in which he embroiled England from 1624–27 had no clear purpose and were inefficiently managed.

In 1628 he was described by MPs as the 'cause of all our miseries', but it has to be said that Buckingham's responsibility for England's troubles was shared with a monarch who identified totally with his favourite's decisions and protected him at the cost of his own relationship with Parliament. When Buckingham was assassinated at Portsmouth in 1628, by an ex-army officer named John Felton, Charles wept alone while his people celebrated.

Spain, but tried to increase his impact, and his value as an ally, by making preparations for war as an alternative strategy. In 1621 he summoned a Parliament, and asked for money to finance intervention in Europe. Aware of the dangers of inflaming an already volatile fear of Catholicism, he stressed the need to prepare for war to secure peace, and redoubled his diplomatic efforts. At first it appeared that his strategy might be successful. Faced with a depression in trade caused by war in Europe, MPs had no wish to incur unnecessary expense. Nevertheless, they voted two subsidies, and then turned their attention to waste, extravagance and corruption at Court (see pages 36–8).

This was not directed at the King – in fact many of the attacks were orchestrated by members of the Lords and Court factions anxious to weaken rivals, especially the Duke of Buckingham. By allowing the Commons to impeach the Lord Chancellor, Sir Francis Bacon, for taking bribes, the Duke survived, and the session ended quietly. In November 1621, when members reassembled, they were directed once again to consider the need for war finance; many MPs did have strong Protestant views and in December they petitioned the King to enter the war against the Habsburgs. At this point, several MPs raised the issue of what kind of war should be fought. The relief of James's daughter and the reconquest of the Palatinate would require a land war and the equipping of an army. Many members were aware of the expense involved, and were equally aware that Spanish strength came from her possessions in South America and the flow of silver from her colonies. To them, it made more sense to consider a naval war, with its echoes of Elizabethan glory and possible financial windfalls from Spanish treasure, and they said so in a Commons' debate.

EUROPE DURING THE THIRTY YEARS' WAR

The map overleaf shows the complicated arrangement of states in central Europe that led to the eruption of war in 1618. The Thirty Years' War was the final stage of the two great rivalries that dominated Europe throughout the sixteenth century – between Catholic and Protestant, and between French and Habsburg monarchies. The Habsburg family controlled Spain and Belgium as well as parts of Italy and Austria, thereby surrounding France. They had also established a tradition of electing Habsburgs to be Holy Roman Emperor, with nominal lordship over the many petty princes who ruled Germany, and to be King of Bohemia (now the Czech Republic). The Habsburgs were devoutly Catholic, and supported the aggressive Catholicism of the Counter-Reformation (see pages 8–9).

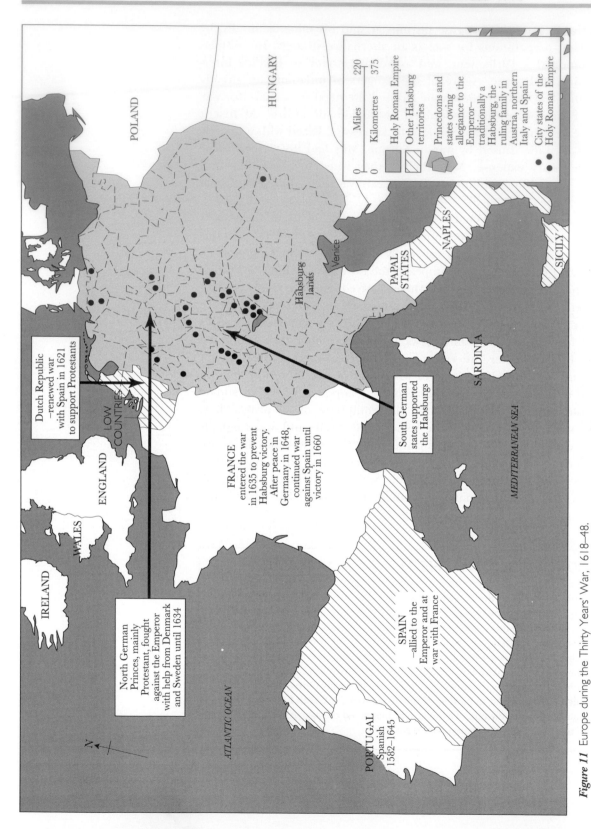

Figure 11 Europe during the Thirty Years' War, 1618–48.

Dutch Republic
–renewed war
with Spain in 1621
to support Protestants

North German
Princes, mainly
Protestant, fought
against the Emperor
with help from Denmark
and Sweden until 1634

South German
states supported
the Habsburgs

FRANCE
entered the war
in 1635 to prevent
Habsburg victory.
After peace in
Germany in 1648,
continued war
against Spain until
victory in 1660

SPAIN
–allied to the
Emperor and at
war with France

PORTUGAL
Spanish
1582–1645

IRELAND

WALES

ENGLAND

ATLANTIC OCEAN

LOW
COUNTRIES

POLAND

HUNGARY

Habsburg
lands

Venice

PAPAL
STATES

NAPLES

SICILY

SARDINIA

MEDITERRANEAN SEA

N

Miles   220
Kilometres   375
0
0

Holy Roman Empire

Other Habsburg
territories

Princedoms and
states owing
allegiance to the
Emperor–
traditionally a
Habsburg, the
ruling family in
Austria, northern
Italy and Spain

City states of the
Holy Roman Empire

b) War, Religion and Parliaments

From James's point of view, this debate overstepped the bounds of parliamentary privilege, and strayed into the formulation of policy, which was the prerogative of the King. Angrily, he reminded members of the limits of their privilege of free speech (see page 24 for Elizabeth's definition of this) and that it came by the will of the sovereign. Provoked in their turn, the Commons set out a Protestation, asserting that the rights of Parliament and the liberties of the subject 'are the ancient and undoubted birthright and inheritance of the subjects of England' – which James tore out of the Commons Journal. In essence, the quarrel was the same as that of 1604, turning on the issue of whether Parliament's privileges existed by right or by gift of the monarch.

In this case, however, MPs were claiming the right to debate royal policy on foreign affairs and religion. Whatever the rights of free speech, these areas of policy came within the King's recognised prerogatives, and the Commons were encroaching on royal powers. James had every right to object, although whether his reaction was politically wise is more debatable. To have allowed the debate would have set a dangerous precedent, but once the issue moved on to parliamentary privileges, there was little chance of agreement. It was clear to James that there would be no grant of taxes, and there had been some attacks on both his policy and his favourite. Accordingly, he dissolved the Parliament and continued his diplomatic pursuit of Spanish friendship and a marriage for his son.

The legacy of the Parliament of 1621 was complex. While his foreign policy had made little progress, the King had defended his prerogative with some success. Nevertheless, there were some worrying signs and precedents. The Commons had been able to bring some government office-holders to account, using the mechanism of impeachment. These proceedings had arisen from rivalries among government factions, but there was no guarantee that the Court or the Lords would always be able to orchestrate their use. The quarrel over privilege and prerogative had sharpened existing fears. Above all, the airing of concerns about foreign policy had alerted Protestant opinion to the Catholic threat and raised concerns about the King's attitude towards Spain. Members had expressed concern about a Catholic marriage, and the concessions that would be required by Spain. The Parliament of 1621 had not precipitated a crisis, but the monarch might well find that it had increased the capacity of later assemblies to do so.

ACTIVITY

'If the papists once attain a connivance, they will press for a toleration; from thence to an equality; from an equality to a superiority; from a superiority to an extirpation of all contrary religions.' (From the Commons Protestation of 1621)

1. What was a Papist?
2. What does the quote reveal about English attitudes towards the Catholic Church?
3. Use your knowledge of the sixteenth and seventeenth century background to explain why these attitudes were widespread.
4. How did they affect relations between King and Parliament?

ISSUE

How important were personalities and individuals in the growth of tension between King and Parliament?

KEY DATES: FOREIGN POLICY

1618 Elector Palatine becomes King of Bohemia;
1621 defeated by Emperor Ferdinand at the Battle of White Mountain and driven from his lands; English Parliament voted subsidies for war;
1623 Charles and Buckingham visit Spain;
1624 war with Spain and marriage of Charles and Henrietta Maria;
1626 failure at Cadiz; war with France;
1627 failure at La Rochelle;
1628 Buckingham assassinated;
1629 peace negotiations bring war to an end.

---

4 Buckingham and Charles, 1623–8

The likelihood of crisis was also increased by the fact that control of affairs was slipping from James to Buckingham and Prince Charles. As the King grew older, and his health deteriorated, he was more content to leave the running of government to his favourite, although he retained control of political strategy. In 1623, however, his strategy was wrecked by the actions of Charles and Buckingham in undertaking a secret visit to Spain to try to secure the proposed marriage. Their motives are not entirely clear – for Charles it was probably a romantic gesture prompted by naivety and youth, for Buckingham the chance to win the favour of the next King. Whatever their reasons, their secret departure and unannounced arrival in Spain wrecked James's plans. His grand diplomatic strategy was reduced to a need to ensure the safety of his son. For Charles and Buckingham, it was a humiliation; the Spanish stalled on marriage negotiations, and then rejected the match. By 1624 they had returned to England, determined on revenge.

Under pressure from Charles and Buckingham, James summoned Parliament to ask for money to finance a war with Spain. His reservations were set aside by an anti-Catholic Parliament in alliance with his favourite and his heir. The King, who was weakened by age and ill-health, was powerless to resist. In order to secure their war, Charles and Buckingham agreed to the naval strategy favoured by MPs but, nevertheless, paid an army to serve in the Palatinate under the command of German mercenary, Count Mansfeld. This deception and the disastrous failure of the expedition infuriated Parliament when it reassembled in 1625, but it was Charles who reaped the bitter harvest, since James had died in March. The brief alliance of Charles, Buckingham and the House of Commons collapsed with a

CHARLES I (1600–49)

The new King, portrayed here by Van Dyck, was the second son of James, a fact that had considerable influence on the events of his reign. Until the age of twelve he had lived in the shadow of his older and more confident brother, Henry. Henry had been physically strong, outgoing, and aggressively Protestant – exactly the kind of heir to the throne that England desired. Until he died of a fever in 1612, little attention had been paid to the small, sickly and reticent Charles. He had therefore grown up to be shy and unable to communicate easily, as well as sensitive and lacking confidence in his own abilities. In fact, he was intelligent and perceptive in certain matters – he became, for example, a generous and discerning patron of artists and architects, and acquired a considerable collection of fine work, which was housed in Whitehall and at Windsor.

This early childhood left its mark on Charles's behaviour as King. He tended to maintain a protective reserve and to place great emphasis on orderly formality. This was reflected in the procedures and rules that he adopted for his Court – immorality was frowned upon, rank and nobility were carefully preserved, and the royal family's privacy respected. Charles had been greatly impressed by the formality of the Spanish Court during his visit in 1623, and sought to emulate its dignity. The same preferences may have influenced his religious views. A devout and conscientious Anglican, he was undoubtedly Protestant in his beliefs, but his appreciation of the 'beauty of holiness' represented in rich decoration and elaborate rituals encouraged his sympathy for the High Church party and even respect for Catholic views. Unfortunately, none of these qualities were likely to endear him to his subjects.

His lack of confidence was also a problem. His response to opposition was to take refuge in the appearance of certainty and to view those who disagreed as motivated by malice. To a degree, his conscientious attention to duty made it more difficult to accept criticism. Perhaps most seriously, it also created a lifelong tendency to rely on the advice of those close to him, as the quote by Edward Hyde opposite illustrates.

Unfortunately the first of these was the Duke of Buckingham, closely followed by the equally determined and equally ill-informed Henrietta Maria.

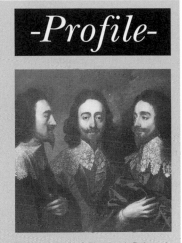

-Profile-

Three Faces of Charles I, Painted by Van Dyke in 1635.

'he will be found not only a prince of admirable virtue and piety, but of great parts of knowledge, wisdom and judgement; and that the most signal parts of his misfortunes proceeded chiefly from the modesty of his nature, which kept him from trusting himself enough, and made him believe that others discerned better, who were much inferior to him in those faculties; and so to depart from his own reason, to follow the opinions of more unskilful men, whose affections he believed to be unquestionable to his service...'

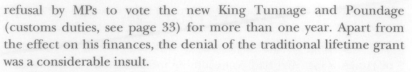

How does the personality of Charles I outlined in the profile on page 45, help to explain the influence of Buckingham and the problems that arose from it?

refusal by MPs to vote the new King Tunnage and Poundage (customs duties, see page 33) for more than one year. Apart from the effect on his finances, the denial of the traditional lifetime grant was a considerable insult.

The new reign therefore got off to a bad start, and it rapidly went downhill. Unlike James, Charles lacked confidence and experience in diplomacy, and relied upon the advice of Buckingham. Freed from the restraints imposed by James, the Duke embarked on an adventurous foreign policy designed to glorify himself and his King. Unfortunately his lack of planning, failure to attend to detail and unrealistic expectations ensured that it was a disaster. An unsuccessful naval expedition to Cadiz was followed by demands for Buckingham to be impeached, and in 1626 in order to save his friend Charles dissolved Parliament without receiving any financial supply. Worse was to follow. In 1624 Buckingham had negotiated a marriage for Charles with Henrietta Maria, the sister of the French King, promising that she would be permitted to practise her own Catholic religion, and that English ships would help to suppress a French Protestant rebellion in La Rochelle. MPs were furious, and became even more so when in 1626 Buckingham's inept diplomacy led to war with France, and an expedition sent in 1627 to help the Protestants in La Rochelle failed miserably because of inadequate planning.

ISSUE

Did Charles threaten the rights and liberties of his subjects?

5 Charles, Parliament, and the Rule of Law

a) The Forced Loan, 1626–7

As complaints about Buckingham mounted, Charles recognised that he would obtain no money from Parliament without sacrificing his friend but, on this, he would make no concession. It was not only a matter of personal loyalty; Charles was also infuriated by the attempt to call his chosen adviser to account in Parliament. Convinced of the need to govern according to his own views, he moved to obtain money by alternative measures. Not only did he continue to collect Tunnage and Poundage without parliamentary approval, he also demanded a **forced loan** to be collected by the JPs, and threatened that any who refused to lend the King money would be imprisoned or conscripted into the army. He was not the first monarch to demand such a loan, but he was the first to carry out his threats against those who refused. In 1627, five gentlemen, who came to be known as the Five Knights, challenged his right to imprison them.

After a good deal of pressure from the King, the judges reluctantly found in his favour. Charles then sought to have their judgement entered as a precedent for the future. While he believed that he was merely asserting his right to govern effectively, in practice he was denying the rule of law (see page 22) and laying a foundation for tyranny.

b) The Petition of Right, 1628

By 1628, Charles had provoked a constitutional crisis, which he lacked the means to handle. Still at war, and in desperate need of money, he was forced to call a new Parliament to ask for supply. Led by the experienced lawyer, Sir Edward Coke, the Commons put together a Petition of Right, which reversed the judgement in the Five Knights' Case and asked the King to declare that in future there would be no more forced loans, no imprisonment without trial, no more use of free lodgings (billeting) for soldiers in civilian households, or use of martial law against civilians. Five subsidies (see page 33, Income and Revenue) were voted, but would not proceed to the House of Lords until the King accepted the Petition. He had no choice but to agree.

The term Petition of Right was carefully chosen to convey the fact the Parliament were asking the King to help them – in this case to define the law – and also asserting a *right* rather than making a request. Hence it maintained an outward respect for the King while also avoiding any implication that such rights were dependent on his goodwill. By claiming that the rights already existed, and that the King was merely redefining the law to correct a mistake by the judges, the Petition avoided asking the King to admit a mistake while also ensuring that, since he was not granting the right to refuse a forced loan, he could not take it away. Once he accepted the Petition, its contents had the force of law.

At this point it was possible that the Petition of Right and the grant of money could provide the opportunity for reconciliation between King and Parliament, and the chances of this improved in August 1628, when Buckingham was assassinated (see the Profile on page 38). However, mistakes by both the King and the more volatile MPs destroyed the opportunity. When Parliament reassembled there were open celebrations of Buckingham's death, which angered the grief-stricken King. In turn, when Parliament began to prepare a bill to extend the King's right to collect Tunnage and Poundage, Charles denied that it was necessary, undermining Parliament's control of taxation. The most serious rift, however, was caused by growing concern about the King's religious views and his policies regarding the Church.

FORCED LOAN

A request from the King for a loan – interest-free and unlikely ever to be repaid – that could not safely be refused. Charles was not the first King to use such a device, and the judges in the Five Knights' Case agreed that he had the right to raise money in this way for the needs of government. There were two problems that created resentment: his need for money arose from his hasty dissolution of Parliament to save Buckingham, and he actually carried out his threat to imprison or conscript refusers.

PARLIAMENTARY CRISIS

1625 accession of Charles I;

1626 Parliament dissolved to prevent impeachment of Buckingham;

1626 –7 Forced Loan levied; King's right to imprison refusers defended by Arminian writers;

1627 Five Knights Case;

1628 Petition of Right presented; William Laud (Arminian) appointed Bishop of London; Buckingham assassinated

1629 King and Parliament quarrel over Arminian appointments and Tunnage and Poundage; leads to the Three Resolutions and Dissolution of Parliament.

ISSUES
How did Charles's religious views differ from James's?
How did his actions regarding the Church add to Parliament's fears?

ARMINIANISM

Jacob Arminius was a Dutch theologian who had challenged John Calvin's views on predestination and argued that God offered salvation to all. The English Arminians had developed a new interpretation of Anglican doctrine that placed the Church much closer to Catholic thinking. For many English Protestants both the Arminians' assertion that the Roman Catholic Church was not the work of the devil but a sister Church that had gone astray, and their emphasis on the authority of the clergy were equally dangerous and offensive.

c) Religion and the Church

The caution and tact used by James in making changes to the Church had resulted in years of relative harmony over its organisation and the role of bishops. While the Puritan ministers and their sympathisers had not given up hope of further reform, and had preached their message with enthusiasm, they had been able to accept the existing rules to the extent of at least partial conformity. Under the leadership of Archbishop Abbot, the majority of bishops used their powers of enforcement with care. Above all, the Calvinist beliefs held by the King himself, and the Calvinist interpretation of the Thirty-Nine Articles of faith accepted by the majority of bishops reassured Puritan minds and established an Anglican identity which most could accept.

This tactful approach came to an end with the accession of Charles I. Unlike his father, Charles placed order and uniformity above tact, and he was not prepared to proceed slowly. His personal beliefs were closest to those of the **Arminian** group, who had recently emerged within the Anglican Church. Their name is derived from the fact that, like Arminius, many of the group rejected the doctrine of predestination. However, the chief characteristic of the English Arminians was their emphasis on ritual and sacraments in place of preaching, and the enhanced role and status that they gave to the Church and the clergy in the individual's search for salvation (see Table 1). Because they regarded the Roman Catholic Church as misguided rather than evil, and respected the common heritage derived from the medieval Church, they traced the power and authority of the clergy back to Christ himself. They hoped that the next thing to happen would be for the King to use his power and authority to establish order, decency, and uniform practice throughout the Church of England.

To a man with Charles's love of beauty and sense of order, Arminian ideas had great appeal. Unfortunately, to many of his subjects both in and out of Parliament, they were uncomfortably close to Catholicism. Oblivious of the fears that he was generating, Charles embarked on a campaign to reform the Church according to his own vision. Where James had promoted and favoured men from all religious factions, Charles exclusively advanced the Arminians, who responded by supporting a heightened royal power. When they defended the King's behaviour over the forced loan of 1627, and argued that subjects had a duty to obey even an unjust King, they reinforced the fears of all those who believed that Catholicism, **absolute monarchy** and tyranny went hand in hand. In 1628 the Arminian leader, William Laud, became Bishop of London. By 1629 there were many who feared that Charles intended to restore

	Puritan view	Anglican	Arminian view	Catholic
Faith and Salvation	Salvation gained as a gift from God to those who were predestined to be saved. Evidence of predestination was the willingness to accept discipline and seek a godly life.	Salvation by faith alone.	The gift of salvation was open to all who would seek it through a true Church. God offers salvation to all – mankind is free to accept or reject it.	Salvation for all but only through the Catholic faith.
Role of the Church and Priesthood	To guide and educate according to the rules laid down in the Bible. The chief function of the minister is to preach God's Word, to allow souls to find their way to Him. Ministers also apply discipline to support the saints and control the sinners.	The Church has authority to guide people to salvation.	The Church guides through a priesthood which has special powers and status. Their authority is symbolised by robes and ceremonies. There is a place for preaching, but teaching through set prayers and rituals is as important.	The Catholic Church and its rituals provide the path to God. Taking part offers salvation.
Ritual and Preaching	Preaching and private prayer, Bible study and reading are the key to salvation. Sacraments like communion are symbolic only. Ritual distracts the ignorant from true religion and creates superstition and idolatry.	There is a place for some ritual to symbolise aspects of faith – for example Holy Communion.	Ritual creates reverence and brings the ignorant to God. If it is beautiful in itself, it is a form of worship. Ritual is essential to promote order and decency.	Ritual is part of salvation – we are saved by our actions and works, such as taking part in a ritual.

Table 1 The religious divide – Arminian and Puritan.

	Puritan view	Anglican	Arminian view	Catholic
Role and Power of Bishops	Bishops have no special power. The parish minister is the true leader of the congregation, and the best organisation would be with committees of ministers, advised by bishops if desired.	Bishops have authority to rule the Church and represent the King.	Bishops have a special place and authority, passed down from Christ himself through St Peter and the medieval Church. They receive power to enforce rules from the King.	Bishops have special authority from Christ passed through the Pope
Attitude to Catholics	Catholicism is evil: the devil seeking to corrupt true faith. The Pope is Antichrist, the devil himself.	Catholics threaten true faith; but many of their errors are not a threat to salvation.	Catholicism represents the early Church, misled by error. It is a sister Church, like those set up by Calvin and Luther, and should be treated as such. There need be no Protestant identity which shuts out Catholics.	The true Church.
Obedience to authority	Obedience should be given to those in authority unless they threaten God's cause and true religion.	Obedience should be given to higher authority except on a few matters vital to salvation.	Obedience to authority in Church and state should be total. If, on rare occasion, conscience makes it necessary to disobey, the subject should surrender to authority and accept punishment.	The authority of the Pope is from God – the Pope is therefore infallible and obedience is essential.

Table 1 Continued.

Catholicism and establish an absolute monarchy in England; or that if he did not, he was being led in that direction by his advisers and his Catholic Queen.

The result was another stormy session of Parliament in 1629, which the frustrated King decided to prorogue (suspend). Fearing that they would have little opportunity to protest in future, a group of MPs ignored the summons to disperse, held the Speaker in his chair to keep the House of Commons in session, and passed Three Resolutions against the growth of Arminianism, the levying of Tunnage and Poundage, and the actions of those who paid it. Angered by such open defiance, Charles dissolved Parliament, and declared that he would not call another until his subjects should 'see more clearly into our intentions and actions' and have 'a better understanding of us and themselves'. What this represented was an open breach between King and Parliament, and a significant breakdown within the system of government.

▼ Working on the Origins of Conflict

The activities within the text were designed to allow you to collect information on the early years of James I and to establish an awareness of the underlying problems facing the monarchy. From 1618 those problems increased because of three new elements in the situation:

1. The outbreak of the Thirty Years' War in Europe
2. The influence of the Duke of Buckingham
3. The personality and actions of Charles I

You should complete your note-making using these headings and the issue boxes.

Making notes is important in providing you with your basic knowledge and understanding, but investigating change and causation requires you to go further than that and begin to analyse the nature and significance of events more deeply. It seems clear that the 1620s marked a new stage in the relationship between King and Parliament. To complete your work on the Origins of Conflict, you need to investigate what was involved in this and how it led to an open breach in 1629. The exercises which follow are designed to help you do so.

ABSOLUTE MONARCHY

A monarchy in which the king has absolute, or complete power and his will and decisions alone make the law. Fear of absolutism was increasing at this time, because the French and Spanish monarchies were moving in this direction by destroying the independence and in some cases even the existence of local assemblies and parliaments. Because these were Catholic monarchs, and the Catholic Church was also organised in this way – the Pope had been declared to be infallible by the Council of Trent – the association of Catholicism, absolutism and tyranny in English minds was deeply entrenched.

Summary of Events and Developments, 1603–29

Date	King and Parliament Finance and Financial Reform	Religion and Foreign Policy
1603	James becomes King	Millenary Petition presented to James by Puritans
1604	Peace with Spain; disputed election leads to quarrel in Parliament and Commons 'Apology'	Hampton Court conference; appointment of Bancroft as Archbishop of Canterbury marks attack on Puritan ministers
1605	Debates over union with Scotland lead to tension and failure of James's plan in 1607	Gunpowder Plot
1606	Bates Case – judges approve the 'imposition' of new duties	
1608	New Book of Rates published	
1610	Complaints in Parliament about 'impositions'; failure of Great Contract	
1611		Appointment of Abbot as Archbishop introduces a more moderate approach to Puritan concerns within the Church
1612	Death of Robert Cecil	
1614	Impositions help to cause chaos in the 'Addled Parliament'	
1618	Lionel Cranfield becomes Master of the Court of Wards and begins to reorganise royal finances	Elector Palatine becomes King of Bohemia
1620	Expenses reduced by 50 per cent	
1621	Impeachment of monopolists and of Lord Chancellor (Francis Bacon) for bribery	Elector Palatine defeated by Emperor Ferdinand and driven from his lands; English Parliament voted subsidies for war but quarrel over Parliament's right to discuss foreign policy leads to Commons Protestation
1623		Charles and Buckingham visit Spain
1624	Fall of Cranfield; Parliament passed an act to restrict the sale of monopolies	War with Spain and marriage of Charles and Henrietta Maria
1625	Accession of Charles I	
1626	Parliament dissolved to prevent impeachment of Buckingham; Forced Loan levied	Failure at Cadiz; war with France King's right to imprison those who refused the forced loan defended by Arminian writers
1627	Five Knights Case	Failure at La Rochelle
1628	Petition of Right presented; Buckingham assassinated	William Laud (Arminian) appointed Bishop of London
1629	King and Parliament quarrel over Arminian appointments and Tunnage and Poundage; leads to the Three Resolutions and Dissolution of Parliament	Peace negotiations bring wars to end

Answering Source-based Questions on the Origins of Conflict

Historians have different views about the nature and significance of the dissolution of Parliament in 1629, raising questions about both its causes and its effects. For some it was part of a steady deterioration of relations between King and Parliament, based on a clash of political ideologies and leading to the English Revolution. For others, it was an unnecessary breach, created by errors and misunderstandings, which led Charles to embark on a period of personal rule that proved ultimately disastrous. The sources here are intended to allow you to develop your own opinion on the issue. Source A provides an example of how to analyse and interpret a source. The questions provided will help you to analyse and interpret Sources B to I in order to decide:

▼ how far Charles's claims were accurate;
▼ why he might feel justified in making them;
▼ what were the main reasons for the breakdown of the relationship between King and Parliament in 1629.

The House hath of late years endeavoured to extend their privileges, by setting up general committees for religion, for courts of justice, for trade and the like ... so as, where in former times the Knights and Burgesses were wont to communicate to the House such business as they brought from the countries; now there are so many chairs erected, to make inquiry upon all sorts of men, where complaints of all sorts are entertained, to the unsufferable disturbance and scandal of justice and government .... In these innovations...their drift was to break, by this means, through all respects and ligaments of government, and to erect a universal over-swaying power to themselves, which belongs only to us, and not to them...

Source A From the Proclamation issued by Charles I after the Dissolution of Parliament, March 1629.

Analysis and interpretation

If we break down what Charles is saying here, he seems to be making three main points.

1. He starts by saying that the House (we can infer that he means 'of Commons') has tried to 'extend its privileges'.
2. They have done this by setting up committees to inquire into all sorts of matters, and his use of phrases like 'unsufferable disturbance' and 'scandal of justice' makes it clear that he does not approve.

3. He suggests that these activities are new, claiming that Parliaments in the past 'were wont' to concentrate on matters related to their own localities.

His final sentence renews and extends point 1 to summarise the crucial accusation – they are trying to gather for themselves a 'universal over-swaying power' in government, which rightly belongs to the monarch.

Source B From the Commons *Apology* of 1604.

> All experience shows that the prerogatives of princes may easily, and do daily, grow [but] the privileges of the subject are for the most part, at an everlasting stand. They may be by good providence and care preserved, but once being lost are not recovered but with much disquiet.

Source C From the Commons *Protestation* of 18 December, 1621

1. What reasons are given in Sources B and C for Parliament's concern with its privileges? (analysis)
2. Do they suggest that parliaments were seeking to extend their powers? (interpretation in context).

> That the liberties, franchises, privileges and jurisdictions of Parliament are the ancient and undoubted birthright and inheritance of the subjects of England; and that the arduous and urgent affairs concerning the King, State and defence of the realm and of the Church of England, are proper subjects and matter of counsel and debate in Parliament; and that in the handling and proceeding of those businesses every member of the House of Parliament hath, and of right ought to have, freedom of speech to propound, treat, reason and bring to conclusion the same. . .

Source D From the Royal Proclamation issued 7 October 1626

3. What reasons does Charles give for levying the forced loan in Source D? (analysis)
4. Use your knowledge of the events of 1626 to assess how far his claims were accurate. (interpretation and evaluation).

> With the advice of our Privy Council, We have resolved, for the necessary defence of our Honour, our religion and Kingdoms, to require the aid of our loving subjects in that way of loan . . .. [there being] no other possible and present course to be taken, nor this to be avoided, if we as a King shall maintain the cause and party of religion, preserve our own honour, defend our people, secure our Kingdoms and support our allies, all of which we are tied to do by that bond of sovereignty, which under God we bear over you.

They made some question whether this course now holden were not against law, and they conceived it was not grounded upon good precedent and they feared future danger by such a precedent. They much insisted that the Parliamentary way of raising money was most equal and most indifferent . . . [and] so did produce good effects, making good law, redress of grievances if anything were amiss, pardons etc. And they did declare that the general opinion was that in a Parliamentary way every man would be willing to contribute to his ability.

Source E Reporting the reaction of the High Constables in Bedfordshire to the Forced Loan

5. What objections were raised against the forced loan in Source E? (analysis) Do they suggest that the ruling class was unwilling to cooperate with the King? (inference)

6. Do the attitudes shown in Source E restrict or threaten the King's power? (interpretation in context).

Whereas . . . we did . . . require the aid of our good and loving subjects of that county by lending unto us such competent sums of money as might enable us to provide for our own and their safeties and for defence of the true religion and our Kingdoms and dominions . . .. We understand that divers of them have obstinately refused to assist us . . .. thereby discovering their disaffection to their prince and county . . .. We think fit that such as neglect us and themselves shall serve in person for the defence of our Kingdoms . . . [and] authorise you forthwith to press or cause to be pressed. . .one hundred and fifty of these persons to serve on foot in our wars.

Source F From a letter sent by the King to the loan Commissioners for Gloucestershire

7. What reasons does Charles give for his actions in Source F? Does the evidence in Sources D and E suggest that he was justified? (analysis, cross-reference, synthesis).

By the authority of Parliament holden in the five and twentieth year of the reign of King Edward the Third, it is declared and enacted, that from henceforth no person shall be compelled to make any loans to the King against his will, because such loans were against reason and the franchise of the land . . . Yet . . . your people have been. . .required to lend certain sums of money unto your Majesty, and. . .upon their refusal to do so. . .have been imprisoned, confined and sundry other ways molested. . .

And where also by the statute called 'The Great Charter of the Liberties of England' it is declared and enacted, that no freeman may be taken or imprisoned or [deprived] of his freeholds or liberties. . .or in any manner destroyed but by the lawful judgement of his peers, or by the law of the land. . ., nevertheless. . . divers [some] of your subjects have of late been imprisoned without any cause showed. . .but that they were detained by your Majesty's special command.

Source G From The Petition of Right, 1628

8. What complaints are made in Source G? (analysis)

9. Do the similarities and differences between Source G, and Sources B and C suggest that Parliament's aims and attitudes had changed in the 1620s? (analysis and cross-reference, inference/interpretation)

10. How far does the evidence in these sources suggest that confrontation between King and Parliament was unavoidable? (synthesis and interpretation).

Answering Extended Writing and Essay Questions

Source-based exercises of this type are very useful in allowing you to focus on particular aspects of a situation and analyse particular elements in depth. However, in order to construct overall explanations of what happened and why, it is necessary to take a wider view and to place the evidence gained from source analysis in a wider context. The approach exemplified in the exercise below is to analyse 'what happened' to establish certain *causal factors*. These are patterns or sets of events, actions and ideas that share a common theme or function in causing something to happen. In this case the 'something' is the breach between King and Parliament that came to a head in 1629, and the factors suggested here are derived from the events of the 1620s. The material that you have read in this chapter shows that, while there were tensions between King and Parliament in the reign of James I, the early years of Charles I saw an increase in the pace and intensity of conflict. This appears to arise from a number of factors – the role of Buckingham and financial problems against a background of war and religious tension; and the personality and actions of Charles, raising concerns about the role of Parliament and the rule of law. Once you have identified the factors, however, you have to explain what they involved and how they worked together to cause the outcome that you are explaining – the breakdown of the relationship between King and Parliament. If you learn these techniques and practise their application, it will help you greatly in planning essays and dealing with issues related to causation. In this case the factors have been identified for you – your task is to analyse and explain how they worked together.

Use the questions to help you consider and explain the role and interaction of the factors listed above in creating an open breach between King and Parliament in 1629.

1. In what ways did Buckingham, as an individual, create problems?
2. How did the financial weakness of the Crown affect:
   (a) the calling and attitude of Parliament?
   (b) the actions of Charles I?
3. List the actions of Charles that showed him to be stubborn, high-handed, or authoritarian.
4. Why did MPs interpret his actions as a threat to Parliament and the rule of law?
5. Explain how the interaction of the personalities of Charles and Buckingham with the financial problems of the Crown created a political crisis, symbolised by the Petition of Right.

6. What factors prevented the Petition of Right and the removal of Buckingham from leading to reconciliation?
7. In what ways were political and religious problems connected?
8. How important was the personality of Charles I in bringing them together?
9. To what extent was the crisis caused by Charles I?

Further Reading

Books in the Access to History Series

The Early Stuarts by Katherine Brice in the Access to History series provides a sensible next stage of reading. The Introduction sets out key themes and explains some of the historical debates related to the period. The chapters that follow explore many of the issues addressed here in greater depth and detail.

General

The best in-depth examination of the period is offered in Derek Hirst's *Authority and Conflict*. There are a number of useful essays in the *Oxford Illustrated History of Tudor and Stuart Britain*; of particular value are Kevin Sharpe's 'Stuart Monarchy and Political Culture', Conrad Russell's 'The Reformation and the Creation of the Church of England', and the relevant sections of 'Politics in an Age of Peace and War, 1570–1630' by Christopher Haigh. Once you have gained an understanding of the period, you will be able to pick out essays that interest you from Conrad Russell's *The Causes of the English Civil War*, and the essays from different contributors in *The Origins of the English Civil War*, ed. Russell. Robin Clifton's 'Fear of Popery' is particularly helpful and accessible. There are a number of interesting biographies of James I and Charles I, but the best starting point for an analysis of their different personalities and impact is Barry Coward's *Stuart England, 1603–1714;* chapters 5 and 6. Angela Anderson's *Charles I* (Longman 1998) also has chapters on the character and personality of Charles, and his early conflicts with Parliament.

CHAPTER 3

THE DEVELOPMENT OF THE CRISIS, 1629–40

KEY ISSUE

Why did the crisis between King and Parliament come to a head in 1640?

WHIG AND REVISIONIST VIEWS

Debates about the causes of the Civil Wars have been long and fierce. By the early twentieth century the prevailing view was based on the writings of Whig historians, who saw Charles as a tyrant seeking to establish absolute monarchy, and saw Parliament as engaged in a conscious struggle for liberty. This was challenged by a number of Marxist historians (see page 101) who argued that economic factors and class rivalries were more important. More recently, some historians produced a revised explanation, and argued that the collapse of authority in the mid-seventeenth century was not caused by long-term problems, but by a clash of personalities and errors of judgement among both supporters and opponents of the King, and could well have been avoided.

POINTS TO CONSIDER

The nature of government between 1629 and 1640 provides important clues about how to interpret the crisis that faced the monarchy in 1640, and about how to understand its causes. The key issue debated by historians in recent years has been whether the crisis arose from deep-seated causes that made it likely, if not inevitable, or whether it was created by individual personalities and specific errors. However, you should remember that these explanations are not mutually exclusive. It is possible to define problems that created the possibility of a crisis, while arguing that individuals and their errors influenced its shape and timing. Whichever approach you consider, you will first need to work out what Charles was trying to do in the situation that faced him, and why his attempts to deal with it led to confrontation rather than agreed remedies.

1 The Personal Rule of Charles I

The dissolution of Parliament in 1629 initiated a period known as the Personal Rule, in which Charles governed without reference to Parliament. This was not, in itself, unusual enough to merit a special title. But the period from 1629 to 1640 was also personal government in that it appears to have reflected his particular view of what good government should be. The Proclamation of 1629 declared that he would summon no more parliaments until his subjects had a better understanding of what he sought to do. This suggests that, in the years that followed, he sought to put his ideas into practice.

Historians have interpreted Charles's actions in this period in different ways. For the Whig historians, his personal rule was an Eleven Years' Tyranny, part of a conscious attempt to establish absolute monarchy in England. If this was the case, then he was remarkably unsuccessful, but his failure should not be presumed inevitable. Recent research by the revisionist historians who challenged the Whig interpretation emphasises how effectively Charles governed until 1637, when he tried to extend his reforms to his more remote kingdom of Scotland. However, if he was not acting like a tyrant, if he only sought to reform and improve his government, why should his plans have created such opposition? The answers to these questions may lie in the nature and effectiveness of government in the years of Personal Rule.

2 The King's Government, 1629–37

ISSUE
Did the dissolution of Parliament create opposition?

a) Reactions to the Dissolution

In 1629 there was very little reaction or resistance to the dissolution of Parliament. A brief refusal by merchants to pay Tunnage and Poundage collapsed when one of them, Richard Chambers, was imprisoned. Nine MPs were arrested for their part in forcing the Speaker to sit after the King had ended the session, but five were quickly released. The three ringleaders, Denzil Holles, Benjamin Valentine, and Sir John Eliot, were held in prison and brought to trial in 1630. There was a measure of vindictiveness in Charles's determination to keep them under lock and key; in 1629–30 they were shifted from prison to prison in order to evade writs of **Habeas Corpus** that would have secured their release until trial. Thereafter, they were imprisoned in the Tower of London, but Holles and Valentine were released within weeks when they apologised to the King. Only Eliot, who refused to do likewise, remained in prison, to die two years later of a fever. His death later provided Parliament's propagandists with a martyr for the cause of liberty, but at the time few remarked on it.

At the time the dissolution of 1629 was considered less significant than it later appeared. Although the events that led up to it, and Charles's declaration that he would call no more parliaments until his subjects had a better understanding of him, indicated that the circumstances were exceptional, it was not unusual for long periods to elapse between parliaments. James had allowed seven years between the parliaments of 1614 and 1621. Parliaments were not an essential part of daily goverment, and it was mainly the financial problems experienced by the Crown in this period, that had led to more frequent sittings. If Charles could finance his government by other means, then he had no need of Parliament.

This was the consideration that worried those who disliked Charles's ideas about reform and about what constituted good government. If he could collect customs duties and other dues without hindrance, and govern without recourse to Parliament, they had no means of preventing the changes that he wished to make.

HABEAS CORPUS
A Latin phrase, meaning 'to have the body'. A writ of Habeas Corpus issued by a court was the standard way of preventing someone from being held in prison indefinitely, without being properly charged and brought to trial. It was regarded as a vital safeguard for personal liberty against the government's power.

The King's prerogatives gave him the right, and the power, to mould government in both Church and State according to his own preferences. In 1629 there was no doubt that those who disliked his preferences had gone too far in openly defying his wishes. Now they could do little but watch and wait.

ISSUE
How personal was the Personal Rule?

b) Organisation and Administration

The centre of administration was the Privy Council, which included key officials and the King's chosen advisers. As well as providing central administration, the Privy Council controlled local government through the choice of Lords Lieutenant in the counties and Justices of the Peace in each locality. In addition, individual privy councillors staffed the prerogative courts of Star Chamber and Chancery, and the regional Councils of the North and the Welsh Marches (see page 19). The effectiveness of administration and the extent of royal control depended entirely on how this structure was used, how much attention the King and his councillors gave to it, and how determinedly they used their powers to obtain local cooperation.

In this area, Charles was generally conscientious. Unlike his father, who had tended to leave business to his advisers, he attended meetings regularly, checked that his decisions were understood and ensured that they were put into effect. When he chose to delegate, he was ably supported by two key figures – Sir Thomas Wentworth (see page 79), and William Laud (see page 61), the Bishop of London and Archbishop of Canterbury from 1633. Both were conscientious and able administrators, whose concern for detail gave their policies the nickname of 'Thorough'. The work of Wentworth in the Council of the North and in Ireland ensured that royal authority was maintained in these outlying areas, while Laud controlled the Church and rapidly became the dominant figure on the Privy Council. His influence in secular, as well as religious affairs, is symbolised by the **Books of Orders** that were issued to local government from 1631.

It would appear, therefore, that as far as administration is concerned, Charles's government was highly effective. It was also, undeniably, Charles's government. After the death of Buckingham he never allowed any adviser to occupy the same place in his affections, moving closer instead to his wife, Henrietta Maria. Their marriage, after Buckingham's death, was remarkably stable and happy, and Charles enjoyed a close family life. In political terms, the Queen's influence was something of a liability, since she understood little of English government and society, and constantly reinforced Charles's tendency to be stubborn and high-handed. Even so, her influence

THE BOOKS OF ORDERS

These consisted of 314 books of instructions to JPs, detailing their duties in the collection of Poor Law rates, treatment of beggars, law enforcement, storage of grain, control of local markets, movement of goods and upkeep of roads and bridges. Under Laud's supervision, the issue of instructions was followed up to ensure that they were carried out.

According to the historian L.M. Hill, 'The poor were better treated and better cared for than ever before. Grain stocks were better administered and waste was curtailed. The quality of local government was markedly improved and little doubt lingered as to the Council's ability to cause the King's writ to run into local parts with considerable authority' (L.M. Hill, 'County government in Caroline England, 1625–40' in Conrad Russell (ed.) *The Origins of the English Civil War,*

WILLIAM LAUD (1573–1645)

-Profile-

Born in 1573, the son of a Reading clothier, Laud was educated at a Free School in Reading and later at Oxford University, which emphasises both his humble origins and his intellectual abilities. By entering the Church he was treading a well-worn path to advancement, but there is no reason to doubt the strength of his faith and commitment. Ordained as a priest in 1601, he served as chaplain to the Earl of Devonshire and Vicar of Stanford (Northants) before a sermon preached before King James in 1608 led to his appointment as a royal chaplain. Thereafter he rose through royal service to become Bishop of St David's (Wales) in 1621, and his close friendship with the Duke of Buckingham ensured him a measure of influence at Court.

Access to real power came in 1625 with the accession of Charles I, for whom Laud's ideas of order, dignity and authority in the Church had great appeal. Although Laud has been called an Arminian, he was less concerned with the details of doctrine than with Church organisation and respect for the appearance and form of worship. His famous phrase 'the beauty of holiness' expressed a desire to see churches that created an atmosphere of reverence and appealed to the emotions rather than the intellect. In pursuit of this he encouraged Charles to promote only Arminians, at the expense of Puritan thinkers, and his own career also flourished. He became Bishop of Bath and Wells in 1626, a Privy Councillor in 1627, Bishop of London (the largest diocese in England) in 1628, Chancellor of Oxford University in 1630, and Archbishop of Canterbury in 1633. In fact he had been acting as Charles's chief religious adviser for some time before this, since George Abbot, the existing Archbishop had found it necessary to live privately after he accidentally killed a gamekeeper while out hunting in 1624.

Throughout the 1630s Laud dominated the Privy Council through his access to the King, his personal attention to administrative matters and the increasing number of his protégés who were given appointments and offices. Although he was genuinely concerned to establish good order in both Church and State, his fussy attention to detail sometimes destroyed the shape of a strategy. In addition, his power was greatly resented by the traditional nobility. His humble origins, his use of the High Commission and the Star Chamber to enforce rules and silence opposition, and his interference in secular (non-religious) affairs made him a natural target for their frustrations and a popular target when Parliament reassembled in 1640. He was impeached in December 1640 and held in the Tower of London until his execution as a traitor to liberty and the Protestant religion in January 1645. In many ways he paid the price for serving his King too well.

was never as great, or as dangerous, as that of Buckingham. Other key advisers, like Wentworth and Laud were kept at arm's length. They were servants and political advisers to the King rather than friends; the architect of the Personal Rule was undoubtedly Charles himself, and it was his attitudes and personality that it reflected.

He was therefore responsible for both the strengths and weaknesses of administration in this period. The effectiveness of supervision was impressive, but it was also demanding and occasionally unpopular. After 1635, when JPs were also involved in the collection of Ship Money, the efficiency with which the Books of Orders were administered began to decline, and after 1637, when preparations for suppressing the Scottish rebellion were added to their burdens, complaints from harassed justices increased sharply. Similarly, the Council itself was unable to maintain such close supervision. While much could be achieved by attention to detail, there were limits to the time and energy of even the most dedicated of councillors. While Charles had brought determination and energy to the business of government, he made few structural changes and did little to alter the basic methods applied. As long as the system was reliant on unpaid amateurs at local level, its scope and effectiveness would be limited.

It would also need to be managed with a measure of political sensitivity, to take account of the concerns and interests of the ruling class whose support was essential. Government attempts to regulate wages and prices to help the poor, for example, were largely unsuccessful when the JPs who were required to set wage levels were also the employers who would have to pay them. While the prerogative courts and councils were respected for their speed and efficiency, they were also resented when they overrode local interests for the benefit of the King or his advisers. The Star Chamber was instructed to uphold the rights of the nobility, for example, and in 1632 awarded huge damages to the Earl of Suffolk because he had been forced to endure 'undeferential behaviour'. There was significant resentment in Yorkshire when Wentworth used his power as President of the Council of the North to further the interests of his family against a neighbour and rival, Sir John Savile. A number of Savile's friends and supporters would eventually support Parliament in the Civil War. It is no coincidence that the prerogative courts were abolished in 1641, and were not restored with the monarchy in 1660.

These resentments were further fuelled by the presence on the Privy Council of a number of bishops and protégés of Laud. While it was normal for the Archbishop to be a member, there was considerable vexation at his dominant role. In 1632 he was able to make his candidate, Francis Windebanke, Secretary of State, and in 1634 he persuaded the King to dismiss the Lord Chief Justice, Sir Robert Heath, because of his Puritan views. In 1635 when Lord Treasurer Weston died, he was replaced by the Bishop of London, William Juxon. The presence of a cleric in an important office of state was bitterly resented for two reasons. In the first place, the bishops were appointed by and dependent on the King, and tended to carry out his wishes without reservation. Lord Brooke expressed the views of many in 1642 when he pointed out that, unlike the landed nobility, bishops had no way of securing the future of their families except by retaining the King's favour, and therefore had no independence in their exercise of power. Secondly, since the Reformation it had become customary for the secular nobility and gentry to manage secular affairs, and the extension of clerical influence carried unfortunate associations with Catholic tradition.

It could therefore be argued that the administration of government in the period of the Personal Rule was in many ways highly effective, but that its effectiveness relied on personalities and a level of central supervision that irritated the political elite. The level of irritation was variable, and in itself would not have created a crisis, but it did add to other concerns. Perhaps most importantly, it did nothing to secure royal power in the long run. When the attention of the King and Council was distracted by more pressing problems after 1637, their control of the machinery of government proved fragile.

c) Finance and Taxation

ISSUE
Could the King finance his government?

The same characteristics can be seen in relation to financial affairs. The King's ability to govern without Parliament depended on securing an adequate income from his 'ordinary' revenue. This meant that he had to address the financial problems that had weakened his father and given Parliament a grip on affairs in the early years of his own reign. The box overleaf sets out the series of financial measures that were undertaken in order to increase revenue, which succeeded in balancing the current budget by 1637, although nothing had been done to settle debts arising from past difficulties. For the most part these gains were made by increasing the efficiency with which finances were managed, rather than by developing new strategies. Only Ship Money could be called a new tax, and even that was based upon a traditional right to aid naval defence.

Nevertheless, Ship Money was significant for several reasons. In the first place it did establish a new style of taxation. Where parliamentary subsidies were levied as a proportion of income and depended on individual assessments which were cumbersome to administer, Ship Money targets were set by the government as a global sum to be levied from the county as a whole. This placed the burden of collection on local justices and cost the government little or nothing. Secondly, in combination with rising customs revenues derived from growing trade, Ship Money offered a long-term prospect of real financial independence for the monarchy. Thirdly, and perhaps for that very reason, it does seem to have created serious and deep-seated opposition.

The Financial Measures of the Personal Rule.

▼ The 'Ordinary Revenue'.

Crown lands – 1630: Commission for Defective Titles set up to examine the titles and leases of Crown tenants. New rents imposed on those unable to prove reason why they should not pay more and fines levied for illegal enclosures of waste or common land, or for any encroachment on royal forests.

1634: Special judicial enquiry set up to detect and fine for any encroachment by farmers/landowners on royal forests.

1635: Second Commission for Defective Titles.

Feudal Duties – in feudal law all men owning freehold land worth £40 a year had to take a title of knighthood (for which they had to pay). In 1630 a commission was set up to contact all who had failed to do so, and arrange for compliance or a fine. This raised £165,000 by 1635. Other duties continued to be levied e.g. Court of Wards and Liveries produced £53,866 a year from 1631–5, and £75,088 a year from 1636–41.

Monopolies – sale of monopolies renewed through loopholes in the 1624 Act against them; exploited by courtiers as well as the King. Charles also sold the same monopolies to different groups e.g. licence to East India Company resold to rival group led by Sir William Courten. The worst example of fraudulent monopolies was the 'Popish Soap' scandal, in which a group of Catholic courtiers obtained a monopoly on soap by rigged demonstrations to prove that it washed whiter!

Justice – fines, court fees, increased by new offences such as proclamations restricting building around London. Buildings were allowed to stand on payment of fines from owners and fees from tradesmen.

▼ Customs Duties.

Tunnage and Poundage – declaration issued in 1630 of the King's right to levy customs duties despite parliamentary refusal of grant. Duties continued to be levied throughout the Personal Rule and their value rose significantly with increased trade.

New impositions – introduced by Elizabeth and James I were also levied as usual, producing £53,091 a year from 1631–5 and £119,583 a year from 1636–41.

▼ Direct Taxes – normally granted by parliament.

Tenths and Fifteenths – n/a

Subsidies – n/a

Poll Tax – n/a

Ship Money – levied from coastal areas in 1634, extended to inland areas in 1635; levied each year thereafter yielding an average of £107,000 a year from 1635–40. All this was done without consulting Parliament.

ISSUE

How serious was opposition to Ship money?

The extent of this opposition has been the subject of considerable debate among historians. The traditional Whig interpretation of the period portrayed Ship Money as an attempt by Charles to finance absolutism, which was recognised and resisted by the political elite in the country. Recent 'revisionists' have challenged these claims, in relation both to the purposes of the tax, and the opposition that it created. According to J.P. Kenyon, 'We are assured by Whig historians...that this aroused the most furious opposition in the provinces, and this "fact" is generally accepted'. In reality, 'there is scarcely any hard evidence for this, and what there is, is associated with predictable individuals like the Earl of Warwick and Lord Saye and Sele [the leaders of the Puritan faction]'. There is certainly some truth in this point – John Hampden, whose refusal to pay the tax in 1636 led to the famous test case of 1637, was a close friend and associate of both Lord Saye and Sele and the Earl of Bedford. His contacts extended through them to John Pym, and his family links covered many of the opposition leaders of 1640–42. Kenyon also points out that the tax was used to build up the navy, and that it was efficiently and successfully collected until after the outbreak of rebellion in Scotland distracted the attention of the Privy Council and many local officials. In 1635 the government received all but £5,000 of the £199,000 demanded, in 1636 all but £7,000 and in 1637, all but £18,000. Only in 1638, when the assessment had been reduced to £70,000 by the government, was there a serious shortfall.

Other historians, such as John Morrill, have supported some of these arguments, at least in relation to how successfully the tax was imposed. It would appear, therefore, that the Whig argument is fatally undermined, or at least shown to be significantly overstated. With regard to Charles's intentions, this may well also be the case. There is no doubt that Ship Money was initially used for naval defence, and its extension to the inland areas was not unreasonable. As with other aspects of Charles's financial policies, it can be seen as a natural and logical desire to maximise the Crown's resources. With regard to the extent of opposition, however, the revisionists' case is less convincing. As early as 1610, the electorate had shown a clear appreciation of the importance of controlling finance in protecting the rights, and indeed the existence of Parliament, in the reservations expressed regarding Salisbury's Great Contract. It would be surprising if they did not now appreciate the significance of the new tax. Certainly the contemporary sources available, including the relatively balanced views of the later royalist, Clarendon, suggest that many of the gentry were both aware of the implications of the tax and opposed to its continued existence in the absence of Parliament.

The issue can be explored further by considering some of the contemporary evidence related to it. The sources set out in the next Activity box are intended to represent a variety of opinions other than those whom Kenyon designated the 'Puritan faction' and to allow you to consider the effect of the tax on a wider section of the ruling elite. In that context, you will be able to make some judgements about the significance of any opposition that you find, as well as the reasons for it.

ACTIVITY

Questions on the sources

1. What does Clarendon (Source A) mean by the phrase 'a spring and magazine that should have no bottom' ? (interpretation)

2. How did this arrangement differ from the kind of taxes levied by parliamentary grants? (interpretation in context)

3. How did Berkeley (Source B) assert and justify the King's right to levy Ship Money? (analysis)

4. Upon what grounds did Croke (Source C) disagree with him? (analysis)

5. What evidence in Source D indicates that Ship Money was a serious cause for concern to the Kentish gentry? (interpretation)

6. Did any of those present accept the views of Judge Berkeley? How does Source F help to explain why? (cross-reference)

7. Why did others feel that 'every man ought to be heard'? How do you think that they wished this to be done? (interpretation in context)

8. Does the evidence in Sources D and F suggest that the Kentish gentry were more worried about the tax, or the way that it was being raised? (synthesis)

How serious was opposition to Ship Money?

Lastly, for a spring and magazine that should have no bottom, and for an everlasting supply of all occasions, a writ is framed in a form of law, and directed to the sheriff of every county of England, to provide a ship of war for the King's service, and to send it, amply provided and fitted, by such a day to such a place; and with that writ were sent to each sheriff instructions that, instead of a ship, he should levy upon his county such a sum of money, and return the same to the Treasurer of the Navy for his majesty's use, and from hence that tax had the denomination of Ship-Money, a word of lasting sound in the memory of this Kingdom.

Source A From Clarendon's *History of the Rebellion*.

Where Mr Holborne [one of Hampden's lawyers] supposed that in case the monarch of England should be inclined to exact from his subjects at his pleasure, he should be restrained, for that he could have nothing from them, but upon a common consent in Parliament.

He is utterly mistaken herein . . . . The law knows no such King-yoking policy. The law is, of itself, an old and trusty servant of the King's; it is his instrument or means which he useth to govern his people by . . .

Source B The Judgement of Sir Robert Berkeley, one of the majority who found for the King in Hampden's Case.

We are not to judge here according to conveniency or state policy, but according to the common law and custom of England we are to judge. We find [it] in our books, records or statutes; if we cannot find it to be law by these we cannot judge it to be law. . . .

The common law of England sets a freedom in the subjects in respect of their persons, and gives them a true property in their goods and estates; so that without their consent (that is to say their private actual consent or implicity in Parliament) it cannot be taken from them.

Source C The Judgement of Sir George Croke, one of the minority who found for Hampden.

When [Judge Weston] came to speak of ship-money, the audience which had before hearkened but with ordinary attention did then. . .listen with great diligence, and after the declaration made I did, in my conceit [belief] see a kind of dejection in their very looks. . . .

Some held . . . that the declaration the judges had made was fully to the point and by that the King had full right to impose it, and all concluded that if a Kingdom were in jeopardy it ought not [to] be lost for want of money . . . . Others argued far differingly . . . that in a judgement that not may, but doth, touch every man in so high a point, every man ought to be heard . . . .

*Source **D*** From an account of the reaction of JPs in Kent to the news that the judges had found against Hampden, in a Memorandum in the papers of Sir Roger Twysden.

It is notoriously known that pressure was borne with much more cheerfulness before the judgement for the King than ever it was after; men before pleasing themselves with doing somewhat for the King's service, as a testimony of their affection, which they were not bound to do. But when they heard this demanded in a court of law, as a right . . . and instead of giving were required to pay, and by a logic that left no man any thing which he might call his own; they no more looked upon it as the case of one man but the case of the Kingdom . . .

*Source **E*** From Clarendon, *History of the Rebellion.*

9. According to Clarendon (Source E), why did opposition to Ship Money increase after the Hampden case? (interpretation)
10. Use the evidence in these sources in the context of your own knowledge to argue for and against the claims by various historians that:
(a) opposition to Ship Money was widespread;
(b) opposition to Ship Money was limited to the 'Puritan faction';
(c) opposition to Ship Money developed gradually.
11. In conclusion, write a short response to the question, 'How serious was opposition to Ship Money?'

*Source **F*** Purpose-built ships like the *Sovereign of the Seas,* built with the proceeds of Ship Money did much to strengthen the navy and lay the foundations of Britain's naval power. In the long run this was essential to the growth of trade and prosperity.

ISSUE
How did Charles and Laud try to improve the condition of the Church?

CATECHISM

The Catechism provided an outline of the key doctrines and creeds of the Anglican Church, as set out in the Prayer Book. It was taught as a set of questions and learned responses, to be recited at particular points during Church services, closely modelled on traditional, Catholic practices.

THE FEOFFEES

A group of Puritan trustees who were empowered to raise money and buy up impropriated parishes in order to provide good preaching ministers for them. Established in 1626, they had acquired a little over thirty parishes, and were looking to extend their work to the purchase of advowsons when Laud banned them and took over the parishes that they had bought. Although they shared his objective of improving the quality of the ministry, their preference for Puritans and emphasis on preaching earned them his disapproval. His action offended Puritans on religious grounds, and many others as an attack on property.

d) Religion and the Church

Whatever resentments may have arisen from Ship Money, there was little scope for them to be expressed in the absence of Parliament. The same can be said of the changes that Charles was introducing in the Church. In 1633 Laud became Archbishop of Canterbury and issued new instructions, which the bishops were to enforce in each diocese. Preaching was to be limited to Sunday mornings and evenings, and replaced by teaching of the **Catechism** in afternoon services. The substitution of catechising for preaching symbolised the Laudian emphasis on ritual, authority and communal worship in place of the intensely personal, Bible-based faith encouraged by Puritan thinkers. Weekday lectures were to be banned, removing a favourite Puritan device that provided preaching opportunities for ministers who objected to the ceremonies and sacraments required by the Prayer Book. A legal challenge was launched against the **Feoffees**, and the parishes that they had controlled were taken into the gift of the King, ensuring that men of orthodox Anglican or Arminian views would be appointed to them. Churches were to be decorated, music was encouraged, and in Hull, for example, the Church bells were restored to Holy Trinity Church despite the objections of the Mayor and Corporation. Most obvious of all, the plain communion tables that occupied the centre of many churches were removed to the east end and covered with richly embroidered cloth, reminiscent of the Catholic High Altar, railed off from the ordinary lay members of the congregation.

From the point of view of Charles and Laud, these changes established order and beauty in the Church. Replacing preaching with set prayers and ceremonies reduced the scope for individuals to express their views and avoided controversy. Music, decoration and ritual encouraged reverence for God and joyful worship, a celebration that appealed to the emotions rather than the intellect. Catechisms and the public recitation of official confessions of faith expressed the unity of a harmonious Christian community. The protection of the altar from abuse by placing it behind rails was a mark of respect. The King and Archbishop were fulfilling their duty in caring for the Church and ensuring that others did the same. The policy was described by Laud himself:

> The inward worship of the heart is the great service of God ... but the external worship of God in his Church is the great witness to the world, that our heart stands right in that service ... Now, no external action in the world can be uniform without some ceremonies; and these in religion, the ancienter they be the better, so [as long as] they may fit the time and place. ...And scarce anything hath hurt religion

more in these broken times than an opinion in too many men, that because Rome had thrust some unnecessary and many superstitious ceremonies upon the Church, therefore the Reformation must have none at all; not considering therewhile, that ceremonies are the hedge that fence the substance of religion from all the indignities which profaneness and sacrilege too commonly put upon it.

Unfortunately, Laud's instructions were interpreted in very different ways by many of the ministers and laity upon whom they were imposed. They thought that restrictions on preaching did the devil's work by leaving people in ignorance and darkness, and that rituals and ceremonies encouraged a mechanical and superstitious emphasis on appearances at the expense of inner faith. They also believed that decorations and statues encouraged the worship of symbols, and that the new placing of the altar recalled the Catholic Mass in which, it was claimed, the communion bread and wine were miraculously transformed into the actual body and blood of Christ (Transubstantiation). For many people, not only of the Puritan faction, this was a return to superstition and idol-worship, attacking the heart of the Protestant faith. It was particularly controversial, and also particularly obvious to the ordinary layman, who saw the physical evidence of the change in his own parish church.

There were also other associations. If the altar was railed off and approached only by the clergy, then this emphasised the status of the clergy as a separate order, above the laity. What was, for Charles and Laud, an attempt to improve the quality of religious provision by creating uniform standards and raising the quality and status of the clergy, appeared to many laymen to be a renewal of the clerical pretensions associated with the Catholic Church. In this context, the presence of bishops on the Privy Council, the claims that they derived their authority from Christ himself, handed down through the Catholic Christian tradition, the emphasis on authority and the special status of the clergy all came together to create fear of absolutism and Catholicism.

The growing evidence that Catholic influence was tolerated at Court increased these fears. The Queen could worship as a Catholic according to her marriage terms, and her priests and confessors sought to gain converts where possible. Catholicism became fashionable in Court circles, and several Privy Councillors, such as Lord Treasurer Weston, were Catholics. In 1637 Charles welcomed an ambassador from the Pope, George Con, and their shared appreciation of art encouraged a growing friendship. Many suspected the King of Catholic sympathies, and even those who accepted that neither he, nor Laud, held Catholic beliefs, feared that by indulging High Church attitudes they were allowing secret Catholics to enter

ISSUE
Why did these reforms create opposition?

LAUDIAN REFORMS AND RELIGIOUS FEARS

1633 Laud appointed Archbishop of Canterbury; new Injunctions issued laying down rules and changes in the Church.

1635 William Juxon, Bishop of London, appointed as Lord Treasurer

1637 George Con, ambassador from the Pope, welcomed at Court and took up residence; Star Chamber trial and punishment of Bastwick, Burton and Prynne.

Figure 12 Church interiors showing the difference between the Puritan influence prevalent before 1630 and the Arminian influence that was imposed after 1633.

(a)

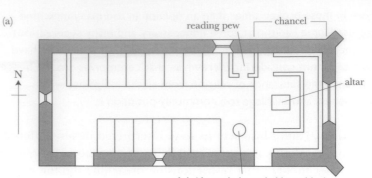

Langley Chapel in Acton Burnell, Shropshire, built as a chapel of ease c.1601.

(b)

St John's Church in Leeds, built 1634.

(c)

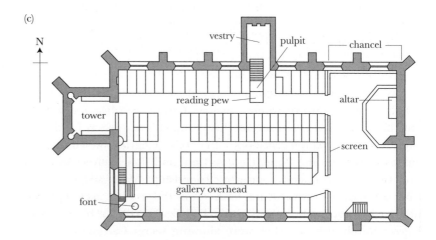

and undermine the Anglican faith. In an era when the Pope was identified as Antichrist, the head of a vast international conspiracy supported by Spain and dedicated to the destruction of true religion, such fears and suspicions isolated the King from many of his subjects.

As with other areas of government, there was little that could be done to prevent the changes being made. Ministers who refused to accept the new rules risked losing their livings, and Laud ensured that the bishops carried out regular visitations to enforce the King's will. Serious acts of defiance were brought before the prerogative court of High Commission, which also imposed censorship through the licensing of books and pamphlets. In more extreme cases, those who defied the law could be brought before the Star Chamber. In 1637 three Puritans named Burton, Bastwick and Prynne, who had published a series of pamphlets attacking Laud and the Queen, were brought to the Star Chamber accused of sedition (encouraging unrest). Burton was a physician, Bastwick was a preacher, and Prynne was a lawyer – all university men of gentry status. Despite this, they were sentenced to be pilloried, branded on the cheeks, and to have their ears cropped.

Such mutilation was rarely inflicted on men of their status, and the sentence was carried out before a shocked and horrified crowd, who sympathised with both their views and their sufferings. Fear of Catholicism, resentment at the pretensions of the Laudian clergy, and a sense that the King was willing to override both law and Parliaments in pursuit of his perception of royal government combined to convince some that he was seeking to create an absolute monarchy. In 1637, faced with Hampden's failure to challenge Ship Money, the prospect that financial independence would enable Charles to dispense with parliaments completely, and the example of Burton, Bastwick and Prynne to show what could happen to those who resisted, leaders of the Puritan interest like the Earl of Bedford considered emigration to New England as a way out. This proved unnecessary because neither Charles's intentions nor his effectiveness were quite what they seemed.

ACTIVITY

Why were the Laudian bishops so unpopular?

The sources overleaf set out a number of contemporary complaints about the changes made by Laud in the Church, and particularly focus on the role and activities of the Laudian bishops. Complaints were made against them on both religious grounds (the policies that they enforced on matters relating to the Church) and on political grounds (their activities in government and their treatment of the laity, particularly those with rank and status). Use the sources and questions to analyse and explain the reasons for the unpopularity of the Laudian bishops.

Questions on the sources

1. Which statements in Source G support the claim that the Laudian Bishops:
(a) tried to increase clerical status at the expense of the laity?
(b) persecuted Puritans and the 'godly'?

ACTIVITY

(c) encouraged the growth of Popery?
(analysis and interpretation)
2. What did the Court of High Commission do (Source H)? Why might its activities be unpopular? (interpretation in context)
3. Why did people like Clarendon disapprove of Juxon's appointment as Lord Treasurer (Source H)? (interpretation in context)
4. Clarendon was a royalist in the Civil War. What does this suggest about the unpopularity of the bishops?
5. What is John Bastwick claiming about Laud (Source I)? (interpretation)
6. How does his attitude help to explain the criticisms suggested in Source H? (cross-reference, interpretation)
7. Explain what was happening in Source K and why. (interpretation in context)
8. How does this explain the meaning of Source J? (cross-reference)
9. Does the content of these sources suggest anything about their authors' attitudes and purpose in producing them? (interpretation in context, reliability)

The humble Petition of many of His Majesty's subjects in and about the City of London, and several counties of the Kingdom, Showeth, That . . . the government of archbishops and lord bishops, deans and archdeacons etc . . .. have proved prejudicial and very dangerous both to the Church and Commonwealth, they themselves having formerly held that they have their jurisdiction. . .of [from] human authority, till of these later times. . . they have claimed their calling immediately from the Lord Jesus Christ . . . .

A particular of the manifold evils, pressures, and grievances caused, practised and occasioned by the prelates [bishops] and their dependents.
1. The subjecting and enthralling all ministers under them and their authority, and so by degrees exempting them from the temporal power; whence follows,
2. The faint-heartedness of ministers to preach the truth of God lest they should displease the prelates. . . .
3. The encouragement of ministers to despise the temporal magistrates, the nobles and gentry of the land;
4. The restraint of many godly and able men from the ministry;
5. The suppressing of that godly design set on foot by certain saints . . . for the buying of impropriations, and placing of able ministers in them, maintaining of lectures, and founding of free schools;
9. The hindering of godly books to be printed;
10. The publishing and venting of Popish, Arminian, and other dangerous books and tenets . . .
11. The growth of Popery and increase of Papists, Priests and Jesuits in sundry places.
14. The great conformity and likeness both continued and increased of our Church to the Church of Rome, in vestures, postures, ceremonies and administrations.

Source G From The Root and Branch Petition, presented to the Commons 11 December 1640.

Persons of honour and great quality, of the court and of the country, were every day cited into the High Commission upon . . . scandal in their lives, and were there prosecuted to their shame and punishment . . . which sharpened many men's humours against the bishops before they had any ill intention towards the Church.

The Treasurer's is the greatest office of benefit in the Kingdom, and the chief in precedence next the Archbishop and the Great Seal . . .. When on a sudden the staff was put into the hands of the bishop of London [William Juxon] a man so unknown that his name was scarce heard of in the Kingdom. This inflamed more men than were angry before, and no doubt did not only sharpen the edge of envy and malice against the archbishop (who was the known architect of this new fabric) but most unjustly indisposed many towards the Church itself, which they looked upon as a gulph ready to swallow all the great offices, there being others in view, of that robe, who were ambitious enough to expect the rest.

Source H From Clarendon, *History of the Rebellion.*

See the prelate of Canterbury ... riding from Croydon to Bagshot, with forty or fifty gentlemen, well mounted, attending upon him .... Behold him, I beseech you ... in his hourly passing from Lambeth to the court, [or] if you should meet him coming daily from the Star Chamber and see what pomp, grandeur and magnificence he goeth in; the whole multitude standing bare[headed] wherever he passeth ... Most certain it is, his most excellent Majesty goeth not in greater state, neither doth he suffer such insolency to be done to his poor subjects ...

Source I From The Letany of John Bastwick, 1637 (a satirical attack on Laud and the bishops using a mock 'litany', a set of prayers recited in churches).

Source J Laud Dining off Prynnes ears, from a pamphlet entitled 'Canterbury, his Change of Diet' (1641).

The Archbishop of Canterbury, being informed by his spies what Mr Prynne said, moved the Lords in the Star Chamber that he might be gagged ... Mr Burton spake much while in the pillory to the people. The executioner cut off his ears deep and close, in a cruel manner. Then Mr Prynne's cheeks were seared with an iron made exceeding hot; which done, the executioner cut off one of his ears and a piece of his cheek with it; then hacking the other ear almost off, he left it hanging and went down; but being called up, he cut it quite off.

Source K From a description of the punishment of Burton, Bastwick and Prynne on 30 June 1637.

10. Do the other sources here help to explain such attitudes?
11. Using the evidence provided by the sources as a whole, explain why the bishops were so unpopular in the late 1630s. (synthesis)
12. What conclusions can you draw from this evidence about the role of religion in causing civil war?

ISSUES
What was Charles
trying to achieve? Why
did his policies create
so much opposition?

3 Assessment – The Nature of the Personal Rule

In 1629 Charles declared that he would call no more parliaments until his subjects understood him better. By 1637 his financial and religious policies had convinced some of them, at least, that his aim was absolute power, and some historians have agreed. In 1649, on the eve of his execution at the hands of a parliamentary faction, Charles wrote to his son urging him to 'be not out of love' with parliaments, which 'in their right constitution' were mainstays of monarchy. Given that he had already chosen to die a martyr, and that this was his last advice to the man whom he regarded as his successor, it seems unlikely that Charles would deliberately lie. Yet this view of parliaments seems to contradict any absolutist ambitions, or any plan to destroy Parliament as an institution.

If Charles planned to establish absolute monarchy, he made surprisingly few changes to the structure of government in this period. The key features of continental absolutism were the concentration of legal powers in the hands of the king, the reduction of local independence in favour of central authority, and the establishment of a professional bureaucracy paid by a financially independent king. On one level, Charles appeared to be pursuing these objectives – he called no parliaments, exercised power over local interests through the prerogative courts and councils, and raised unparliamentary taxes to finance his government. Only in the last of these, however, did he try to exercise new powers or greatly extend the old, and even there it could be argued that his extension of Ship Money was no more revolutionary than James's use of 'impositions' to extend customs duties in 1606–8 (see page 34). The hallmark of Charles's government was attention to detail in order to make the existing system more effective, or to exploit existing sources of revenue more completely. While it could be argued that he had little time to bring in extensive changes before 1637, the time and energy devoted to making the existing system work was considerable. If there had been a coherent plan to destroy parliaments and make monarchy absolute, such time would have been better given to establishing a standing army and a system of salaried officials.

If Charles did not therefore plan to create absolutism, what where his aims? Some clues can be found by looking at the nature of his Court and the image of monarchy that he sought to establish there. The royal Court was the heart of government, the centre of society and the pinnacle of the social hierarchy on which government was based. The style and behaviour of the Court reflected the personality and aims of the monarch who shaped it. Where Elizabeth and her father had created public magnificence, and James permitted licence and indulgence, Charles sought dignified formality. Access to the monarch was limited, and strictly according to rank. Ceremonial was carefully staged, and often conducted at Windsor, away from the public gaze. A strict code of behaviour was enforced and entertainments took the form of plays and masques, in which the King and Queen sometimes appeared in a symbolic role to restore order and end confusion. This indicates the kind of king that Charles tried to be. Reserved, dignified, aloof and personally chaste, he tried to shape the monarchy and the kingdom in his own image. Even his critics, like the fiercely Puritan Lucy Hutchinson, recognised some of his virtues.

This image reveals Charles's view of monarchy, and symbolises what he tried to achieve across all aspects of government. Administration was to be efficient and well-ordered, and the Church was to be beautified and dignified by ceremonial. Hierarchy was to be upheld by insisting on respect for rank – of bishops in the Church and nobility in the State. At the head of both was the King, his authority accepted and exercised for the benefit of his people. The results would be peace and harmony, a well-oiled machine with all parts working in their place.

Q

What image of Charles does this portrait attempt to promote?
How does it disguise the fact that he was less than five feet tall?

Figure 13 Charles I on horseback, by Van Dyke, 1638 (National Gallery, London). 'King Charles was temperate, chaste and serious; so that the fools and bawds ... of the former court grew out of fashion .... Men of learning and ingenuity in all the arts were in esteem and receiving encouragement from the King, who was a most excellent judge and a great lover of paintings.' (from Lucy Hutchinson, *Memoirs of Colonel Hutchinson*).

If this is the case, then it is necessary to explain why such a vision would give rise to significant opposition within a governing class that shared the King's belief in hierarchy and order. The reasons seem to lie partly in the nature of Charles's beliefs, and partly in the methods by which he sought to pursue his aims. In relation to religion and the Church, his beliefs raised fears that he does not seem to have understood. The changes that he introduced into the Church offended Puritans at every level, but Puritans never constituted a majority among his subjects. What offended a far wider number was the fear and suspicion raised by the respect shown to Catholics. Charles never understood that for many Protestants, not only those with Puritan sympathies, the Pope was Antichrist, the servant of the devil. To allow Catholics into positions of power and to make it easier for them to be accommodated within the Church was to undermine the defences of true religion and liberty. Against the background of militant Catholicism and war in Europe, Charles appeared to be furthering the cause of an international Catholic conspiracy by giving a foothold in Protestant England to its most dangerous enemies.

Dramatic though these images may be, they reflected the anti-Catholic prejudice in English thinking, which encompassed political as well as religious fears. Catholic monarchs were thought of as absolutists and destroyers of parliaments. Catholic bishops were seen as enforcing the Pope's will, persecuting other faiths and interfering in the affairs of governments. The architect of absolutism in France was a cleric, Cardinal Richelieu – and rumour had it that Laud had been offered a cardinal's hat by the Pope himself. Laud claimed that bishops in the Anglican Church inherited their power from Christ himself, encouraged the pride and pretensions of the clergy, dominated the Privy Council and gained appointments for his protégés, both clergy and laymen. The similarities were too close to ignore.

In this context, Charles's personal rule took on a more sinister appearance than he could imagine. Historians who suggest that there was little reaction to the dissolution of 1629 are probably correct; opposition grew with the development of Charles's policies and the apparent hardening of his intentions after that date. To some extent this was a matter of the cumulative effect of his policies in different areas, but it was also the result of his personality. Charles was no more autocratic in his political beliefs than his father, but he lacked James's grasp of political reality and suffered from a dangerous combination of naivety and determination. Because he had no plans to destroy Parliament he was incapable of understanding the fears that he generated. Faced with opposition for which he could see no justification, he assumed that it was maliciously intended. Feeling himself under attack, he responded with a determination to assert his authority that included vindictive punishments of those who opposed him. While Charles was not an autocrat by belief, he was certainly autocratic in temperament; for many of his subjects, the effect was much the same.

4 The Failure of the Personal Rule, 1637–40

It is clear, therefore, that by 1637 a combination of political and religious grievances had created opposition among a far wider spectrum of public opinion than the 'Puritan faction'. That opposition, however, had few opportunities to express itself in the absence of a parliament. If Charles could maintain his control of the situation, there was no reason why he could not continue to impose his will. A combination of growing trade and Ship Money offered the prospect of financial independence, and if that were the case, then even if he chose to call a parliament, it would have little prospect of influencing the King's decisions. Without a need for parliamentary taxes, Charles could dissolve any parliament that obstructed him as and when he chose. The apparent growth of parliamentary influence and independence that had occurred since the Reformation could be rapidly reversed by a King whose administrative grip and financial position was secure.

In these circumstances, Charles's decision to extend his programme of reform into his outlying kingdoms exposed his fatal lack of political awareness. In Ireland he had already withdrawn the royal proclamations known as the Graces, which had given Irish Catholics a measure of religious freedom, and Strafford's iron grip as governor appeared to have suppressed any resistance. In Scotland, however, the independence and strength of the Presbyterian **Kirk** created difficulties for the monarchy, as well as an encouragement to English Puritans.

James I had already taken some cautious steps towards greater uniformity, but Charles lacked his father's understanding of Scottish politics and culture, and he made little effort to acquire it. He had visited Scotland only once and tended to rely on advice from a small group of Scots living in London rather than from the Scottish Privy Council in Edinburgh. James had attempted to create stronger links between the English and Scottish churches, persuading the Scots to restore the office of bishop, although their role was to advise rather than to enforce conformity as in England. In 1621 he had proposed the establishment of a formal order of service, similar to the English Prayer Book. The fierce opposition that it aroused convinced him to withdraw the plan. Charles, however, was not only less aware of Scottish concerns than his father, but also considerably less tactful.

THE KIRK
The Scottish Kirk was a Presbyterian Church, founded by John Knox in 1560. When Mary, Queen of Scots, returned to Scotland from France in 1560 she found a Protestant Reformation already completed. The result was that the Kirk, run by committees of ministers and elders rather than bishops, was in many ways independent of the monarchy. Worship was based on preaching and improvised prayers, both provided by ministers who had little hesitation in speaking their minds. From the point of view of the Monarch, this independence needed to be curbed, but for many Scots, the Kirk was a symbol of both their religious and cultural identity.

STEPS TO CRISIS 1637–40

1637 At Charles's insistence a new Prayer Book is imposed on the Scottish Church;

1638 Scottish nobility and leaders of the Church sign the Covenant;

1639 First Bishops' War ends in Treaty of Berwick;

1639 –40 Scottish Assembly votes to abolish both Prayer Book and bishops;

1640 Charles recalls Strafford who advises calling Parliament; April–May: the Short Parliament; June–October: Second Bishops' War, ending in the Treaty of Ripon; November: the Long Parliament meets.

COVENANT

A contract or agreement in which the parties bind themselves to carry out certain obligations. The Scottish Covenant was a national treaty in which those who signed it agreed to come together to defend the existing Kirk, if necessary by force of arms, and to remain together until its safety was assured. It was therefore an act of rebellion, which Charles could not ignore.

In 1637, he ordered that a new prayer book, based on the one used in England, should be formally adopted and read in Edinburgh churches. The order was imposed by proclamation and without reference to either the Scottish Parliament or the Assembly of the Kirk. When the book was read in St Giles's Cathedral in Edinburgh, a woman named Jenny Geddes was so incensed that she threw her stool at the bishop who was reading it. The service erupted into a riot, which rapidly sparked off riots elsewhere among a people who were infuriated by both the book and the manner in which it was imposed. The Scottish Council withdrew the book but Charles insisted that his orders were carried out. The Scottish clergy and nobility united in anger at such arbitrary English domination, and early in 1638 they met to draw up a **Covenant** to defend the Kirk. Predictably, Charles was outraged by their defiance especially as the Covenanters claimed to be acting in God's name.

It was not surprising that Charles responded to this defiance by raising an army. He regarded the Covenanters as rebels, and had no hesitation in using military force to put down such a rebellion. Unfortunately, he was in no position to do so. Lacking the money to employ mercenaries, he had to rely on English support. Many of the nobility had no wish to fight, and the JPs were half-hearted in their preparations, perhaps alienated from the King or preoccupied with the need to collect Ship Money. The militia was locally based, and men were reluctant to move from their home areas. When they did, the number who became involved in attacking Church ornaments or joining local rioters in pulling down **enclosures** demonstrates their lack of enthusiasm for the cause for which they were asked to fight.

The Scots, on the other hand, were committed to their cause. The Covenanters saw the Kirk as the embodiment of both their religion and culture, and regarded the King as unwittingly serving the cause of Antichrist by restoring devilish ceremonies in the Church. They would fight to defend their religion and felt justified in resisting their sovereign in the name of God. Even Charles realised that he did not have the strength to win, and signed the Treaty of Berwick in 1639. This allowed the Scots to decide on their own religious settlement, and they immediately exercised their freedom by abolishing both the Scottish Prayer Book and the Scottish bishops.

If Charles had ever intended to respect the Treaty, this action ensured that he would not do so. His political isolation was clear. The London merchants refused to lend him money to raise a new army, and some of the English nobility among the Puritan faction, such as Lord Saye and Sele and his son Nathaniel Fiennes, were already in contact with the Scots to encourage them to intervene in England. Charles, however, was unaware of the depth of resentment that he faced, and determined to reassert his authority. To do so, he recalled Sir Thomas Wentworth, now Lord Strafford, from Ireland.

THOMAS WENTWORTH, EARL OF STRAFFORD (1593–1641)

-*Profile*-

Sir Thomas Wentworth was a gentleman of south Yorkshire with wide connections of blood and marriage. Knighted in 1611, he became MP for Yorkshire in 1614. His election as a county MP (rather than a borough representative) indicates his influence and status within the county. As an MP he was initially associated with the defence of parliamentary rights against royal encroachments, being imprisoned in 1627 for refusing to pay the forced loan, and playing an important role in the presentation of the Petition of Right. Much of his opposition, however, was directed at the influence and inefficiency of Buckingham, and when the King offered him the post of President of the Council of the North after Buckingham's assassination in 1628, he accepted. This decision was regarded as a betrayal by some MPs, a perception that increased with his active role in the Personal Rule of Charles I. In 1629 he was appointed to the Privy Council, where he shared with Laud the responsibility for the administration of 'Thorough'. In 1632, however, he was appointed Lord Deputy of Ireland, and was absent from England for the next eight years.

Strafford was an able and energetic governor, a good administrator and a man of iron determination. In Ireland he promoted trade, reformed the administration and built up the army, but he was resented for his harsh control and dictatorial methods. This led Charles to recall him in his time of need, and promote him to an earldom and the role of chief adviser. It was Strafford who recommended Charles to call Parliament, believing that he could manage it by exploiting anti-Scottish sentiment. This was a mistake, arising possibly from his long absence, or possibly from his dislike of Puritan ideas. Whatever the reason, he soon paid the price. When Parliament reassembled in November 1640, he was a primary target for the opposition, who may have desired revenge for his betrayal and certainly feared his abilities. Strafford was aware that the opposition leaders were in contact with the Scots, and planned to impeach them for treason, but was himself accused of having plotted to bring over an Irish army to use against Parliament. While he may have been willing to do this, there was little evidence to support the claim. He defended himself brilliantly against impeachment proceedings in the House of Lords, and his accusers were forced to introduce an Act of Attainder in April 1641, by which he was simply declared to be guilty. He was executed on 12 May 1641.

Strafford advised Charles to call Parliament, hoping that traditional anti-Scottish feeling would enable him to rally support. This was a dangerous strategy, but there was probably little alternative. The previous war had forced the government to anticipate revenue, and the financial gains of the Personal Rule had already been wiped out. Generous concessions on grievances might have enabled the King to win over his critics, although the number of petitions sent to

ENCLOSURES

Enclosures were a cause of significant popular unrest in this period. They involved the rearrangement and fencing of land into individual units, which enabled and encouraged new farming methods. Problems arose where previously common or waste land was included, depriving poorer villagers of rights to collect fuel or graze animals, or where such lands had provided homes for squatters or customary tenants. Even where these poorer villagers were given a share of the land, they were often unable to afford fencing, or development costs, and so were forced to sell their holdings and work as landless labourers.

Westminster to greet the MPs who assembled in April 1640 suggests that it may already have been too late. In any case, Charles's handling of the situation destroyed any chance of success. Without offering any concessions, or even perhaps realising that they were needed, he demanded money to defend the kingdom from a crisis that he had created.

The result was a chaotic session in which the 'opposition' began to assume shape and structure. The key figures in the Lords were the Earl of Bedford, Lord Saye and Sele and Lord Montague, later Earl of Manchester. In the Commons the dominant figure was John Pym, Bedford's legal adviser. Nathaniel Fiennes was already in touch with the Scottish army and awareness of these contacts may have encouraged Charles to dissolve Parliament very quickly; had he had proof of these activities, it is likely that Fiennes would have faced a treason charge. As it was, the April Parliament, which became known as the Short Parliament, achieved nothing for the King.

In spite of all, Charles was determined to restore his authority. His actions in this period highlight the best and worst aspects of his character – courageous and determined, stubborn and high-handed, and, most dangerous in political terms, seriously out of touch. His lack of political awareness is revealed by his willingness to borrow from Catholics and use Catholic officers, while the rank and file busied themselves in burning altar rails and other Catholic symbols. Not surprisingly, the under-equipped and unenthusiastic English army proved unable to match the Scots, who had by now entered England. After a brief battle at Newburn-on-Tyne it disintegrated, leaving the Scots in control of Newcastle and able to force their terms on the King once more in October 1640, in the Treaty of Ripon. Their conditions – a further truce, payment by Charles of their expenses at £850 a day and the postponement of further negotiations until a Parliament met – were designed to give that Parliament the advantage. In fact, Charles had already accepted the need to call a new Parliament, and had concluded, somewhat late in the day, that some concessions would be needed to gain support. He had little idea of just how many!

ACTIVITY

The material in this chapter analyses Charles's political beliefs and his personal temperament. Consider his handling of the affairs of Church and state as a whole, and explain which factor was more important in creating opposition and undermining his plans – his beliefs or his personality.

▼ Working on The Development of the Crisis

You have now read through a substantial body of material, which should enable you to explain the causes of the crisis that had developed through the seventeenth century, and come to a head in 1640. The tasks below are designed to bring together and draw on the information in Chapters 1 and 2 as well as this chapter. The first step is always to ensure that you have understood and recorded the key points of what you have read, in the form of linear notes based on the sections and headings provided in the chapters. Advice on how to set these out was offered on page 32, and if you have not done so already, you should read and make notes on Chapters 2 and 3 before attempting any further tasks.

Essay questions on the development of the crisis focus on two key questions – *how* did it develop, and *why* did it happen. These questions are different, but there are links between them. If you understand how the crisis occurred, it helps you to explain why. *How* asks you to look at what happened and organise it into stages of development. When you do this, you will see that certain *factors* seem to cause problems in each of the stages, although perhaps in different ways at different times. These factors enable you to explain *why* the crisis developed.

You may have already looked at factors and how they worked together in the tasks at the end of Chapter 2. If you are to be able to write essays explaining the crisis as a whole, you now need to widen your perspective and look at the factors that were present across the whole period 1603–40. Different essay questions will require you to deal with these factors in different ways, but the first stage is to define what they were, and how they worked together to build up the crisis. It could be said that the factors provide the building blocks of your explanation, and the stages of development define the pattern in which you lay them out.

For example, the explanation of what James inherited in Chapter 1 defined four key areas where problems existed. This gives you four factors that help to explain why there was a crisis – religious divisions, financial problems, relations between King and Parliament, and the problem of governing three kingdoms. You also know from your study of Chapter 2 that these problems were made worse in the 1620s by the addition of two new factors – the Thirty Years' War in Europe, and the personality of Charles I. The interaction of these six factors created a breach between King and Parliament in 1629, which increased tensions during the Personal Rule. Hence we can see that problems were building up during three stages of development. However, the crisis would not come to a head until something occurred to destroy Charles's control of the situation and bring the different factors together. The Scottish rebellion, brought together the problem of religion in different kingdoms and the King's financial weakness. This combination forced him to recall Parliament and address their accumulated grievances.

One of the best ways to express this process is to set it out in a diagram. While linear notes are good for recording detailed information about each factor, diagrams and flow charts can be more effective in expressing the links between them and how they worked together. The summary diagram on page 83 sets out the process that we have just described, to provide you with a basic explanation of how and why the crisis of 1640 developed. It shows what factors were involved, and how they worked together in different stages.

Planning and Writing Essays on the Development of the Crisis

Once you have your building blocks in place, writing essays is merely a matter of applying them to different questions you are asked. Before you ever attempt to write an essay, it has to be planned so that you know what you want to include, and it is your building blocks of factors which enable you to plan it. There are many different ways to plan essays, but what is suggested here provides a method that you can practise and apply to the questions below.

Begin with a straightforward question such as 'Why did Charles I face a crisis in government in November 1640?'

▼ Using the diagram on page 83 to help you, write out a summary that answers the question. This would probably provide the conclusion to your essay. For example:

'Charles inherited *financial problems* from his father, made worse by the adventurous foreign policy and inefficiency of his favourite and adviser, the *Duke of Buckingham*. This caused *friction with Parliament and led to an open breach in 1629*. Relations were made worse by his *religious policies*, which involved promoting Arminians in the Church and raised *fears of Catholic influence*. The resulting grievances grew during his Personal Rule, but it was his attempt to *extend these reforms to Scotland that brought the crisis to a head in 1640*, and brought him face to face with a Parliament that was determined to restrict his powers for the future. Although all of these factors played a part in the crisis, it was *Charles himself who brought them together in this way*.'

▼ Review your summary, and set out the key factors that you will have to explain. These will provide the main sections of your essay. For example: Charles inherited financial problems (explain in detail), made

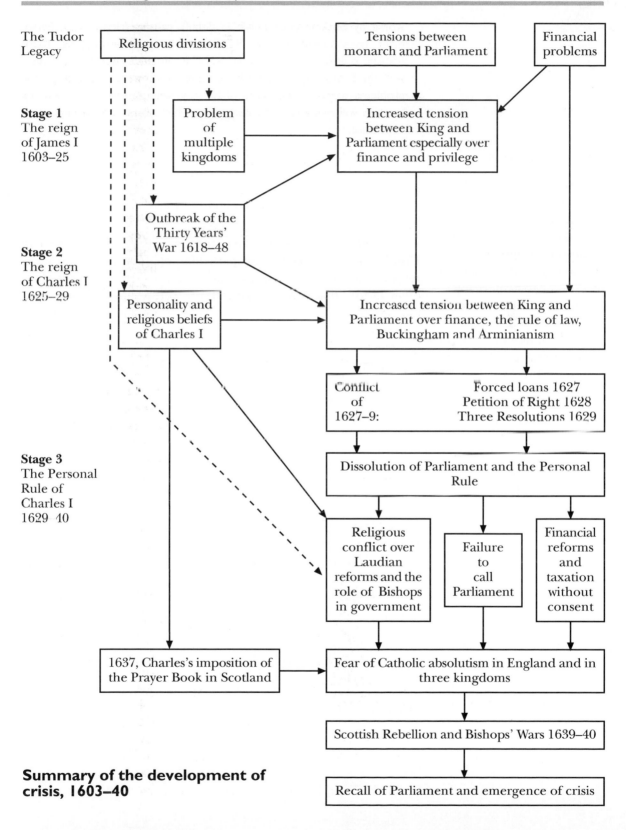

The Tudor Legacy

Religious divisions

Tensions between monarch and Parliament

Financial problems

Stage 1
The reign of James I 1603–25

Problem of multiple kingdoms

Increased tension between King and Parliament especially over finance and privilege

Outbreak of the Thirty Years' War 1618–48

Stage 2
The reign of Charles I 1625–29

Personality and religious beliefs of Charles I

Increased tension between King and Parliament over finance, the rule of law, Buckingham and Arminianism

Conflict of 1627–9:

Forced loans 1627
Petition of Right 1628
Three Resolutions 1629

Stage 3
The Personal Rule of Charles I 1629–40

Dissolution of Parliament and the Personal Rule

Religious conflict over Laudian reforms and the role of Bishops in government

Failure to call Parliament

Financial reforms and taxation without consent

1637, Charles's imposition of the Prayer Book in Scotland

Fear of Catholic absolutism in England and in three kingdoms

Scottish Rebellion and Bishops' Wars 1639–40

Recall of Parliament and emergence of crisis

Summary of the development of crisis, 1603–40

worse by Buckingham (explain in detail), causing friction with Parliament (give examples 1625–9). Relations worsened in the 1630s (explain religious policies and fear of Catholicism) and came to a head with the Scottish Crisis (explain how). It was Charles who brought the problems together (examples of his role and personality). These six sections will give you a coherent essay, which you can draw into a final conclusion.

Essay Questions

1. 'The main factor in causing a crisis for the monarchy in 1640 was Charles I himself'. How far do you agree?
2. To what extent was the crisis of 1640 inevitable?
3. How far were contemporaries correct in blaming 'evil counsellors' for the problems faced by the monarchy in 1640?

You will see that the starting point for this plan was the question that was asked. The building blocks that you have can provide you with the material that you need to answer a variety of questions, but you will need to arrange them differently, and explain the links between them in a different way. For example, if the question was 'To what extent did religious issues cause the crisis that Charles faced in 1640?', you would need to pay particular attention to the impact of religious divisions, but you would also need to set them against the other factors that played a part. Hence you would rearrange your building blocks to respond to the particular question, but you would still use them all.

▼ Using the diagram to help you, write out a summary/conclusion to the question 'To what extent did religious issues cause the crisis that Charles faced in 1640?'
▼ Divide the summary into key factors required for the essay.
▼ Write out a plan using the factors, the effect of each one and the important links between them.

Now practise the method on the questions in the margin before choosing one essay to write.

Further Reading

Most of the books and essays recommended at the end of Chapter 2 are also useful for the issues raised by this chapter; in particular, you should look at Katherine Brice's *Early Stuarts* for further information and A. Anderson's *Charles I* for the role of Charles. Barry Coward's *Stuart England* is useful for a clear analysis of key issues, once you have established your basic knowledge of events. In addition, *The Nature of the English Revolution*, a collection of essays by John Morrill includes some useful analyses of the causes of the crisis that had developed by 1640. See also a useful collection of documents with a helpful commentary, edited by J. Morrill and C.W. Daniels *Charles I* CUP 1988.

FROM CRISIS TO WAR, 1640–42

KEY ISSUE
Why did the crisis of
1640 lead to civil war?

CHAPTER 4

POINTS TO CONSIDER

In 1640 those who assembled in the Long Parliament expected to achieve a settlement with the King. At that point, war was not possible, because the King had neither the money nor the support to create an army. However, in the year that followed the unity of the Commons crumbled and Charles was able to rally enough support to make a military solution to his problems a possible option. It is therefore necessary to consider why this happened – what issues divided MPs in 1641, when they had been apparently united in 1640? However, the fact that war was possible does not make it inevitable, and the reluctant drift to military action that occurred in the early months of 1642 suggests that it was unwanted. It is therefore also necessary to explain what issues divided men so deeply that a settlement was impossible, and they chose to fight rather than submit.

1 The Collapse of Parliamentary Unity, 1640–42

ISSUES
What was the attitude of MPs towards the King?
Why did Charles face an organised opposition?

a) The Long Parliament and the Nature of Opposition to Charles I

Explanations of how the crisis of 1640 became a civil war in 1642 can most easily be made intelligible to a modern audience by the use of terms such as 'opposition', 'sides' and 'parties', although they do not actually match the reality of what was happening in seventeenth-century parliaments. While factions among the nobility and rivalry between ministers were normal, the idea of opposition to the King was close to treason. Yet it is undeniable that Charles did face a coherently organised group of MPs, linked to certain members of the Lords, with a planned strategy for defeating his most cherished plans and imposing their own. This group has been described by the historian Conrad Russell as **'Pym's Junto'** reflecting the leadership of John Pym and the somewhat conspiratorial nature of the group. Its activities in opposing Charles and his 'evil counsellors' encouraged some historians to accept the contemporary royalist view that its

PYM'S JUNTO
Junto refers to a small, organised group who work together to gain or maintain power. The group associated with Pym in 1640–42 was not formally organised, and it is difficult to draw a distinction between members and associates, but it is clear that Pym had a number of trusted allies.

Figure 14 John Pym, 1583–1643. Born in Somerset, son of a wealthy landowner, educated at Oxford. Spent his early manhood managing his estates in Somerset, and was first elected to Parliament in 1621. Sat in every Parliament thereafter until his death from cancer in 1643. By 1640 he was an experienced parliamentarian, an able speaker and a clever tactician, enabling him to lead and manage the opposition campaign in the Commons.

members plotted and schemed to manipulate Parliament in pursuit of their own ambitions. This is supported by the evidence that they were in touch with the Scots in the spring and summer of 1640, and that part of their strategy was to replace Charles's advisers with their own men. In May 1641 a scheme to appoint the Earl of Bedford as chief adviser to the King, with Pym as Chancellor of the Exchequer was aborted by the death of Bedford from a fever.

Against these claims it can be argued that there was nothing unusual or underhand in planning to replace bad advisers with good ones, and that a willingness to contribute to the King's government was perfectly natural among those who wished to influence it. This was precisely what Strafford had done in 1628. It can also be argued that the manipulation of Parliament was a necessary strategy if the King was to be pressurised into redressing grievances and abandoning his plans for government in Church and State. The majority of members came to Westminster with a desire for change but little understanding of how to achieve it. What requires explaining in relation to 'Pym's Junto' and its associates is not the willingness of its members to use political tactics in pursuit of their cause but their ability to do so.

Three factors seem to have been important in this – their previous experience of Charles I, their personal and political links, and the outstanding political skills of John Pym. Most of the opposition leaders had been MPs in the 1620s, many of them being supporters and protégés of Sir Edward Coke (see page 47). Pym, in particular, learned a great deal from Coke's management of parliamentary opinion over the Protestation of 1621 and the Petition of Right. After the dissolution of Parliament in 1629, some contact had been maintained through business and family links. Pym was employed as a lawyer and agent by the Earl of Bedford. In 1629 Bedford, Lord Saye and Sele, Lord Brooke, and the Earl of Warwick founded a privateering company named the Providence Island Company to attack Spanish ships and property in the West Indies, and included as co-directors both Pym and John Hampden. There is little doubt that these men helped to organise the Ship Money case, in which Hampden employed as his counsel another of Bedford's agents, Oliver St John. Hampden himself had wide contacts of blood and intermarriage in Buckinghamshire and East Anglia, including the MP for Cambridge in 1640, Oliver Cromwell.

While these contacts provided a core that contributed to the coherence of the group, they are not sufficient to explain its effectiveness or its impact. The adherence of others such as Sir Arthur Haselrig whose family home was in Durham, Sir Henry Vane and Denzil Holles, son of the Earl of Clare, was based upon political and religious conviction. It is significant that all of the central group and most of their associates held Puritan views in religion. Equally important was their experience in the Short Parliament of April 1640. The brief period of its existence gave them occasion to meet and awareness of the tactics that would be needed, as well as useful contacts with the Scots brought by Nathaniel Fiennes, MP, son of Lord Saye and Sele, who had been in touch with the Covenanters since 1639. It is probably fair to say that the opposition group, as such, took shape at this time, and that their planned strategy for the Long Parliament was based on the experience of its predecessor of April. When Parliament assembled in November, Pym launched an attack on existing grievances and established the group in positions of influence by proposing various committees with his associates as members and chairmen. From that base, they were able to put forward proposals and influence debates.

It is important to consider the relationship of this group to other members of the Long Parliament. It is difficult to support the royalist perception that they tricked and manipulated an assembly of innocents into supporting strategies that they did not understand. Nevertheless, it is clear that there was a difference in political perception between men like Pym and the average country member. According to Clarendon, he met Pym in Westminster 'some days before the Parliament' and was told by Pym that 'they must now be of another temper than they were the last Parliament [the Short Parliament of April 1640] ...that they now had an opportunity to make their country happy, by removing all grievances and pulling up the causes of them by the roots, if all men would do their duties'. This suggests more radical measures than those envisaged by the Yorkshire MP, Sir Henry Slingsby, who left home on the 2 November commenting that 'Great expectance there is of a happy Parliament, where the subject may have a total redress of all his grievances'. While the two men shared a concern for the redress of grievances, there was a significant difference in their political awareness of what it would take to achieve it.

It could be argued, therefore, that the opposition leaders differed from the majority of MPs in their political experience, the depth and intensity of their opposition, and possibly the importance of religion in their concerns. But it should be remembered that it is difficult to make effective generalisations because the Long Parliament was, above all, an assembly of individuals and local factions rather than a coherent political body. The county petitions that accompanied them to Westminster show that there was a widespread concern with grievances and a demand for the reversal of Charles's policies in Church and State. To this extent the opposition leaders were a part of, and in tune with, the electorate that they represented. In terms of strategies for achieving their aims, however, they were far more advanced and radical in their thinking than the majority of members, on whose support they had to rely. They would therefore need to proceed carefully, at a pace, and in a direction that they could make acceptable to the varied and often cautious representatives of the ruling class around them.

b) The Redress of Grievances, 1640–41

i) Politics and the Constitution

When MPs assembled for the meeting of what was to become the Long Parliament in November 1640, they did so in a mood of optimistic expectation. The obvious weakness of the King's position and his desperate need for financial support seemed to guarantee the opportunity to gain redress for the accumulated grievances of the Personal Rule and to ensure that it could not be repeated. The table of events on page 89 indicates the extent to which they were successful. By the summer of 1641, the future of parliaments had been secured by the Triennial Act, the 'evil counsellors' had been replaced and punished, and the machinery (such as Ship Money and the prerogative courts) by which Charles had raised money and silenced opposition, had been dismantled and abolished.

This record of success, however, disguised a number of problems. While the King had given his assent to the Triennial Act, the obvious reluctance and resentment with which he did so raised fears that he might later seek to reverse the decision, and possibly punish those whom he regarded as responsible. In a speech made to Parliament on 16 February 1641, the day on which he gave his assent, he complained that Parliament had 'hitherto done what concerns yourselves' rather than attended to the needs of the kingdom (and King). 'You have taken the government almost to pieces' he concluded, 'and, I may say, it is almost off the hinges.'

These concerns were greatly increased by the execution of Strafford, which followed in May. The dangers of openly criticising the King had led the opposition leaders to place the blame for the events of the Personal Rule on the shoulders of the King's 'evil counsellors', especially Strafford and Laud. Proceedings for the impeachment of both had begun in November 1640, but those against Strafford ran into difficulty. Since he had, in fact, been carrying out the wishes of the King there was little evidence to support a charge of treason, and it soon became apparent that he had every chance of successfully defending himself in the Lords. 'Without question they will acquit him' wrote the MP Sir John Coke in April 1641.

However, to many MPs the removal of Strafford was a political necessity rather than a judicial matter. The opposition leaders therefore introduced an Act of Attainder, by which Strafford was simply

ISSUES
What constitutional changes were MPs seeking to achieve in 1640?
To what extent were they successful by the summer of 1641?

ISSUE
Was the execution of Strafford a turning-point in the relationship between King and Parliament?

The Constitutional Reforms of the Long Parliament, 1640–41

The events and reforms listed below are those which were successfully established by the Long Parliament in 1640–42, and for the most part, not reversed in the Restoration of 1660.

November 1640 – Impeachment proceedings begun against Laud and Strafford in order to remove the King's 'evil counsellors'; this was not a new procedure, but an extension of the use made of this device in the 1620s.

February 1641 – The Triennial Act passed through Parliament and received the King's assent. It ensured that Parliament would be called at least every three years, and made provision for a Parliament to assemble even if the King had not called it. The Act survived the Restoration, but in 1664 it was replaced with a weakened version, which lacked this provision.

May 1641 – An Act of Attainder declared Strafford to be guilty of treason, and he was executed on 12 May. This use of Parliament's legislative powers to punish a minister without trial was doubtful on grounds of justice and equity, but did provide an alternative means of calling the King's advisers to account.

July 1641 – The Abolition of the Prerogative Courts of Star Chamber and High Commission removed the King's capacity to deal with legal cases directly through his prerogative powers. They were important steps in dismantling the machinery of Personal Rule, but did not remove the possibility of such courts being re-established in future under a different name. However, the prerogative courts were not revived with the Restoration.

August 1641 – An Act was passed declaring Ship Money to be illegal. Again, this removed an important element of government during the Personal Rule, but did not guarantee that a future King might not try to establish a similar tax. In practice, however, none did.

declared to be guilty and condemned to death. It passed the House of Commons by 204 votes to 59. To ensure its passage through the Lords, Pym stirred up fears by revealing a plot to dissolve the House of Commons and release Strafford by force. Concocted in March–April by a group of army officers, it had all the ingredients required to induce panic. Some of the participants were Catholics, and although there was no evidence to implicate the King, his refusal to dismiss those involved raised serious questions. To protect the Parliament, Charles was forced to agree to an Act declaring that this Parliament could not be dissolved without its own consent. When the Bill of Attainder moved to the House of Lords, the London mobs appeared in Westminster and threatened any who opposed it. Many who opposed the bill chose to stay away, and those who attended voted in favour. However, the attainder required the King's assent, and Charles had promised Strafford that he would never agree. But, faced by angry demonstrations and fearing for the safety of his family, Charles gave in. Strafford was executed before a jubilant crowd of several thousands on Tower Hill on 12 May 1641.

GROWTH OF MISTRUST 1640–41

1640 December – Root and Branch debates reveal religious divisions;

1641 February – King's response to the Triennial Act shows reluctance to make real concessions;
April/May – trial and execution of Strafford shows opposition use of intimidation and popular support; first Army Plot raises fears that the King will use force; Act against the dissolution of the Long Parliament raises fears of Catholic plots and reduces Charles's non-military options;
June – King's visit to Scotland raises fear of attack on Parliament; Ten Propositions raises fears that opposition seeks further power.

The measures used to destroy Strafford had a number of effects. Such devices undoubtedly disturbed a few MPs who had previously supported the opposition campaign, but the main impact was on the King. Having lost the capacity to dissolve this Parliament, he was more likely than ever to consider other strategies, including force. More immediately, he was angry and humiliated; a King who had been intimidated into breaking his word and betraying his chief adviser was unlikely to feel obliged to deal gently with those who had forced him into this position. As long as the opposition leaders had the support of a united Parliament, he was in no position to punish them, but if they should lose that support, they would not only endanger the rights and liberties of Parliament, but their own liberty and lives as well.

By the summer of 1641, therefore, the opposition had attained many of their initial objectives, but at the price of alienating the King and placing themselves at risk. It was no longer enough to dismantle the machinery of the Personal Rule and remove those responsible for it; there was also a need to ensure security for the future. Hence these developments forced the opposition leaders to formulate new demands and place further restrictions on the King. The first example of this came with the Ten Propositions of June 1641. In the aftermath of Strafford's execution, Charles had announced his intention to visit Scotland and finalise the treaties that had ended the Scottish rebellion. For the opposition leaders, this posed problems. If Charles could escape the financial burdens imposed by the Treaty of Ripon, he would gain much greater freedom to manoeuvre with Parliament. Worse still, if he could conclude a different agreement with the Scots and build up his support there, he might well be able to use an experienced Scottish army to impose his will in England. To prevent this, the opposition put forward a list of ten points, including parliamentary control of the King's choice of advisers, and asked the King to delay his visit until after he had considered and agreed to them.

Such demands were a clear encroachment on the King's existing powers, and there was little chance that Charles would agree to them. More importantly, many MPs also had reservations about such demands. The majority were not professional politicians, but country gentlemen who regarded the King's authority as their guarantee of order and the main pillar of the social hierarchy upon which they themselves depended. They had come to Westminster in November with a conviction that the King had overstepped his powers and infringed both law and the rights of parliaments. They were therefore united in demanding the removal of such abuses and securing parliaments for the future. To go further and make significant changes that would alter the balance of the constitution was something that they had not considered. To make matters worse, many were already concerned about other changes that had been put forward to deal with religious grievances and the difficult issue of reforming the Church.

ii) Religion and the Church

As with other grievances, the changes introduced by Charles and Archbishop Laud in the Church had created widespread and apparently united opposition. In December 1640 the Commons had accepted a petition from London and the surrounding counties, which called for the reversal of Laud's reforms and the abolition of episcopacy (government of the Church by bishops). When the petition was debated, it became clear that many MPs were reluctant to go so far, but the issue was laid aside to deal with more urgent matters, and caused little damage to the unity of Parliament. By May 1641, however, those other matters had been dealt with, and MPs turned their attention to the matter of the Church.

It was quickly apparent that the widespread unpopularity of the Laudian bishops disguised a variety of different ideas about the future of the Church. While the majority of MPs disliked the pretensions of the clergy, the inquisitions of the Church courts and the interference of bishops in affairs of state (see the source-based exercise on religious grievances on pages 72–3), this fell far short of the Puritan schemes for wholesale reform of the Church. While most were willing to see the removal of the rituals imposed by Laud and restore a distinctively Protestant identity based on a preaching ministry, few were committed to any Presbyterian model, and even fewer to the complete abolition of bishops. While Laud was in power and the threat of Catholic influence immediate, Protestants of many shades of opinion could agree on the need to remove him. When it came to deciding on how to replace him, such unity quickly dissolved and the underlying divisions were revealed.

These problems were illustrated by the varying success of the religious measures introduced in 1640–41. By January 1641 the King had agreed to remove the bishops from his Privy Council, reducing their role in administration and government. In May the opposition introduced a bill to exclude bishops from the House of Lords, which rapidly passed the Commons only to be defeated in the Lords by a combination of the bishops themselves and the King's influence. In June the Puritan faction attempted to bring in a Root and Branch Bill, to abolish the office of bishop completely and reform the Church along Presbyterian lines. Although this was now the only means of removing their political influence, it was clear that it would fail and its supporters laid it aside. The attitude of many moderate

> **ISSUES**
> How were religious problems addressed? Why were religious issues so contentious?

members was expressed by the Yorkshire MP, Sir Henry Slingsby of Scriven, as recorded in his Diary:

> I went with the Bill for their taking of [the Bishops'] votes in the House of Peers and for meddling with temporal [non-religious] affairs, but I was against the Bill for taking away the function and calling of Bishops . . . I could never be of that opinion that the government of the Church, as it is now established by Bishops and Archbishops to be of absolute necessity, so that the taking of them away should quite overturn the state and essence of the Christian church; but I am of the opinion that the taking of them out of the Church . . . may be of dangerous consequence to the peace of the Church . . . considering that this government hath continued from the Apostles . . . it were not safe to make alteration from so ancient a beginning.

For men like Slingsby, the issue of Church government was not simply a matter of religious belief, but also of social order. While some MPs, particularly among the opposition leaders and their supporters, were deeply committed to reform of the Church along Puritan lines, there were many who regarded this as dangerous innovation, threatening the vital role of the Church in teaching the lower orders to obey and defer to those in authority. Others, like Edward Hyde, later Lord Clarendon, had a genuine affection for the traditional Anglican services practised since the time of Elizabeth. Others again, like Lord George Digby, disliked any clerical pretensions to power over the laity. Hence, while they opposed the activities of the Laudian church courts and clergy, they had no intention of replacing them with a Presbyterian clergy who would claim similar powers. It is no coincidence that all the men mentioned here ultimately fought on the side of the King. More than any other issue, the religious divide of June 1641 foreshadowed the eventual divisions of the civil war itself.

c) The Shaping of the Conflict

ISSUES
Why did communication between King and Parliament break down?
How did two 'sides' take shape?

By the late summer of 1641 the situation between the King and his critics had reached something of a stalemate. Charles's initial strategy of regaining control through limited concessions had clearly failed, and his alternative of building a separate power base in Scotland had achieved little. Although he had brought the rebellion to an end, he had neither weakened the power of the Covenanters nor built up a royalist party among the nobility. At the same time, the opposition in England had lost much of the momentum of 1640. While able to maintain parliamentary unity in redressing the grievances of the past – the prerogative courts were finally abolished in July 1641 – they were aware of concerns about further encroachments on the King's power, and had failed to find an agreed way forward in reforming the Church. While neither party, therefore, had a clear strategy for progress, there was still no reason to expect anything other than further compromises of some kind.

What changed this situation was the outbreak of rebellion in Ireland. In October, when MPs returned to Westminster after the summer recess, they were met by rumours of a rising among the Irish Catholics and attacks on Protestant settlers. Wildly exaggerated stories circulated, claiming that as many as 200,000 had been murdered, many of them tortured before death. There were reports that an Irish army had landed in England and that the English Catholics would rise to join them. The reality was much less dramatic, but the rebellion was real enough and there were undoubtedly atrocities committed. Most terrifying of all, the leaders of the rebellion claimed to have the King's approval and support.

Nothing could have been more effective in stirring up panic among MPs and people alike than the conjunction of Irish influence, Catholicism and a King who was already mistrusted. According to the Puritan minister, Richard Baxter, 'there was nothing that with the people wrought so much [had such an effect] as the Irish massacre and rebellion. This filled all England with a fear both of the Irish and of the Papists [Catholics] at home.... And when they saw the English Papists join with the King against the Parliament, it was the greatest thing that ever alienated them from the King'. To make matters worse, Charles seems to have reacted remarkably slowly. He remained in Scotland until late November, returning to a sumptuous welcome from the corporation of the City of London on 25 November. By that time, steps had already been taken in Parliament that proved both divisive and dangerous.

The rebellion posed a difficult problem for the opposition leaders. On the one hand, they wanted to take action to deal with the rebellion and rescue their fellow Protestants. They were ready to vote supply to the King to provide an army to go to Ireland. On the other hand, they were unwilling to entrust such an army to a King whom they feared might be in league with the rebels, and who might even use it against Parliament instead. The suggestion that Parliament should maintain control of the army itself was an infringement of the King's powers, and a considerable insult to him, infuriating a growing number of MPs who believed that the opposition had gone too far. Since the Ten Propositions and the religious debates of June 1641, a number of moderate MPs led by Edward Hyde and Sir John Culpepper, with the aid of Lord Falkland, had been arguing the case for the King. Any attempt to make further inroads into the royal prerogative would undoubtedly create the kind of divisions in Parliament that the opposition most feared.

ISSUE
What was the impact of the Irish rebellion?

STEPS TO WAR 1641–42

1641 October – outbreak of rebellion in Ireland; Pym revealed a second Army plot in England; November – King slow to return to London fuelling fears; triumphal welcome in city of London; Pym introduces the Grand Remonstrance; rejected by Charles; December – decision taken to publish Grand Remonstrance; Militia Bill introduced giving choice of commander to Parliament; London council elections favour opposition; public demonstrations for Parliament and attacks on bishops; King appoints Lunsford to Tower of London;
1642 January – attempt to arrest MPs; riots and demonstrations; King leaves London.

The Division of Parliament, 1640–42

In 1640 a civil war was impossible because the King faced a virtually united Parliament, and both believed in the possibility of a compromise settlement. In the year that followed, this possibility grew fainter, largely because of the attitude of the King, while the growing extremism of the opposition in response undermined the trust that would be required for it to work. At the same time, war would have remained impossible had Parliament remained united. Figure 16 traces the process by which these two developments – the growth of mistrust and the division of Parliament – took place.

a) construct a brief explanation of how civil war became the most likely outcome of the crisis; b) explain the significance within this process of the execution of Strafford, the Irish rebellion, and the attempted arrest of the Five Members.

Under pressure and deprived of time to manoeuvre, Pym devised a strategy that he hoped would reunite the Commons. On 22 November he introduced a Grand Remonstrance to be forwarded to the King, which reviewed the events of the previous year and reminded the House what had been achieved by their united efforts, before setting out the challenges that remained. This was presented to the King on 1 December. Six days later a Militia Bill providing an army for Ireland was introduced, with an amendment from Sir Arthur Haselrig proposing that Parliament should be given the right to approve the King's choice of commander. The result was uproar, and many of the uncommitted MPs rallied to the King. The division in Parliament had been revealed by the Grand Remonstrance, which passed the Commons by only eleven votes, and the Militia Bill was an additional offence. For the first time in a year, Charles was able to watch opinion in Parliament moving in his favour.

The response of the opposition was to take an even more radical step and appeal to public opinion. On 15 December the decision was taken to publish the Grand Remonstrance, to the fury of royalist MPs. In the words of Sir Edward Dering, 'when I first heard of a Remonstrance. . . I did not dream that we should remonstrate downward, tell stories to the people and talk of the King as of a third person'. In London, however, the strategy was effective. The elections to the City's corporation on 20 December produced a large majority for the friends of the opposition, and new demonstrations against the bishops. Charles responded by appointing a new Warden to the Tower of London, in the person of a brutal and aggressive soldier, Colonel Thomas Lunsford. When this provoked further demonstrations, Lunsford had the demonstrators beaten and arrested.

By late December, therefore, the Irish rebellion and the reaction of the opposition leaders had destroyed the parliamentary unity on which the opposition relied. There were now, quite clearly, two opposing sides, and a military solution to the King's problems was a growing possibility. Had Charles waited and allowed the tide of opinion to flow more strongly in his favour, he might even have gained the upper hand through purely legal means. At this point, however, a number of factors led him into rash action. In late December a quarrel erupted between the bishops and the lay nobility about the validity of business transacted in the Lords when demonstrations in London had prevented the bishops from attending. Such a reminder of the arrogance of the Laudian bishops was likely to provoke MPs as well as the Lords. At the same time, rumours reached the King that Pym was planning to impeach the Queen – the rumours had possibly been started by Pym himself to provoke the King. If this was the case, the strategy worked. On 3 January the King

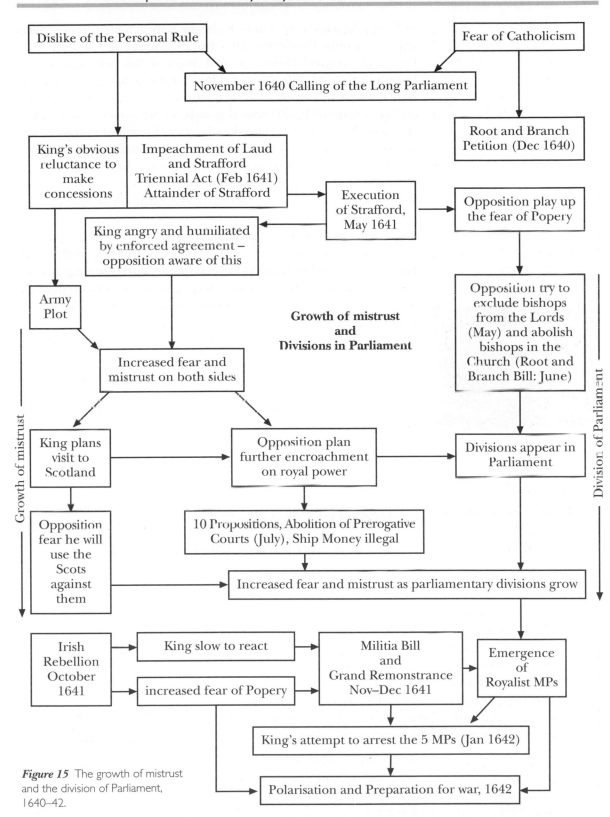

Figure 15 The growth of mistrust
and the division of Parliament,
1640–42.

ordered the House of Lords to begin impeachment proceedings against Viscount Mandeville (later Earl of Manchester) and five MPs, including Pym and Hampden. Still angry at the behaviour of the bishops, the Lords failed to act. On 4 January Charles appeared in the House of Commons, bearing a warrant for the arrest of the MPs and accompanied by 300 armed guards, whose presence was a clear threat to the members involved and a gross breach of parliamentary rights. To complete his embarrassment, the members were absent, having been warned in advance and taken refuge in London.

Charles's action undid much of the good work carried out by Hyde and Culpepper, and turned moderate opinion against him. Had he succeeded in arresting the opposition leaders, his gamble might have paid off, but to have been seen to use force and fail was disastrous. Fury erupted in and outside Parliament, and on 10 January the King left London for Hampton Court, claiming that he feared for the safety of his family. Despite hasty concessions over the militia and the exclusion of bishops from the Lords, Charles was unable to recover support, and in February he moved the Court to his northern capital of York. By now, effective communication with Parliament had ceased, and as increasing numbers of those loyal to Charles joined him in York, control of the Commons passed ever more securely to the opposition. The existence of two sides, both aware of the threat and possibility of using force, could no longer be doubted.

ISSUES

Why did Charles attempt to arrest the five members? Why was this a mistake?

ACTIVITY

Using the Evidence – Why Did Parliament Become Divided, 1640–42?

Mr Hyde [Clarendon himself, then Edward Hyde MP] met Mr Pym in Westminster Hall some days before the Parliament, and conferring together . . . [Mr Hyde] discerned that the warmest and boldest counsels would find a much better reception than those of a more temperate nature; which fell out accordingly; and the very first day they met together, in which they could enter upon business, Mr Pym, in a long formed discourse, lamented the miserable state and condition of the Kingdom . . . and then named the Earl of Strafford [as] the principal author and promoter of all those counsels, which had exposed the Kingdom to so much ruin.

Source A From Clarendon, *History of the Rebellion.*

Questions on the Sources

1. Read Source A. How does Clarendon describe the role and attitude of Pym in the early days of the Long Parliament? (comprehension and analysis)

The Parliament consisted of two sorts of men, who . . . were united in their votes and endeavours for a reformation. One party made no great matter of these alterations in the Church; but they said that if Parliaments were once down . . . and arbitrary government set up, and law subjected to the prince's will, we were then all slaves . . .. The other sort were the more religious men, who were also sensible of all these things, but were much more sensible of the interest of religion; and these most complained against the innovations in the Church.

Source B From Richard Baxter, *Autobiography*, ed. N.H. Keeble (Dent 1974), pp 21–2.

We all agree upon this; that a Reformation of Church government is most necessary. . .but. . .[not] to strike at the root, to attempt a total alteration. . . I am confident that for every Bishop we put down in a diocese, we shall set up a Pope in every parish.

Source C From Lord George Digby's speech during the debate on the Root and Branch Petition, February 1641.

The next day the Lords did throw the [Bishops' Exclusion] Bill quite out, and so left the Bishops in the state they were before. This bred much murmuring in the City [of London]. The discourse of all men is that they must now strike at Root and Branch.

Source D From a letter from Sir Henry Slingsby to Sir John Penington June 1641.

When they [Pym and his associates] found the heat and distemper of the House. . .in any degree reduced by some gracious act of the King, [they would] warm and inflame them again with a discovery, of some notable plot and conspiracy against themselves, to dissolve the Parliament by papists, or some other way, in which they would be sure that somewhat always should reflect upon the Court.

Source E From Clarendon, *History of the Rebellion*.

2. What different motives does Richard Baxter ascribe to MPs in Source B? (analysis and interpretation)

3. There was no question of allowing Catholics to worship openly. Use your knowledge of the period to explain what Digby really means in Source C by 'a Pope in every parish'. (interpretation in context)

4. What does Slingsby mean when he says in Source D, 'they must now strike at Root and Branch'? (interpretation in context)

5. What is Clarendon accusing Pym and his associates of doing in Source E? (analysis and interpretation)

6. Using all five sources together, explain: (a) What evidence suggests that the Long Parliament was not as united as it appeared in the early months of its existence? (b) How far is Clarendon's evidence about Pym, written after 1646, likely to be affected by hindsight? (c) In the light of this, whether religious differences or personalities were more serious causes of division within the Long Parliament? (evaluation and synthesis)

7. How accurate is Lucy Hutchinson's account of events in the autumn of 1641? How does this source (Source G) help to explain the widening divisions in Parliament? (reliability, interpretation in context)

8. Why was Sir Edward Dering (Source H) so shocked by the decision to publish the Grand Remonstrance? How does this help to explain the growing support for the King and the widening divisions in Parliament? (inference and interpretation in context)

9. Using evidence from all the sources, evaluate the argument that the unity of the Long Parliament was always more apparent than real, and that the emergence of two sides was therefore inevitable. (synthesis and application)

> While the King was in Scotland, that cursed rebellion in Ireland broke out, wherein above 200,000 were massacred in two months space . . . As soon as this sad news came to the Parliament, they vigorously set themselves to the work of relieving them; but then the King returned from Scotland, and being sumptuously welcomed home by the city, took courage thereby against the Parliament, and obstructed all its proceedings for the effectual relief of Ireland . . . . The Parliament . . . were forced for their own vindication to present the King with a petition and a remonstrance on the state of the Kingdom.

Source F From Lucy Hutchinson, *Memoirs of the Life of Colonel John Hutchinson*, ed. J Hutchinson (Dent 1968), pp. 75–6.

> Mr Speaker, when I first heard of a Remonstrance, I. . .imagined. . . we should hold up a glass. . . to represent unto the King the wicked counsels of pernicious councillors, the restless turbulency of practical Papists. . . the bold innovations and some superstition brought in by some pragmatical Bishops and the rotten part of the clergy. I did not dream that we should remonstrate downward, tell stories to the people and talk of the King as of a third person.

Source G From Sir Edward Dering's speech during the debate on the Grand Remonstrance and the decision to publish it, 22 November 1641.

ISSUE
How did the military conflict begin?

2 The Drift to War, 1642–3

'It is strange to note' declared the Parliamentarian lawyer Bulstrode Whitelocke in a speech to the Commons in the summer of 1642, 'how we have slid into the beginnings of a civil war by one unexpected accident after another. . . .From paper combats, by Declarations, Remonstrances, Protestations, Votes, Messages, Answers and Replies, we are now come to the question of raising forces. . . . Yet I am not for a tame resignation of our Religion, Lives and Liberties into the hands of our adversaries who seek to devour us.' Whitelocke's view of how war began, which could be matched by similarly puzzled and distressed commentaries from some supporters of the King, reveals three important elements in the outbreak of civil war – that it was unintended, unwanted, and initially fought for defensive purposes. The development of military action and the taking of sides occupied almost a year between the King's departure from London and the beginning of effective military campaigns. Although the first major battle took place at Edgehill in October 1642, attempts to secure treaties of neutrality and prevent the war from spreading were still being actively pursued in December 1642.

The point is illustrated by the table on the Outbreak of War, which sets out the major steps taken in pursuit of war and peace in 1642 and 1643. What is also significant is the defensive nature of many of the military measures that were taken – the acquisition of arms, the securing and fortification of strong points and houses – rather than any positive deployment of troops or planning of strategy. The fear of military action had been apparent, especially on Parliament's side, before the end of 1641. Reactions to the Irish rebellion were increased by the revelation of a second Army Plot in October, and one reason for the anger provoked by the appointment of Lunsford to the Tower of London was the fear that it was the first step in a military coup. The King's departure from Whitehall was hastened by the action of the citizens in taking up arms and closing the gates of the city. On both sides, thinking and action in the early months of 1642 were dominated by fear of attack and the need to take precautions – and each precaution helped to convince the other that a military strategy was being planned.

In the meantime, both sides embarked on a propaganda war, designed to increase their own support and to discredit the other side. In April, when Sir John Hotham forestalled the King's attempt to seize control of the port and arsenal of Hull, the King declared him a traitor and Hotham appealed to Parliament for support. A paper war followed, in which each side defended their actions and accused the other of acting illegally. In June Parliament followed this up with Nineteen Propositions offering terms for negotiation. Since they included parliamentary control of the King's choice of advisers and of the militia, there was little chance that Charles would accept them, and they are more appropriately regarded as a declaration of Parliament's aims. Similarly, the King's reply, drafted by Hyde and Falkland, was a statement of his legal rights and a defence of mixed monarchy. It was also a claim to stand for order, justice and the rule of law.

Everywhere men sought escape in neutralism ... Sir John Hotham's fear lest 'the necessitous people...set up for themselves to the utter ruin of all the nobility and gentry' was widely shared. In county after county gentlemen shunned both the militia ordinance and the commission of array. ... Towns like Leicester shut their gates ... But zealots could be found everywhere and the neutralists could not build quarantines against them.

Source H Derek Hirst, historian, describing the situation in the summer of 1642.

THE OUTBREAK OF WAR, 1642–3

1642

January   Parliament reorganised the London Militia to defend Parliament and the City after the King left London; Charles sent the Earl of Newcastle to secure the port and arsenal of Hull, but the Mayor refused to accept an external governor; Charles accepted Parliament's choice of Sir John Hotham as Governor to avoid open confrontation; the King accepted the exclusion of bishops from the House of Lords.

February   Henrietta Maria sailed for France to seek help and raise forces. Charles set up Court in York

March   Parliament issued a 'Declaration of fears and jealousies' and took control of the Militia.

April   The King attempted to seize control of Hull and declared Hotham a traitor for denying him entry; Hotham's appeal to Parliament sparked a propaganda war, which continued throughout May.

May   Henry Parker issued his *Observations*, a pamphlet in which he justified Parliament's right to preserve itself against the King's authority, effectively claiming a right to take arms against the King.

June   Parliament issued the Nineteen Propositions as an attempt to negotiate a settlement; however, since it included parliamentary control of the militia, the right to approve the King's advisers and reform of the Church with Parliament's advice, it was a declaration of Parliament's aims rather than a serious attempt at negotiation. The King's reply, drafted by Hyde and Falkland was a similar statement, staking his claim to represent legal power and order. The King also issued Commissions of Array to all counties; Parliament responded by sending out Militia Commissioners; the King and the Earl of Linsay tried to seize Hull after a token siege; Cromwell secured Cambridge Castle for Parliament.

July   The navy declared for Parliament; both King and Parliament appointed commanders.

August   22 August: the King raised his standard at Nottingham and called for volunteers; Staffordshire JPs declared the county to be a neutral zone; gentry in Yorkshire agreed a treaty of neutrality.

September   Parliament appointed Lord Fairfax commander in the north; at first he did not act, but under pressure from Parliament, he began to raise forces in Yorkshire.

October   Battle of Edgehill: first major battle of the war.

November   King's march on London halted by London Trained Bands (militia).

December   County Associations set up to coordinate defence in groups of counties; Cheshire JPs concluded a neutrality treaty at Bunbury.

1643

January–May   Failed peace negotiations at Oxford marked a new phase of war.

ISSUES
Why did war break out?
What factors influenced those who took up arms?

3   The Causes of the Civil War

In view of all this, it is necessary to ask why war started at all. The answer seems to lie in three main factors. The first is the fear and mistrust that existed on both sides, made worse by military preparations of any kind. Arising from this is the fact that there was no mutually trusted arbiter to stop it. While both sides postured and propagated their own interpretations of the situation, they not only weakened the prospects of serious negotiation, but also set in motion a series of developments whose only logical end was war. Despite the efforts of Royalist moderates and a Parliamentarian 'peace party' to renew negotiations into the spring of 1643, the military actions and preparations continued, and ultimately took over when alternatives ran out. Mutual mistrust meant that both sides sought to negotiate from a position of strength and that depended on military success. Even more importantly, the reluctance and confusion in which the war began should not be allowed to disguise the third factor, that great issues were at stake. Derek Hirst has described the failure of neutrality pacts (see Source H) at the hands of 'zealots', whose commitment to their cause overpowered their more lukewarm neighbours. The key point about such zealots is that they represented the fact that, for some, the war arose from a clash of ideologies involving political and religious issues for which they were prepared to fight and die.

However, historians such as Christopher Hill, who were influenced by Marxist arguments about the importance of economic trends in shaping political history, saw economic rivalries rather than politics or religion as the major cause of the Civil War. They argue that changes in population and price inflation created economic opportunities for rising gentry, who found the monarchy to be an obstacle to their political and economic development. Hence they explain the war in terms of a class struggle. Recent research has shown that the situation was more complex, and that there was little correlation between the economic fortunes of the gentry and their support of either King or Parliament. Nevertheless, some links between economic and political changes can be identified.

I undertook not this service for private interest, revenge or pay. I had an estate left by my ancestors; the office of a justice of peace I long had executed in my country; and I wanted not [did not lack] solicitations to adhere to the King's party ... But upon assembly of the gentry that were that way affected, hearing some discourse that tended both to the dishonour of God and the overthrow of the common liberty, I ... fully resolved with my utmost to promote the purity of religion and the public [by raising a regiment for Parliament].

Source I From the Apology of John Weare – a Devonshire Parliamentarian.

The Marxist View

The term Marxist is derived from the nineteenth-century philosopher, Karl Marx, whose ideas created Communism. Marx argued that changes in government and society were shaped by major economic trends, which gradually transferred economic power from one class to another until the resulting stress produced political changes in the form of revolutionary upheaval. Marxist historians have tended to interpret the Civil Wars as a revolution transferring power from a feudal monarchy and aristocracy to a 'bourgeois' gentry and merchant class who introduced a capitalist economy. In turn, capitalism created an Industrial Revolution, which produced a working class, capable in time of seizing power from the bourgeoisie (middle class) and establishing Communism.

In the first place, the overall trend of economic development does suggest that the number of the gentry as a social group increased. The effect of the Reformation and the dissolution of the monasteries was to expand the market in land, allowing more landed estates to be purchased and to remove the clerical administrators who had served the Crown, increasing the role of the nobility and gentry as an administrative class. The Protestant religion encouraged literacy, and the demands of administration and pursuit of office encouraged university and legal education. The result was that the gentry in the early seventeenth century was probably more numerous, more articulate and more confident than ever before. This produced several results. If there were greater numbers of gentry, then by the early seventeenth century there were more men chasing and competing for a fixed number of posts and offices. This placed greater stress on the working of patronage, at precisely the time that the aristocracy, who formed the vital link between the Court and the localities, were weakened by inflation and fixed rents. As a result, they were unable to satisfy the demand for 'places' in the Court and administration and less able to provide leadership and management in Parliament. A more confident and articulate House of Commons was therefore more able and more likely to obstruct the Crown in its exercise of power.

If these arguments are correct, and they are difficult to document with any accuracy, they may well have contributed to tension between Crown and Parliament. Nevertheless, they do not explain the outbreak of a war, let alone a revolution. At most they could explain a level of tension and destabilisation that interacted with other factors. Similarly, the more widespread popular unrest arising from high prices and unemployment created a problem for government, but not a breakdown of either government or society. From the mid-sixteenth century a growing concern with vagrancy led to harsh laws by which vagrants could be flogged, branded and hanged, and the provision of parish poor rates and houses of correction. In 1598–1601 these were codified in two major Poor Laws, which provided support in their own parish for the old, sick and under-employed, along with harsh punishment for those who left without permission. Thereafter, although trade depressions and bad harvests led to local rioting and attacks on enclosures, there was little sign that governments were unable to cope. In the bad harvests of the early 1630s the Books of Orders demonstrated the government's ability to respond. While economic stress could, and did, create unrest among the lower classes and tension among their betters, there is little to suggest that either was revolutionary in its impact.

Historians therefore continue to disagree about the causes of the war, but the role of different issues in the outbreak of war can be

---

Before the flame of the war broke out in the top of the chimneys, the smoke ascended in every country. The King had sent forth commissions of array, and the Parliament had given out commissions for their militia ... Between these, in many places, there were fierce contests and disputes ... for in the progress every county had the civil war (more or less) within itself. Some counties were in the beginning so wholly for the Parliament that the King's interest appeared not in them; some so wholly for the King that the godly (for those generally were the Parliament's friends) were forced to forsake their habitations and seek other shelters.

Source J From Lucy Hutchinson, *Memoirs of the Life of Colonel John Hutchinson*, 1660.

examined more fully by considering the factors that influenced men to take sides. It is important, however, not to oversimplify this process. The sources below offer a number of contemporary views of how the country divided, and the distribution of support across class boundaries and geographical areas. They must be handled with caution on two counts. The first is the element of prejudice that is likely to arise in the interpretations of those who were actively involved in the struggle, the second is the piecemeal way in which it developed. As Lucy Hutchinson explains, before the major campaigns began each county community struggled within itself to decide which side should dominate, and individual choices were always influenced by practical considerations such as the prevailing weight of opinion, fear of attack, and older rivalries. While the distribution of support and the motives of the committed minorities can reveal a great deal about the issues and ideologies behind the war, they should be viewed through a filter of local and circumstantial pressures, so that any general conclusions allow for the many exceptions and complexities that existed.

In Leicestershire leadership was divided between Henry Hastings [Royalist] and the Puritan Lord Grey of Groby. This division was much more than a rivalry between Puritan and Cavalier, however. The division between the two families went back to personal feuds and rivalry for control of the county since the mid-sixteenth century. According to Clarendon the whole county was divided between the Greys and the Hastingses. Local circumstances forced the gentry to take sides.

Source K From A. Everitt, *The Local Community and the Great Rebellion.*

ACTIVITY

The Causes of War and the Distribution of Support

Use the Sources in Section 3 and those below to decide:

1. What evidence suggests that support for King and Parliament was influenced by:
   (a) class divisions;
   (b) religion;
   (c) geographical area?   (analysis and interpretation)
2. How can you begin to assess the reliability of the evidence?   (interpretation in context, cross-referencing)

3. What evidence suggests that the distribution of support was influenced by local conditions and loyalties?   (analysis and interpretation)
4. How do these conflicting motives help to explain why the early stages of the war were so complex?   (interpretation in context, synthesis)
5. What evidence of neutralism is there in these sources?   (analysis and interpretation)
6. How far do they support Derek Hirst's opinion in Source H?   (synthesis, evaluation)
7. Using all the information that you have, explain how England divided in 1642–3.

   (synthesis, application)

A great part of the Lords forsook the Parliament and so did many of the House of Commons, and came to the King; but that was after Edgehill fight, when the King was at Oxford. A very great part of the knights and gentlemen ... adhered to the King; except in Middlesex, Essex, Suffolk, Norfolk, Cambridgeshire etc., where the King with his army never came. And could he have got footing there, it is like that it would have been there as it was in other places. And most of the tenants of these gentlemen, and also most of the poorest of the people, whom the other called 'the rabble' did follow the gentry and were for the King. On the Parliament's side were (besides themselves) some of the gentry in most of the counties, and the greatest part of the tradesmen and freeholders, and the middle sort of men, especially in those corporations and countries which depend on clothing and such manufactures.

Source L From Richard Baxter, *Reliquae Baxterianae*, 1696.

In Yorkshire over one third of the Royalist gentry were Catholics and over a half of the Parliamentarians were Puritans. To put it another way, of those who took sides, 90% of all Catholics became Royalists, and 72% of all Puritans became Parliamentarians. All the Parliamentary leaders in Yorkshire had a previous record of strong Puritan sympathies. There is reason to think those who had opposed the crown on purely constitutional and political grounds in the 1620s and 1630s tended to swing back to the King with Sir Edward Hyde in 1642, while those who had also opposed the crown on religious grounds were far more likely to stick to Pym and fight for the Parliamentary cause.

Source M From Lawrence Stone, *The Causes of the English Revolution*, 1529–1642 (1972) p. 143.

Training as volunteers for Parliament began ... only in those corporations and by those inferior people who were notorious for faction and schism [divisions] in religion ... The people generally (except in great towns and corporations where, the factious lecturers and emissaries from Parliament had poisoned the affections) were loyally inclined.... [In the west] most of the gentry were engaged [against the Parliament] as they were in truth throughout the Kingdom; yet the common people, especially in parts of Somerset, were generally too much inclined to them ... [Their leaders were] for the most part clothiers [who] had gotten very great fortunes; and by degrees getting themselves into gentlemen's estates, were angry that they found not themselves in the same esteem and reputation with those whose estates they had ... Those, from the beginning were fast friends to the Parliament ... [In Gloucestershire] the yeomanry [have] been most forward and seditious, being very wealthy ... [In Lancashire] men of no name ... and the town of Manchester opposed the King. ...[In Yorkshire] besides the Lord Fairfax ... few of good reputation and fortune ran that way. ...Leeds, Halifax and Bradford [three very populous and rich towns which, depending wholly upon clothiers naturally maligned the gentry] were wholly at their disposition.

Source N From Clarendon, *History of the Rebellion*.

There was in this county [Cornwall] . . .a full submission and love of the established government in Church and State, and especially to . . .the Book of Common Prayer, which was a most general object of veneration with the people. And jealousy and apprehension that the other party intended to alter it was the principal advancement of the King's service.

Source O From Clarendon, *History of the Rebellion.*

The greatest family was the Earl of Newcastle's [commander of the King's northern armies]. He had indeed, through his great estate, his liberal hospitality and constant residence in his country, so endeared [the gentry and their dependents] to him that no man was a greater prince in all that northern quarter . . . Most of the gentry . . . were disaffected to the Parliament. Most of the middle sort – the able substantial freeholders and the other commons who had not their dependence upon the malignant nobility and gentry – adhered to the Parliament . . . Mr Henry Ireton . . . was the chief promoter of the Parliament's interest in the county. But finding it generally disaffected, all he could do when the King approached it was to gather a troop of those godly people which the cavaliers drove out, and with them to go into the army of my lord of Essex.

Source P From Lucy Hutchinson, *Memoirs* (referring to the county of Nottinghamshire).

They who were most inclined to the Parliament, whereof the Lord Fairfax and his son were the chief . . . [preferred] to look on [rather] than engage themselves in the war. [And the royalist commander, Sir Thomas Glemham] was not . . . able to infuse fire enough into the phlegmatic constitutions of [his] people. Who did rather wish to be spectators of the war than parties in it, and believed, if they did not provoke the other party, they might all live quietly together; until Sir John Hotham, by his excursions and depredations out of Hull, and their seditious neighbours, by their insurrections, awakened them out of that pleasant dream.

Source Q From Clarendon, *The History of the Rebellion* (this passage describes neutralism among the county gentry of Yorkshire.

▼ Working on From Crisis to War

Before attempting any exercises or essays on this chapter, you should ensure that you have accurate linear notes that record the information that you need. If you have not already done this, reread the chapter and make notes, using the headings and issue boxes to help you.

Summary of the causes of the Civil War

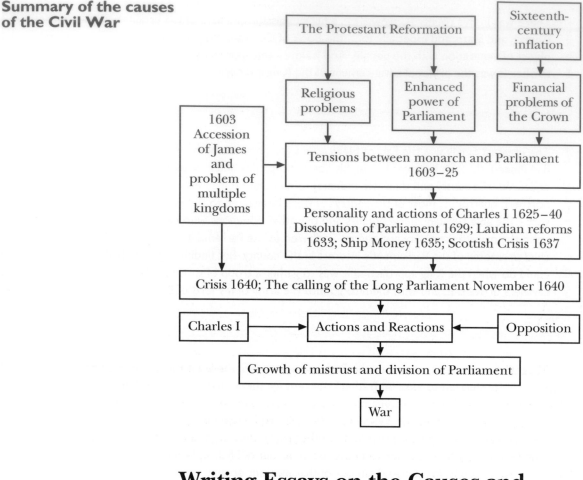

Writing Essays on the Causes and Outbreak of the War

The issue of why civil war broke out in England in 1642 is a favourite with examiners. Although the phrasing of the question may vary (see below), the essential issue is to decide what factors helped to bring about war, and how they worked together to do so. The study guide at the end of Chapter 3 suggested a way of defining factors and establishing how they built up to cause the initial crisis; you could now apply and extend that to explaining the war of 1642. The summary charts at the ends of Chapters 3 and 4 will help you to define your factors and outline your explanation.

Chapter 4, however, suggests that the transition from crisis to war was not a simple or inevitable process, and an approach to essay writing that ignores these complexities may well gloss over some key issues. It is suggested that what destroyed parliamentary unity and the chances of a negotiated settlement was *the growth of mistrust* and extension of *opposition demands*, combined with *divisions over the future of the Church* and its social role (see Figure 17). What heightened tension and brought problems to a head was the *Irish rebellion*, interacting with an *existing fear of Catholicism*. Yet all of these factors, except the rebellion, existed before 1640. We are therefore faced with two possible interpretations of the causes of the war.

▼ It could be argued that war was inevitable at some time in the reign of Charles I. There were serious and deep-seated divisions in society over religion and the need to reform the machinery of government, which Charles had inherited from his predecessors. These revealed themselves in the form of *religious divisions, financial problems, tensions between Crown and Parliament, and the relationship between three kingdoms. The personality of Charles I* made conflict inevitable, because in crucial areas, he allied himself with one faction rather than maintaining a balance, driving those who opposed that faction into opposition to the King himself. Charles did not stand above the conflicts as a king, but acted as a party leader. *All of these factors* were in place before November 1640, *creating the essential conditions for war*. They can therefore be defined as **conditional factors**. What occurred thereafter was that the *attempt to find a settlement brought the problems into the open, and thereby intensified hostility and mistrust, so that a single event such as the Irish rebellion could act as a trigger* to begin the slide into civil war.

▼ An alternative argument would define the factors in the same way, but would argue that war was not inevitable. Although the **conditional factors** (creating conditions for war) were in place in 1640, the desire for settlement was also present. Although the King's personality made a settlement difficult, he did make concessions in 1640–41, and the remaining difficulties might have been resolved by moderates in both factions. What prevented this was the *combination of errors and actions by Charles, the opposition leaders, and their Scottish allies, and the rebellion in Ireland*, which robbed them of time to manoeuvre. It was therefore these **contingencies**, or **contingent factors** that were most important in causing the war.

These explanations both use the idea of conditional and contingent factors to organise an explanation and define what part different factors played in causing war. The assumption behind this is that events happen because certain *factors work together to make them likely to happen*, while other factors influence how and when the likely outcome actually occurs. It is therefore possible to break down the main question into series of sub-questions that provide structure to the essay. Having defined the factors involved, it is possible to ask:

▼ Which factors created conditions in which a conflict of some kind was possible?

▼ Which factors caused these conditions to build up and make conflict probable?

▼ Which factors dictated the nature and timing of the conflict?

The approach allows factors to be explained within a broad chronological framework and also provides a basis upon which the essay writer can make judgements about the importance of particular factors by weighing up and comparing the part that they played in the overall process. This is the main area of debate in the explanations offered above.

Using these ideas to help you organise and structure an essay plan, you should now consider the questions here. Some questions that refer to the war are actually focusing more on the crisis that led up to it; others are focused on why it broke out when it did. You will probably need to refer to the same factors for each question, but will give greater importance, and therefore depth of explanation, to different factors according to the precise phrasing of the question.

▼ Analyse each question and define its key focus. It may be useful to discuss this with others, and to break the main question down into sub-questions like those above.

▼ Use your notes and knowledge of the period to construct an essay plan. This should list the factors involved in the order in which you will explain them, establish links between them, and summarise their part in causing the war.

▼ Having planned and discussed all the essays, choose one to write.

Essay questions

1. Why did civil war break out in England in 1642?

2. 'A conflict of some kind between King and Parliament was always likely in the seventeenth century, but it was the personality of Charles I that brought it to civil war.' How far do you agree with this statement?

3. In 1640 most MPs wanted and expected to redress grievances and settle the problems created by the Personal Rule of Charles I. Why, then, did they find themselves at war in 1642?

Further reading

Books in the Access to History Series

The relevant volume of the Access to History series is A. Anderson *The Civil Wars, 1640–9*. Chapter 2 reviews the different historical interpretations of the war while Chapter 3 explores the issues related to its outbreak in greater depth. Chapter 4 may also be of use, since it considers the nature of the divisions across the country that influenced the taking of sides.

General

There is a very large number of valuable works that examine the causes and outbreak of war. It is impossible to provide an exhaustive survey of others, but it is worth glancing at Anthony Fletcher's detailed analysis of the events of 1640–42 in his *Outbreak of the Civil War* (Arnold 1981). Few students will find time to read it all, but there is a helpful conclusion, which explains his view and students who have already gained a clear view of events will be able to dip into chapters of particular interest. Of the shorter surveys of the period, Ann Hughes, *The Causes of the English Civil War* (Macmillan 1991) is perhaps the most useful and accessible.

WAR AND REVOLUTION, 1642–9

KEY ISSUES
Why did Parliament
win the first civil war?
Why did this lead to
the execution of the
King?

CHAPTER 5

POINTS TO CONSIDER

The execution of Charles I was not the intended outcome of the Civil War. Parliament's aims were to force him to agree to their terms, and even those MPs who wanted to achieve outright victory rather than a compromise peace were merely trying to ensure that they could negotiate from a position of strength. In 1647 the emergence of the army as a political force introduced a more radical element into the situation, but the army leaders also sought to negotiate terms with Charles. This defines three areas of investigation – the difficulty of finding a settlement, the emergence of radical forces, and the interaction of these factors to create a revolution that none had expected or intended to happen.

1 The Victory of Parliament, 1643–6

The campaigns and main battles of the first civil war in England are outlined on the maps in Figure 16. Broadly speaking, in 1642 the King held the north and west, while Parliament controlled the south-east, and the campaigns of 1642–3 focused on the Royalist effort to attack and take London. At the end of 1643, the entry of the Scots on the side of Parliament tipped the balance in the north, but weaknesses within the Parliamentarian command strengthened the Royalist hold on the west and led to the restructuring of Parliament's armies in the winter of 1644–5. In 1645, after a decisive battle at Naseby, near Leicester, the Royalists began to weaken, and Parliament's New Model Army was able to mop up resistance in the final year of war.

Various reasons have been put forward to explain Parliament's victory, including criticisms of the King's leadership, the indiscipline of Royalist troops and the weakness of Royalist administration. In fact, recent studies suggest that the two sides were remarkably similar in their methods and approach until late 1644. Both relied at first on locally-based forces, run by county committees, and both experienced difficulty in persuading them to release forces for duty elsewhere. Both experienced internal divisions and rivalries. The

King's advisers disagreed over war aims, and there was considerable rivalry among his military commanders, while Parliament was divided between a 'peace' party who wanted a negotiated settlement and a 'war' party who sought outright victory first.

Ultimately, the Parliamentarian victory was based on three main factors – the failure of the Royalists to capitalise on their early advantage, the superior resources enjoyed by Parliament, and the military and political restructuring in 1644–5 that enabled those resources to be effectively exploited.

a) The Failure of the Royalists

In the early stages of the war, the advantage lay with the King. Although the gentry divided between the two sides, the greater number joined the King, bringing with them their tenants, horses and military expertise, at least in terms of the ability to ride and fight. Many were quick to donate money and plate. The King was also able to call on the professional soldiers, mainly officers, who had been fighting abroad in the Thirty Years' War, and in his nephews, Rupert and Maurice of Nassau, he had two experienced and battle-hardened commanders. Some of these advantages were revealed in the battle of Edgehill in October 1642. It ended in a stalemate that left the road to London open, and the King's forces were only pre-vented from reaching the capital by the London Trained Bands (vol-unteers from the city) under the command of Philip Skippon, and by the approach of winter.

ISSUE
Why did the Royalists fail to build on their initial advantages?

PRINCE RUPERT OF THE RHINE (1619–82)

-Profile-

Prince Rupert, one of the leading Royalist generals, was the son of Charles's sister, Elizabeth and the Elector Palatine (see Chapter 2). Already experienced through service in the Thirty Years' War, he and his brother Maurice joined Charles at Not-tingham in 1642. Both served him well as military commanders, and Rupert was justly famed for his skill and courage as a leader of cavalry, but his abrasive personality led to quarrels with other Royalist generals and a bitter feud with Lord Digby. This con-tributed to the fatal decision to attack at Naseby. Later in 1645 Rupert was forced to surrender Bristol, for which the King never forgave him. In 1646 he left England, but returned with Charles II and served with distinction in the navy and became First Lord of the Admiralty (1673–9).

Portrait of Prince Rupert by William Dobson.

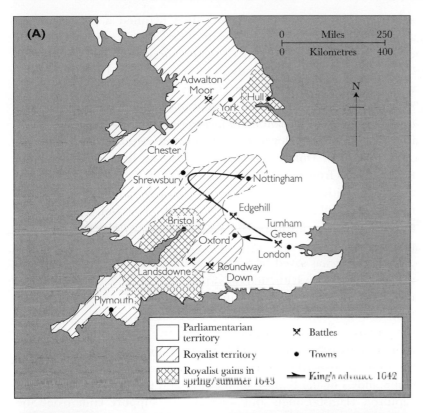

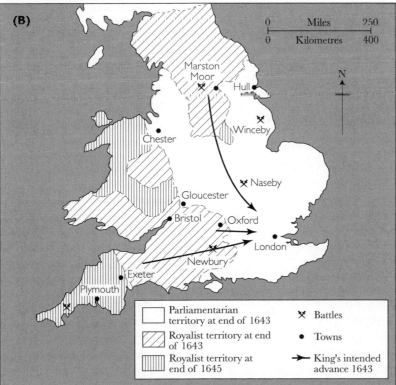

Figure 16 The Civil War campaigns, 1642–6

Map A shows the Parliamentarian campaign at its weakest point in 1643. Map B shows the King's planned attack on London in 1643, and the vital importance of the Parliamentarian strongholds of Hull, Gloucester and Plymouth. The threat of attack from these garrisons in the rear of the advancing Royalist armies prevented his strategy from being successfully carried out.

After wintering at Oxford the Royalists planned a three-pronged attack. The northern army under the Earl of Newcastle extended its control from a secure base in York, and succeeded in defeating Parliament's Yorkshire army at Adwalton Moor in June 1643. The southwestern army under Sir Ralph Hopton had secured Cornwall, and much of Devon, and was ready to march east. In July, Prince Rupert took Bristol while his brother, Maurice, defeated the Parliamentarian forces at Roundway Down in Wiltshire and captured Dorchester to gain control of Dorset. There seemed to be little to prevent the King's armies from approaching London from Newbury, Oxford and the north. With a peace party in Parliament demanding negotiation, they would probably not need to attack the city, but could rely on internal pressures to force the Parliamentarian leaders to sue for peace.

Parliament was saved by a combination of factors. Its control of the navy helped Parliamentarian strongholds at Hull, Gloucester and Plymouth to hold out, preventing the Royalists from concentrating their strength on London. In particular, Hull provided a safe refuge for the remains of Parliament's Yorkshire army, and Newcastle refused to march south with hostile forces at his back. In East Anglia, the Eastern Association (of counties) had developed a strong force commanded by the Earl of Manchester and Oliver Cromwell, which captured Gainsborough and was able to support Hull from the south. Finally, in September, the Earl of Essex was able to march from London to relieve Gloucester, and succeeding in defeating a Royalist force at Newbury on his return. In military terms the year ended in a stalemate, similar to that with which it began, but in political terms, significant changes had taken place.

b) The Turning Tide, 1643–4

These changes were the work of John Pym. In the early part of the year he concentrated his efforts on building up an effective system of taxation and administration in Parliamentarian areas, introducing an **excise tax** in May 1643 which gave Parliament a sound financial base. With great skill he maintained a balance between peace and war parties, securing a precarious unity among MPs. Finally, in the autumn of 1643 he persuaded Parliament to sign a Solemn League and Covenant with the Scots, by which Parliament would receive the help of the Scottish Covenanters' army. This was no mean achievement. The price demanded by the Scots was the introduction of a Presbyterian system into the Church of England. While many MPs held Puritan views and wanted to see further reform in the Church, few were committed to a full Presbyterian system and certainly not the rigid version used in the Scottish Kirk. Pym's tactics were to avoid

ISSUE
What factors helped Parliament to hold out?

EXCISE TAX
The Excise Tax was placed on home-produced beer and cider, and on a range of imported goods. It was easy to collect and, in principle, no different to customs duties. But it was unprecedented in England, and was highly unpopular.

divisions and satisfy the Scots by calling an Assembly of Divines (ministers) to discuss and devise a suitable model for England. The Assembly met in December 1643, the same month in which Pym died.

The Solemn League and Covenant

The Solemn League and Covenant was a treaty between Parliament and the Scottish Covenanters of 1638 (see pages 77–8). It secured Scottish aid at the time of Parliament's greatest need, but it also made Scottish pressure for religious uniformity a significant factor, and brought into the open the various conflicting views on religious reform that existed among Parliament's supporters. The Assembly of Divines was dominated by ministers who favoured some form of Presbyterianism, but there were already some among MPs and in Parliament's armies who were unwilling to accept any national establishment. In early 1644 five members of the Assembly issued a public appeal for a limited measure of religious toleration, and when this was denied, sought to prolong debates and delay reform. As a result, the Assembly was unable to complete its scheme, the Directory of Worship, until 1646. In the meantime, religious separatists of all kinds had mounted a campaign for toleration that changed the whole political situation (see below), and the Directory was never fully implemented.

By the time that military campaigning was renewed in 1644, therefore, the balance of forces had changed. The King's early advantages had begun to fade, and the superior resources provided by Parliament's control of the south and east were beginning to take effect. More immediately, the Scottish alliance began to produce results. In February Parliament established a Committee of Both Kingdoms to coordinate the war effort, in April and May the Earl of Newcastle was forced back into York, while Manchester's Eastern Association army extended its control of Lincolnshire. In June, Prince Rupert joined Newcastle with a force of 8,000 men, and they left York to meet the combined forces of Manchester, the Yorkshire army under Lord Fairfax, and the Scots led by Lord Leven, at Marston Moor. After a bitter day's fighting the Royalists were defeated, in part because of the superior discipline and tactics of the Parliamentarian cavalry led by David Leslie and Oliver Cromwell. Within a fortnight York had surrendered to Parliament, and the King's control of the north was ended.

What might have been a decisive victory for Parliament, however,

PARLIAMENT'S VICTORY

1642 Battle of Edgehill followed by victory of the London Militia at Turnham Green, prevented the King from entering London;

1643 sieges of Hull and Gloucester prevented Royalist march on London; Scottish alliance with Parliament;

1644 Battle of Marston Moor secured the north for Parliament;

1644 The Self-Denying –5 Ordinance and establishment of the New Model Army transformed Parliament's military organisation;

1645 Battle of Naseby destroyed the King's main army;

1646 Charles surrendered to the Scots.

was negated by the Earl of Essex in the south. Marching west from Lyme Regis, where he had lifted a Royalist siege, he sought to relieve Plymouth and then to march into the Royalist stronghold of Cornwall. Hopton simply parted his forces to allow the Parliamentarian army through, then closed again behind them. The result was a serious defeat for Essex at Lostwithiel in Cornwall, followed by an even more disastrous surrender of 6,000 men with all their cannon and supplies. While Essex took a ship back to London, what was left of his army was forced to walk, devoid of weapons, through hostile country. Fewer than 600 men reached London alive. To make matters worse, Waller, Manchester and Cromwell allowed the King to return safely to Oxford after an indecisive battle at Newbury.

This disaster, combined with successes for the Royalists in Scotland, did much to restore the military balance but it was the political effects that were most important. The humiliation of Essex brought into the open a simmering dispute between the peace and war parties in Parliament over how the war should be fought. Complaints were partly based on military considerations – Sir William Waller, for example, had been arguing for a mobile, professional army to replace the locally-based forces – but there were deeper concerns about the attitudes and aims of Parliament's commanders. Men like Essex and Manchester had, in the normal seventeenth-century manner, been appointed to command because of their noble status rather than their military talent, and both their social position and political outlook made them cautious. They were accused of seeing the war only in defensive terms and of seeking to avoid defeat while hoping for negotiations, rather than pursuing victory. The issue had already led to open conflict between Manchester and his commander of cavalry, Oliver Cromwell, and the conflict was complicated by political and religious rivalries. By December 1644 it was clear that a way had to be found to resolve the differences and avoid disaster.

ISSUES
How did Parliament gain the initiative? How important was the establishment of the New Model Army?

c) The Victory of Parliament

The solution adopted became known as the **Self-Denying Ordinance**, in which all members of Parliament agreed to give up their military commands. By separating the military and political commands, it allowed the failed commanders, who were members of the House of Lords, to be removed without losing face. It permitted a reorganisation of Parliament's forces and the creation of a single, mobile and professional army of 22,000 men, a New Model, to fight the war more effectively. Its commander was to be Sir Thomas Fairfax, a man of proven military talent with little awareness of politics, whose aim was to achieve military success and to leave the politics to others. An unexpected bonus for the war party was that, unable to agree on a new commander of cavalry, MPs appointed Cromwell to fulfil the role until a replacement could be found – he was to continue in this position on a series of temporary commissions until after the war ended.

In many ways the creation of the New Model Army in the early months of 1645 was a military revolution (see Profile and Further Reading), but its full effects were not felt immediately. It took time to train and prepare the force, and time for its unity and identity to become established. Nevertheless, it was to play a crucial role in Parliament's victory. Its first success, at Naseby in June 1645, was helped by rivalries and misjudgments among the Royalist commanders, but thereafter it proved its value in the speed with which Fairfax could move around the country to mop up the remaining Royalist forces. In June he defeated Goring's army in Somerset, in September Rupert was forced to surrender Bristol, and by the end of the year the Royalists had been driven back into Wales and the south-west. In early 1646 the New Model took control of Devon and Cornwall, and in May the King accepted defeat, surrendering to the Scots at Southwell in Nottinghamshire on 5 May.

In fact, Naseby had proved decisive. Not only had it destroyed the main Royalist army, but the capture of the King's baggage-train had provided Parliament with a significant political victory. The baggage-train contained the King's correspondence, and when this was published it revealed his determination to secure victory on his terms, the lack of good faith with which he had approached peace negotiations since 1642, and his willingness to take help from any source, including the Irish Catholics and the Pope. Royalist support was further weakened by the increasing demands laid on Royalist areas for taxes, men and provisions. The result was the outbreak of Clubmen risings in many counties, where local forces and residents combined to oppose all military activity in an attempt to defend what was left of their property and livelihoods.

2 The Impact of War

a) The Emergence of the Radicals

By 1646, therefore, Parliament had secured the victory that MPs hoped would force the King to accept a settlement on their terms. The Nineteen Propositions of 1642 were quickly revived and presented to the King with some amendments while he was still with the Scottish army at Newcastle. Nevertheless, the situation in which MPs began the task of finding peace was already very different from that of 1642. The process of war and the steps taken to secure victory had altered attitudes and expectations in a way that could not have been

SELF-DENYING ORDINANCE

Proposed by a member of the war party, Zouch Tate, and supported by Cromwell. The military failures of late 1644 led to recriminations among Parliament's generals, revealing their political and religious differences. While Cromwell accused Manchester and Essex of preferring negotiations to victory, Manchester and the Scots accused Cromwell of favouring political and religious radicals. By separating military and political functions, the Ordinance allowed the political and religious divisions to be set aside while a new and more effective army was created.

CLUBMEN

Although this resurgence of neutralism was not confined to Royalist areas, the strongest Clubmen organisations were in the west and west Midlands where the Royalist armies had been based. In Somerset the Clubmen joined with Fairfax to drive out Goring's army, which was notorious for its lack of discipline and brutality towards civilians. But most Clubmen groups were strictly neutral. Their effect on the Royalist war effort was greater because the King's armies were more dependent on provisions seized from the land, and because their crumbling effectiveness and morale made them more vulnerable to such external pressures.

THE NEW MODEL ARMY – SOLDIERS OR SAINTS?

-Profile-

Officially formed 4 April 1645, under the command of the Lord General, Sir Thomas Fairfax of Nun Appleton, near Tadcaster.

Consisting of:

12 regiments of Foot (14,000 men) under the command of Major-General Philip Skippon, previously commander of the London Trained Bands under service with the Earl of Essex.

11 regiments of Horse (6,600 men) under the command of Lieutenant-General Oliver Cromwell, previously Lieutenant-General to the Earl of Manchester in the army of the Eastern Association.

1 regiment of dragoons (1,000 men) armed with muskets.

▼ The character of the New Model Army has been the subject of much debate. There is no doubt that it became a highly effective fighting unit, contributing significantly to Parliament's victory. Opinions differ, however, as to the reasons for its effectiveness.

▼ Historians like Sir Charles Firth who published a study of 'Cromwell's Army' in 1904 explored the religious radicalism of the army, described in more hostile terms by critics like Thomas Edwards. Firth argued that the religious separatists recruited and protected by officers like Oliver Cromwell dominated the army. Its effectiveness came from their discipline and dedication in pursuit of what they regarded as God's cause, which also explains the political role of the army after 1647.

▼ More recent research has challenged this view, and argued that the effectiveness of the army came from thorough training, regular pay and professional discipline rather than religious fervour. The 'Army of Saints' was, in fact, an army of well-trained soldiers.

▼ The likelihood is that both factors played a part. The army was not made up of religiously motivated volunteers, but there were a number of them, especially among the cavalry regiments. Such men set a tone of restraint and good discipline, which enabled these standards to be more easily enforced. They also made egalitarian policies such as promotion by merit more effective, and this contributed to the spirit of comradeship that held the army together. Regular pay, effective training and a habit of victory helped to maintain this spirit, and establish mutual respect and loyalty between officers and men. The result was a formidable fighting unit, and a potential political force.

When I came to the Army among Cromwell's soldiers I found a new face of things, which I never dreamt of: I heard plotting heads very hot upon that which intimated their intention to subvert both Church and State ... I found that many honest men of weak judgements and little acquaintance with such matters, had been seduced into a disputing vein, and made it too much of their religion to talk for this opinion and for that; sometimes for State democracy, and sometimes for Church democracy.

Source A From Richard Baxter, *Reliquae Baxterianae.*

foreseen at its outset. On the one hand, there was an overwhelming desire for peace, which acted to the benefit of the King. The country had endured levels of taxation that dwarfed Charles's demands before 1640, and a dislocation of trade, physical damage and personal suffering that translated into a desire for the return of pre-war normality. In Parliament this was reflected in a resurgence of support for the peace party. On the other hand, the war effort and the propaganda required to maintain it had encouraged the development of new ideas and new expectations among some who had fought most enthusiastically for Parliament. It was this effect, the emergence of new and radical ideas, that caused most immediate concern to those involved in the search for peace.

ISSUES
How had the experience of war changed the political situation?
Why had religious and political radicalism developed by 1646?

The Emergence of Radicalism

Figure 19 traces the emergence of religious radicalism from its roots in mainstream Protestant thinking. It illustrates a number of important points including the common origins and links between religious and political radicalism:

▼ Radical ideas and groups had existed in England before 1640, but their illegal status forced them to be secretive and they left little evidence of their existence.

▼ Their roots and origins lay in the same Protestant ideas as the mainstream reformers, especially the emphasis on private faith, the authority of the Bible, and Calvinist predestination.

▼ The first separatists were therefore only 'radical' in their desire to separate, that is, to set up separate churches outside the Church of England, whose members had voluntarily chosen to join.

▼ Some had done this because they found the Anglican Church inadequate and despaired of reform, others because they believed that the 'saints', the godly minority whom God had predestined to salvation, should withdraw from contact with sinners and work together to find their way to God.

▼ This meant that the first separatists were not seeking rights for all, but privileges for the saints; their interests were religious, not political.

▼ However, separation was in practice a political act, threatening to a government and society that believed religious uniformity to be an essential part of political unity.

▼ This meant that the separatists had to develop in isolation and secrecy. In those circumstances they tended to become more radical and eccentric, drawing new enthusiasms from the Bible and their own interpretations of it (For an example, see the Profile of Smyth and Robinson on page 242).

▼ The collapse of authority, especially of the bishops who were responsible for censorship and control of preachers and the press, in 1640–42 allowed the radicals to emerge from hiding, to debate in public, and to develop their ideas in new forms and directions. By 1644 a coherent campaign in favour of religious toleration had developed in London.

▼ In turn this led to the emergence of political radicals like the Levellers and to an explosion of new ideas. The execution of the King in 1649 convinced many that a new world was opening up, and even that God himself would soon return to earth to rule in person.

▼ In these conditions, new and even more eccentric groups emerged, arguing for complete freedom and the authority of individual conscience above all else. The nature and development of radical ideas is explored in greater depth in Chapter 8, pages 236–252. The focus here is on the political impact of the radicals and their effect on the search for peace.

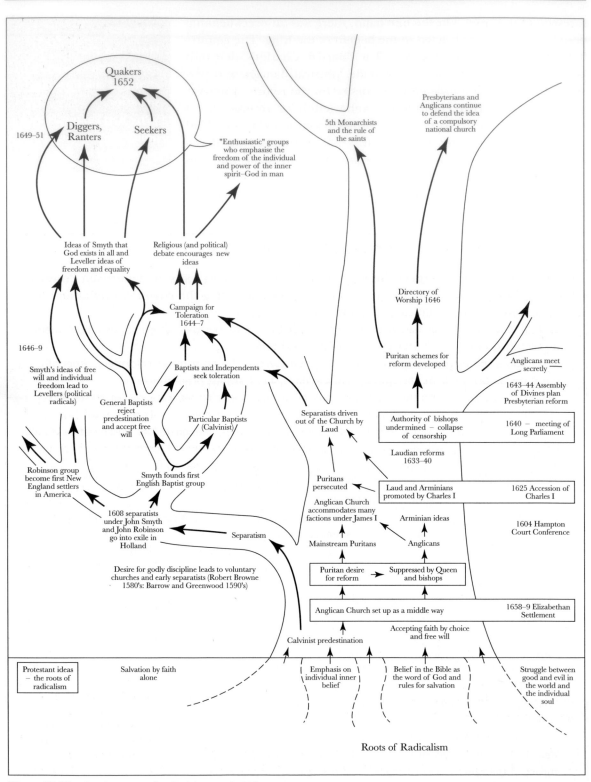

Figure 17 The development of radical groups and ideas.

b) The Effects of Radicalism

ISSUE
How did the radicals affect the war effort and the search for peace?

The impact of radicalism was significant in a variety of ways. As early as 1641 the emergence of separatist groups and 'tub-thumping' lay preachers in London frightened many of the more conservative MPs into supporting the King's power as the guarantee of authority, a tendency that increased in 1642 as social disruption and popular unrest followed the breakdown of authority. At the same time, the radicals and their preachers provided many of Parliament's most dedicated supporters and activists. The preachers argued that Parliament's cause was God's cause, part of the great struggle between good and evil, which would end with the return of Christ to earth and the rule of his saints. The clearest, but not the only, example of this can be seen in the army of the Eastern Association, where Oliver Cromwell deliberately recruited troopers who 'knew what they fought for and loved what they knew'. The image of his cavalry, and of the New Model Army that they later created, as a disciplined body of psalm-singing saints has been considerably exaggerated (see above, page 116), but there is no doubt that men of this kind formed an influential core, which contributed a great deal to the dedication and effectiveness of Parliament's forces. In the House of Commons and on the battlefield the radicals contributed much to the victory of Parliament.

For many of the conservative Parliamentarians who celebrated this victory, however, they constituted a new and disturbing threat to their vision of a reformed monarchy and Church. The experience of war and success against the King encouraged more radical and **millenarian** dreams, and the breakdown of authority provided the chance to express them. The result was a tendency to look for a new earth as well as a new heaven – to believe that society could be transformed according to God's word and that the saints need not wait for salvation. The first sign of this came in 1643–4, at the time when the Solemn League and Covenant threatened the imposition of a Presbyterian uniformity that would be no more acceptable to some radicals than the Anglican Church and the bishops.

In early 1644, five members of the Assembly of Divines published an Apologetical Narration, arguing for the right of orthodox Protestant saints to establish their own congregations outside the Church and to exercise discipline over their members. It was a cautious and limited appeal, but it was quickly followed by bolder spirits who began to argue for extensive religious toleration. By the end of 1644 there was an organised campaign for toleration and for freedom of speech and the press, which brought together figures such as Roger Williams, the founder of the American colony of Rhode Island, John Milton, the Puritan poet, and the later leaders of the Leveller move-

MILLENARIANISM
The belief that the struggle between good and evil would end in the physical return of Christ to rule on earth. Not confined to radical eccentrics, but they tended to pursue it in its most enthusiastic and literal forms. Millenarian thinking was based on the Bible and particularly on the book of Revelations, a collection of prophetic visions. Radical groups debated and disagreed about when it would happen, and what part the 'saints' should play in bringing it about. However, even scientific scholars like Sir Isaac Newton spent time and energy trying to interpret the 'evidence' to discover when Christ would return.

EMERGENCE OF RADICALISM

1608 John Smyth and John Robinson take their separatist congregations to Holland, where they develop the first Baptist and Congregationalist groups;

1616 first Baptist church in England;

1641 breakdown of censorship; separatists emerge in London; seven Baptist churches publish joint statement of doctrine;

1644 Assembly of Divines – Independent ministers call for toleration; first Independent (Congregationalist) church established in England, at Hull;

1644 –5 press campaign for toleration brings Leveller leaders together;

1645 –6 emergence of Leveller political movement.

ment, John Lilburne, Richard Overton and William Walwyn. These men had begun to argue as a matter of principle, that religious beliefs were private, personal and no concern of governments and magistrates. The Puritan vision of godly uniformity was being threatened from within its own ranks.

By 1645, therefore, a division had become apparent both within and outside Parliament. The majority of MPs and their supporters, the City of London authorities and the Scots remained committed to a single, national Church and a rapid peace to restore the King and his authority. They tended to be labelled Presbyterian, although not all of them were committed to a fully Presbyterian organisation. A minority of MPs, including influential leaders like Cromwell and Sir Henry Vane, were sympathetic to some of the radical demands, and favoured a limited toleration for 'tender consciences' who sought spiritual support in 'independent' congregations of like-minded souls. Labelled Independents, they also wanted to pursue the war vigorously. They were prepared to restore the King, but only from a position of strength, with significant limitations being placed on his powers. They had the support of radical groups and a strong base in the newly created New Model Army.

Presbyterian and Independent

The use of religious labels such as Presbyterian and Independent can be confusing, because not all members of either group adhered strictly to the religious beliefs that they implied. It is probably easiest to define the political Presbyterians by their concern with order and hierarchy, and hence desire for a reasonably strong monarch to work alongside Parliament, and the return of a compulsory national Church. Some preferred a form of Presbyterianism, others would have accepted bishops with reduced powers, but both emphasised compulsion and authority. The Independents are defined by their insistence on allowing a measure of religious freedom, which would also involve restricting the powers of the King.

ISSUE
How did divisions among Parliament's supporters widen?

The victories of the New Model Army were therefore a mixed blessing to the conservative MPs. As long as the Royalists were in arms, they depended on its successes throughout the country, and could do little but fret about the radical churches that sprang up wherever it went. By 1644 the Baptist groups were already strong in London and in parts of East Anglia, and in that year the first Independent Church was formally constituted in Hull, helped by the presence of the army chaplain, John Canne. By 1646, there were six such

JOHN LILBURNE AND THE EMERGENCE OF THE LEVELLERS

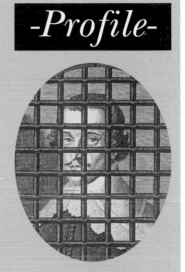

-Profile-

Lilburne's life story is in many ways the story of Puritan development in this period, from its enthusiastic but ill-defined beginnings to the fragmentation and internal dissension that undermined hopes of godly reform. In the process, the godly reformers created something far more significant and radical in the long term – a demand for fundamental human rights and political influence for the people as a whole. While the Leveller movement, which formulated and published the demand, was short-lived and easily crushed in this period, its ideas were able to survive as a radical tradition and inspiration for later reformers. The profile set out here outlines the development of a man, and of a movement that he, above all, created. Both were unique in their time.

John Lilburne was the second son of a gentleman from County Durham, a member of the minor gentry, who was apprenticed at the age of fourteen to a cloth merchant named Thomas Hewson in the City of London. It is likely that his family and his master were Puritan in their outlook, and John regularly attended sermons preached by the ministers of the day. He and a number of other apprentices were in the habit of attending a morning sermon, and meeting later to discuss and debate its meaning. Through these activities, John became acquainted with John Bastwick [see pages 71–3]. Lilburne seems to have visited Bastwick in prison, and concocted a scheme to have Bastwick's 'Letany' (an illegal tract written against the bishops) printed in Holland and smuggled back for resale. The likelihood is that he hoped both to serve the Puritan cause and provide himself with enough money to establish his own business on completing his apprenticeship. Instead he was arrested, brought before the Star Chamber in 1638, and sentenced to be whipped and pilloried.

When the sentence was carried out he protested loudly that this was an abuse of his rights as a free-born Englishman, and harangued a gathering crowd so effectively that Laud had him gagged. Removed to the Fleet prison, he was placed in solitary confinement, but continued to petition for release and deny the power of prerogative courts to punish free men. It is clear that he had already established a reputation as a radical and trouble-maker – when fire broke out in the Fleet, local residents believed that Lilburne had set it in order to escape. He remained in prison, however, until the meeting of the Long Parliament, when friends persuaded the MP for Cambridge, Oliver Cromwell, to secure for his release. This initiated a friendship between the two men.

The story of Lilburne's early troubles illustrates the variety of opinion held by 'puritans' at this stage. Lilburne was already moving towards the General Baptist view that God offered salvation to all, a denial of the Calvinist belief in predestination, held and defended by men like Bastwick, Prynne and Cromwell. Conflicting ideas could be glossed over or set aside while there was a common enemy to fight in Laud and the bishops, and ideas did not need to be fully explored and defined until the opportunity existed to put them into practice. That moment did not arrive until 1643–4, in the Solemn League and Covenant with Scotland, and the calling of the Assembly of Divines.

By 1644 Lilburne had served in the army under Lord Brooke and later the Earl of Manchester. Taken prisoner by the Royalists, he had survived because he argued so fiercely against their right to punish him, even challenging Prince Rupert to a duel, that they had concluded that he was insane. He was released during an exchange of prisoners, and continued both to serve with distinction and to fall foul of both authority and Presbyterians. He seems to have been kept in the army by respect and loyalty to Cromwell, but in early 1645 he refused to join the New Model because it involved accepting the Covenant, with its commitment to a compulsory Presbyterian Church.

Returning to London he became engaged in a pamphlet war and campaign for religious freedom that had begun in 1644. It is at this point that he began to work with William Walwyn, a prosperous merchant, and Richard Overton, a shadowy figure who made a living through printing and publishing political tracts. Lilburne also found himself engaged in a vitriolic war of words with his old friends, Bastwick and Prynne. In July 1645 his activities led him to be imprisoned in Newgate by the House of Commons, on a charge of slandering the Speaker. Released in October, he continued his campaign for toleration, but now began to extend it by questioning the behaviour of MPs in imprisoning men without proper trial. An examination before a Commons committee, conducted behind closed doors, did not constitute a court of law, and John had no intention of allowing his own rights, or those of others, to be so abused. In 1646 he was campaigning against a similar imprisonment of Overton and his wife, when a combination of Presbyterian enemies from his army days and his London activities succeeded in having him brought before the House of Lords. Lilburne pointedly ignored their warrant, but presented himself at the bar of the House to tell their assembled lordships that they had no right to try him, no status other than that derived from William the Conqueror's robber barons, and no valid cause beyond their own interests. Not surprisingly, he found himself in prison in the Tower of London.

Lilburne's clash with the Lords marks the beginning of the Levellers as a coherent political movement. Although it had been taking shape over the previous year, it was his challenge to Parliament in the name of the people, and the subsequent public campaign for his release, that defined its aims and shaped its methods. His stand against the Lords raised serious issues regarding individual rights under the law, and he had widened that issue to question what Parliament stood for and what the war had been fought to achieve. While Overton (now released) and Walwyn organised petitions and demonstrations calling for Lilburne's release, John began to formulate and develop the argument that Parliament's power was derived only from the people, and that the people could and should call them to account.

Against a background of economic distress, high taxation and the dislocation of trade, the Leveller leaders drew on the support of the 'middling sort' in London, and channelled their concerns and grievances into a demand for social justice, economic freedom, and political rights. In a flood of pamphlets, letters and petitions they evolved a theory of popular sovereignty and individual freedom. Over the two years between Lilburne's imprisonment by the Lords and the beginning of the second civil war, they formulated a democratic constitution in the 'Agreement of the People'. The nature of seventeenth-century society, and their own errors denied them the opportunity to put it into effect, but in historical terms their failure is outweighed by the significance of their thinking.

churches in Yorkshire alone. Although many were not specifically created by army men, the army's mobility, the contacts created by soldiers drawn from many areas, and the protection provided to radical preachers by leading officers like Cromwell, made it a powerful influence in spreading radical ideas. Although the radicals never constituted more than a tiny minority of the population, they were quite sufficient to frighten those who believed that social harmony and their own social position depended on the restoration of authority in Church and State.

The result was a conservative overreaction that widened divisions and drove some radicals to new heights. In 1645 an attack was launched against radical leaders, especially the outspoken and uncompromising John Lilburne. An account of his troubles, and how they led to the formation of the Leveller movement is contained in the Profile. Meanwhile, conservative complaints about the army increased in volume and intensity. In 1645 the Presbyterian minister, Richard Baxter, complained of the talk of 'church democracy and state democracy' that he heard among soldiers, and in 1646 the less moderate Presbyterian, Thomas Edwards, published a book entitled *Gangraena*, a vicious and vitriolic account of radical groups and ideas, likening them to a poison in the blood of the body politic. When Parliamentarian victory and the desire for a rapid peace strengthened the influence of the conservatives on the parliamentary committees, they determined to use their position to ensure that the search for peace included the destruction of radical influence.

3 The Search for Peace, 1646–8

a) The Aims of Parliament

By early 1647 the Presbyterians in Parliament appeared to be close to success. The King had been handed over to their custody by the Scottish army, which had withdrawn to Scotland shortly afterwards. The Scottish commissioners had hoped to work with Charles to ensure a conservative settlement, and would have supported the restoration of most of his powers, but had found him unwilling to compromise on the future of the Church. He was held at Holdenby House in Northamptonshire, where he appeared to be considering his response to Parliament's revised propositions, put to him at Newcastle in 1646. The key demands were that he granted control of the militia to Parliament, sought its approval of his choice of advisers and allowed a reformed Church of England. The Westminster Assembly had finally produced a scheme for reforming the Church, the Directory of Worship, which was broadly Presbyterian even if

ISSUES
What were the aims of the majority of MPs in 1646?
Why did their search for a settlement fail?

POLITICAL PRESBYTERIANS

Used by many historians to describe the more conservative Parliamentarians, as opposed to the political Independents who sympathised with the army and some of the radicals. The use of religious labels to indicate political views arises from the key issue of the future of the Church and the kind of religious settlement that the different groups favoured. While the Independents favoured a measure of religious toleration, the political Presbyterians were determined to re-establish a compulsory national Church along Presbyterian lines, not because they were religious Presbyterians, but because it offered the best hope of restoring religious authority and social control.

INDEMNITY

The protection of ex-soldiers from legal proceedings for any action undertaken as part of the war. For example, troopers who had requisitioned horses as part of their wartime duties might find themselves sued or accused of theft if they did not have the protection of a legal indemnity. Given the range and type of actions that they might well have carried out under orders, this was a serious matter for soldiers of all ranks.

the Scots considered it insufficiently rigorous in its discipline. Parliamentary elections held in 1646 to 'recruit' numbers of MPs to a more nationally representative level had strengthened conservative support. With a clear majority in Parliament, the leaders of the **political Presbyterians**, Denzil Holles and Sir Philip Stapleton, could expect to create a peace settlement that reflected their aims.

In the meantime, they sought to deal with the legacy of war. Popular complaints of high taxation and economic dislocation made it logical to consider disbanding Parliament's forces now that they were no longer needed. Accordingly, MPs voted in February 1647 to disband the New Model Army, retaining only a force of volunteers to go to Ireland, where rebellion still lingered, under the leadership of new officers. The decision was perfectly logical, although there were signs of an ulterior motive in the plan to remove the old, radically-minded officers and replace them with good Presbyterians. Nevertheless, the plan would probably have been accepted if MPs had not, in their haste to get rid of the radical threat, neglected to make provision for either arrears of pay or **indemnity** for the disbanded troops.

b) The Politicisation of the Army

Faced with such ingratitude for the hardships and sacrifices that they had endured, several regiments petitioned their general, Sir Thomas Fairfax, to intercede on their behalf, while Cromwell and his son-in-law, Henry Ireton, who were both officers and MPs, put the army's case in Parliament. The refusal of the conservatives to reconsider was probably a result of their fear of radical influence in the army, but in fact it opened the way for that radical influence to increase. In March and April the soldiers elected representatives called Agents or Agitators to speak on their behalf, and many of those elected had radical views and connections. Experience of **sectarian** worship, with its emphasis on godly debate and lay preaching, encouraged ordinary troopers to become both articulate and confident, and it is not surprising that such men should have been the ones chosen to speak for their companions. While the radical activists were never a majority, especially among the infantry who tended to be less educated than the cavalry, their ability to lead gave them significant influence in shaping the army's protests.

Under their leadership, the complaints about disbandment without arrears and indemnity began to widen into concern about the nature of the settlement that such MPs would establish. There has been considerable debate among historians about how far the emergence of the army's political demands stemmed from within, and how far it was the result of outside interference. The answer is, probably, that it was a combination of both. By early 1647 the

Levellers in London were despairing of persuading Parliament to reform, and saw the army as a potential power base. Infiltrating the military was not difficult for men who, like Lilburne, had been soldiers, and shared contacts among the sectarian churches. There is little doubt that by May, when the army threatened open mutiny, the Agitators were in touch with, and influenced by, civilian Levellers. There is also little doubt that the existence of religious radicals within the army was a crucial link between the civilian radicals and the majority of soldiers who were concerned first and foremost about their indemnity and arrears.

Whether or not the army itself was dominated by radicals, the threat of army mutiny arose, therefore, from the interaction of radical ideas and conservative fears. The existence of radicals within the army drove conservative MPs to act hastily in trying to get rid of it, and their overreaction drove the army into resistance, which, in turn, allowed civilian radicals to gain influence within it. What finally shaped the army into a political force was the decision by certain leading officers to join with their men in a campaign to influence the outcome of any settlement. In April and May 1647, Cromwell and Ireton found their pleas for better treatment of the army ignored in Parliament with the same determination as their desire for a religiously tolerant settlement. By the end of May it was clear that the army would act, with or without them. They were therefore faced with the choice between betraying the Parliament in whose name they had fought, or seeing the army and their religious allies embark on a strategy that could end in chaos.

On 27 May 1647, Parliament ordered the army to disband without arrears. On 28 May the Agitators informed Fairfax that the regiments would not obey, and on 29 May a council of officers agreed to support them. On the orders of the Agitators, and possibly with Cromwell's knowledge, Cornet (Second Lieutenant) George Joyce and an armed escort left for Holdenby House to secure the King. Joyce visited Cromwell in London, but it is unclear whether this was to gain his support or merely to inform him of the plan. Whatever the purpose, the visit seems to have been decisive, since a few days later both Cromwell and Ireton left London to join the army while Joyce brought the King from Holdenby to the army at Newmarket. On 5 June the army met in a general rendezvous led by Fairfax and Cromwell, and agreed on a Solemn Engagement to hold together until a fair settlement was assured. It was agreed to establish a General Council of the Army, made up of the leading officers and the Agitators, to coordinate strategy. On 14 June an Army Representation (Declaration), written by Ireton, set out the army's case and its determination to oppose Parliament until its rights were secured in a fair and just settlement. What this meant is analysed in

ISSUE
Why did the New Model Army mutiny in 1647?

SECTARIANS
Sectarians or 'sectaries' was the word used to describe the Puritan separatists. The forms of organisation and worship used in sectarian meetings tended to encourage open discussion and blur the distinction between the minister and other members of the congregation. Within the army, the frequent absence of any ordained clergy encouraged talented speakers among the soldiers to lead worship and preach in their place. The whole experience of radical religion helped to produce men of the 'middling sort' who were both willing and able to challenge the assumptions of their social superiors.

ISSUE
How did the Army emerge as a political force?

the next activity. The army had become a third political force in the English search for settlement, alongside the existing elements of Parliament and King.

THE ARMY GENERAL COUNCIL

The Army General Council was unusual in that it contained representatives of the rank and file as well as officers. It was a symbol of army unity, but it was used by the Levellers to try to pressurise Fairfax and his leading officers into adopting Leveller policies. They came closest to success in the Putney debates of October/November 1647, but were defeated by the determination of Cromwell and Ireton and the King's escape from custody. With a second war imminent, Fairfax was able to disband the Council in January 1648. After the second civil war, the army reverted to a council of officers, although some of these kept radical influence from disappearing completely.

Figure 18 A meeting of the Army General Council. What is the significance of the way that the members are presented, with the officers seated and drawn as larger figures?

ISSUE
How did the politicisation of the army affect the search for peace?

The effect was to greatly complicate the search for a settlement. With Parliament and army divided, the King was encouraged in his belief that he could play for time, widen the conflicts among his enemies, and win the peace in spite of losing the war. Believing that there could be no settlement without him, he was determined to hold out for a settlement of his choosing, and that would involve the restoration of his powers as well as the Anglican establishment in the Church. He therefore listened to proposals from both army and Parliament, without any intention of accepting either. In the meantime he maintained contact with the Scots, and cast around for other opportunities, such as the Queen's continued efforts to raise forces abroad. Given Charles's stubborn nature, sincere convictions, and refusal to accept the reality of his position, the search for settlement would always have been difficult. The divisions in Parliament that developed in 1646–7 and the emergence of the army as a third political force rendered it well nigh impossible.

ACTIVITY

Use the evidence skills that you have practised in earlier chapters to analyse the Army Representation and explain:
▼ what the Army was seeking to achieve, and
▼ how it justified such interference in political matters.

We were not a mere mercenary army, hired to serve any arbitrary power of a state, but called forth and conjured by the several declarations of Parliament to the defence of our own and the people's just rights and liberties. And so we took up arms in judgement and in conscience to those ends . . .

All authority [being] fundamentally seated in the office and but ministerially in the persons . . . we cannot but wish that such men and such only might be preferred to the great power and trust of the commonwealth as are approved at least for moral righteousness, and of such we cannot but in our wishes prefer those that appear acted [motivated] thereunto by a principle of conscience and religion in them . . .

[And by this means] justice and righteousness shall flow down equally to all . . . in its ancient channel . . .

The House of Commons [shall have] the supreme power . . . of final judgements. [It is] a mere tyranny that the same men should sit during life or at their own pleasure . . . The people have a right to new and successive elections unto that great and supreme trust at certain periods of time . . . [so that] if they have

made an ill choice at one time they may mend it at another . . . [There should be a] general act of oblivion . . . whereby the seeds of future war or feuds, either to the present age or posterity, may be better taken away, by easing that sense of present and satisfying those fears of future ruin or undoing to persons or families which may drive men into any desperate ways for self-preservation and remedy.

There being no design to overthrow presbytery or hinder the settlement thereof and to have Independent government set up . . . We only desire that according to the declarations promising a privilege for tender consciences, there may be some effectual course taken, according to the intent thereof, and that such who upon conscientious grounds may differ from the established forms may not for that be debarred from the common rights, liberties or benefits belonging equally to all men and members of the commonwealth, while they live soberly, honestly, inoffensively towards others and peacefully and faithfully towards the state.

Source B From The Representation of the Army, 14 June 1647.

To complicate matters still further, the summer of 1647 saw an internal struggle for control of the army between the leading officers who sought moderation and compromise and the Levellers who sought to use the army for revolutionary purposes. The effects of this, and the complex events of the summer and autumn, are set out in Figure 21. There has been considerable debate among historians about some of the relationships and issues involved, although the key developments are largely undisputed. Historians of the Levellers, for example, have followed the Leveller leaders themselves in claiming widespread support within the army and a major influence on the army's proposals for peace. Others have challenged the extent of radical influence within the army, and emphasised the role of the leading officers (known as the Grandees) in exploiting the army for their own political purposes. These issues need to be investigated in greater depth than is possible here, and suggestions for further reading are included at the end of this chapter. What is clear is that the efforts of the four parties to find an acceptable settlement in 1647 were ended by the King's Engagement to [treaty with] the Scots in December and the ensuing outbreak of a second civil war.

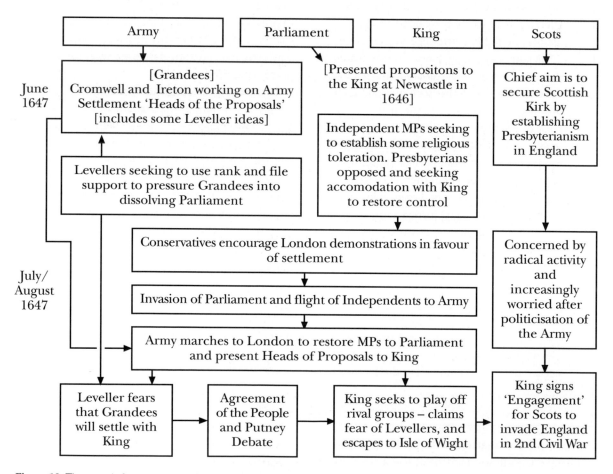

Figure 19 The search for peace, June–December 1647.

Figure 19 reveals a number of key points related to the search for a settlement, which help to explain why it failed, and why it ended in the execution of the King.

▼ The army leaders had no intention of removing the King at this stage. The Heads of the Proposals, drawn up by Cromwell and Ireton, were the most flexible plans for settlement ever offered to Charles. Although he would have lost control of the militia and his choice of advisers for ten years, there was considerable emphasis on reconciliation. Only seven royalists would have been excluded from a pardon (as compared to 58 in Parliament's Newcastle Propositions) and the Proposals included the restoration of bishops in the Church, albeit with only advisory powers.

▼ There is also evidence of Leveller influence in the Proposals, for example, in the plans to reform Parliament by redistributing seats according to taxation and holding elections every two years. Legal and economic reforms were proposed, as well as a measure of religious toleration. This undoubtedly reflected Leveller views, but there is no reason to believe that the Grandees objected to them.

▼ It is also clear that the army leaders were determined to limit Leveller influence and maintain the social and political hierarchy. Their plans were a compromise, and they consistently refused to agree to Leveller demands for a dissolution of Parliament. When the army did march to London in July, it was to restore the Independent MPs who had been chased out by conservative supporters, and only eleven conservative MPs were named as responsible for the divisions among Parliament's supporters. It was Leveller fears that they were about to be outflanked that led them to propose the Agreement of the People in October.

▼ Surviving records of the debates suggest that the Levellers may have had the best of the argument. However, in the rapid ending of discussion after the King's escape, the General Council accepted three rendezvous, rather than a single rendezvous of the army as the Levellers wanted. This, and the ease with which Cromwell dealt with the mutiny at Corkbush Field suggests that Leveller support among the rank and file was never as great as it appeared. The impression of widespread support owed much to the soldiers' grievances over arrears and indemnity, and to the outspoken and articulate views of the Agitators. It should also be remembered that the leading officer could call on a loyalty based on shared religious views as well as shared victories and dangers.

▼ Above all, what is revealed by the events of 1647 is the bad faith with which Charles approached the search for a settlement. On one level, this is understandable. He was a King forced to negotiate with rebels, and few monarchs of this age would have felt any obligation to be honest with them. He was also being asked to compromise his most deeply held convictions. For the most part, he did not lie as such – he

THE FAILURE OF THE PEACE SETTLEMENT

1646 Parliament presents adapted version of the Nineteen Propositions to the King at Newcastle (Newcastle Propositions); King delays response and later rejects them;

1647 Army mutiny leads to Heads of Proposals, presented to Charles in August: response delayed, then rejection; November: King escapes to Isle of Wight and signs Engagement with Scots in December;

1648 Second Civil War; November: army demands trial and execution of the 'Man of Blood'; December: Parliament votes to renew negotiations; Pride's Purge.

merely stalled and played for time in the hope that his situation would improve. Such hopes were greatly encouraged by the obvious divisions among his enemies. Only in secretly negotiating with the Scots and inviting them to invade England can he be accused of serious betrayal.

4   The Army Revolution, 1648–9

a) The Second Civil War

By January 1648 it was clear that renewed war was imminent, and the army prepared itself. In January 1648 the Agitators apparently ceased to sit in the army council, and military discipline was restored along with army unity. Parliament voted 'No Further Addresses' to Charles Stuart, and in an emotional prayer-meeting of the Council of Officers in April the King was condemned as a 'man of blood'. By then scattered Royalist risings had developed in England and Wales, while the Scots prepared to invade in accordance with their commitment to Charles. While Fairfax besieged Colchester, the centre of royalism in Essex, Cromwell advanced into Wales. Unfortunately for Charles, the Scots invasion was delayed, and Cromwell was able to deal with the Welsh risings and then cut off the Scots at Preston, before advancing into Yorkshire to mop up Royalist resistance there. Although the siege of Colchester was long and bitter, dragging on until September, the outcome was never in doubt. By the autumn of 1648, the military crisis was over.

While the second civil war was of little significance in military terms, its political impact was enormous. Most of Parliament's supporters viewed the first war as unplanned, and more importantly as a trial of strength between the King's cause and that of Parliament, in which God gave his judgement for Parliament. In neither context was Charles judged to bear all blame. In 1648, however, he deliberately waged war on his people, using a foreign army to do so. Moreover, by doing so he rejected God's judgement and God's will. Not only was he a man of blood, in the **providential** thinking of many Protestants he had rejected God – and in the view of the army, he must be brought to account for his crimes.

By November 1648 the army was virtually united in a demand that the King should be brought to trial. The strategist in this case was not Cromwell, who remained in Yorkshire to complete military operations, but his son-in-law, Henry Ireton. On 20 November he published an Army Remonstrance, demanding that the King be brought to justice. Meanwhile, he renewed negotiations with the Levellers to ensure their quiescence, if not their support. The army was now represented by a Council of Officers rather than the old

PROVIDENCE
Providential beliefs were widespread among seventeenth-century Protestants, although they tended to appear in their most extreme forms among the radicals. They were based on the belief that God intervened directly in the affairs of men to ensure that the outcome of events conformed with His will. Matters such as the victories of the New Model Army, or Charles's refusal to compromise, were therefore interpreted as acts of Providence, evidence of God's judgement and purpose. Men like Cromwell therefore sought to read these providential signs in order to know God's purpose, before deciding what action to take.

General Council, significantly reducing Leveller influence and support. At the same time, the army's allies in Parliament, the Independent MPs, pressed the case for dealing with the King according to Parliament's **vote of No Addresses**.

b) Pride's Purge and the Execution of the King

In Parliament, however, the mood had changed since January. The scattered uprisings in support of the King had not been the work of old Royalists as much as an expression of popular desire for peace and a return to normal government. Aware that a tide was running in favour of a conservative settlement, the majority of MPs supported renewed efforts to negotiate. For most, the concept of a settlement without the King was unthinkable, and many feared their radical allies far more than their Royalist enemies. In September 1648 parliamentary commissioners were sent to the Isle of Wight to renew negotiations with the King. In early December they returned with the King's answers to four key bills which formed the first stage of a treaty. While one, Sir Henry Vane, made it clear to the House that the King remained unwilling to make real concessions, most MPs were now so desperate for negotiations that his views were ignored. On 3 December a bill was passed to give Parliament direct control of the militia (a first step to disbanding the army), and on 5 December the vote of No Addresses was repealed.

In these circumstances, the army was bound to act. If negotiations followed, the King would be returned to London and a wave of Royalist enthusiasm would leave little scope for extracting the concessions that he was so clearly unwilling to make. At best, the conservatives were giving up the advantages of victory – at worst, they were deliberately working with the King to destroy the army and its allies. There was little doubt that any settlement that emerged would restore most of the King's powers and, above all, a compulsory national Church. It was not only the army's interests that were threatened, but the religious rights and freedoms that civilian and military radicals enjoyed. For many also, this was a betrayal of God's cause. The fruits of victory and the interests of a significant minority in and outside Parliament were about to be thrown away. Ironically, the behaviour of the conservative MPs does much to vindicate the King's assumption that peace could not be achieved without his agreement. What he had failed to recognise was that the emergence of the army as a political force had introduced a new, and ultimately revolutionary, element into the equation.

On 6 December the regiment of Colonel Pride surrounded the Houses of Parliament and refused entry to those who were known to support the negotiations with the King. A few of the conservative

VOTE OF NO ADDRESSES
A vote in the House of Commons on 3 January 1638 that no further addresses (i.e. offers to negotiate) be made to the King.

ISSUE
Why did Parliament try to renew negotiations with the King?

ISSUE
Why did the army purge Parliament?

THE TRIAL AND EXECUTION OF CHARLES I

1648

6 December   Pride's Purge; that evening, Cromwell returned to London and signified his agreement.

1649

1 January   Ordinance establishing a High Court to try the King was passed by the Rump of the Commons, but rejected by the House of Lords.

4 January   The Rump passed Three Resolutions, claiming sole authority to make law.

20 January   The King's trial began; Charles denied the right of the Court to try him, and refused to enter a plea.

27 January   Charles found guilty and sentenced to death.

30 January   The execution of the King.

13 February A Council of State was appointed to govern in his place.

17 March   Abolition of the monarchy.

19 March   Abolition of the House of Lords.

19 May   England declared a Commonwealth.

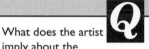

What does the artist imply about the attitude of contemporary observers to these events? How reliable is this as historical evidence?

Figure 20 The execution of Charles I.

-*Profile*-

That Charles Stuart hath acted contrary to his trust in departing from the Parliament . . . making a war against them, and thereby hath been the occasion of much bloodshed and misery to the people whom he was set over for good . . . and since was the occasion of a second war, besides what he has done . . . tending to the destruction of the fundamental laws and liberties of this Kingdom.

Source C From the charge of treason drawn up by Parliament against the King, 28 December 1648.

I do stand more for the liberty of my people than any here that come to be my pretended judges. And therefore let me know by what lawful authority I am seated here.

Source D The King's reply.

Having refused to plead he remained silent until the sentence was announced. He was then refused permission to speak, replying:

'I am not suffered to speak – expect what justice others will have'.

leaders were arrested and imprisoned, but most (about 186 MPs) were simply excluded. Another hundred or so who heard of what was happening chose to stay away, leaving a minority of around seventy MPs who remained in Parliament to carry out the procedures involved in bringing the King to trial. Although Ireton had originally intended to dissolve Parliament, he had been persuaded by Sir Arthur Haselrig that this 'rump' of MPs would represent legal authority and maintain stability in this crisis period. On 7 December Cromwell returned to London and took his seat in Parliament after expressing his approval of what had been done. Having agonised and 'waited on the Lord' for a sign as to how to proceed, he interpreted conservative provocation and the actions of the army as the sign that he sought, and thereafter, he drove the business forward with his usual energy and determination. The results can be seen in the profile on page 132.

5 Conclusion – Was the Execution of Charles an English Revolution?

To paraphrase the words of the historian Barry Coward, if there ever was an English Revolution, then it surely took place on 30 January 1649 with the execution of Charles I. Certainly the King's public trial and execution can be regarded as a revolutionary act. He was placed on trial in the name of his people, and charged with treason because he had waged war against them. The crime of treason had always related to an action against the King – the embodiment of the State. It was now being interpreted as action by a King against the people, implicitly claiming that the people, not the King, represented the State. This was followed up by publications such as John Milton's *Tenure of Kings and Magistrates* in 1649, which explicitly argued that power belonged originally to the people and was given to Kings in a social and political contract in order to provide for government. By this contract the King was obliged to use his powers for the benefit and safety of the people, and if he abused them, the people (or their representatives) had the right to remove him. Although Charles refused to plead and challenged the legality of the proceedings, the fact that he was executed and that it was justified in these terms amounts to a political revolution and the destruction of divine right monarchy.

At the same time, however, it is clear that the action was taken by an armed minority, against the wishes of the majority both inside and outside Parliament, and then only as a matter of necessity. The army and its allies were forced to act in defence of the liberties for which they had been fighting, because the parliamentary majority was about to restore an untrustworthy King to a position from which he could destroy them. Even if Charles made promises to protect and respect their rights (and there was no reason to think that he would) he could not be trusted to keep them. In fact, experience suggested that, once restored to power, he would ignore his promises and pursue with vindictive energy those who had defied him. If he could not, therefore, be restored to power, he would have to be killed; alive, he would always be a threat. His beliefs would never permit him to abdicate (resign the throne) and if he did not, there was no possibility of a peaceful replacement. His sons would not be willing to take his place, and there were no other viable candidates. If removed from the throne and left alive, Charles would simply try to raise a new army to regain his throne. Those who could not accept Charles as King had little choice but to destroy him. What remains revolutionary, however, was that they chose to do so by public trial, and to try him as King. As Cromwell put it 'We will cut off his head with the crown on it'.

The English Revolution therefore displays a number of contradictions. It was carried out, reluctantly and out of necessity, by a minority whose conscious choice was to act in public. In the name of a Parliament that they had purged by force, they created a political revolution that was largely motivated by religion. The charge against Charles was presented in the name of the people, but those who presented it also saw themselves as the instruments of God's will. The men who made the revolution were members of the social and political elite, while the radical revolutionaries who had called for popular rights and freedoms were left in impotent isolation. Above all, it was unintended. It occurred only because circumstances made it necessary, which explains not only the inherent contradictions of 1649, but also the divisions and uncertainties that emerged thereafter and suggest why it was unlikely to prove permanent and lasting.

Summary of Events and Developments: War and Revolution

1642

August	The King raised his standard at Nottingham (August 22)
October	Battle of Edgehill; King able to move towards London
November	Royal forces stopped at Battle of Turnham Green; King retreated to winter in Oxford

1643

May	Peace negotiations at Oxford failed
June	Battle of Adwalton Moor; defeat of Parliamentarians in Yorkshire, Fairfax retreated to Hull; Solemn League and Covenant (alliance) concluded between Parliament and Scots; Assembly of Divines set up to plan reform of the Church
July	Royalists began the Siege of Hull; Prince Rupert captured Bristol; Charles began the siege of Gloucester (July/August)
September	Earl of Essex relieved Gloucester and defeated Royalists at Newbury; Solemn League and Covenant ratified by both Houses; Charles signed Cessation treaty with Irish rebels
October	Siege of Hull broken; Parliamentarian control of Lincolnshire and East Yorkshire secured
December	Death of John Pym

1644

February	Independents in the Assembly of Divines published arguments in favour of limited religious toleration; toleration campaign grew throughout the year
July	Parliamentarian victory at Marston Moor
September	Essex trapped in Cornwall; surrendered entire army at Respryn Bridge
September/ November	Parliamentary crisis; religious and political divisions symbolised by Manchester/Cromwell quarrel
December	Self-denying Ordinance introduced, finally passed in April 1645

1645

January/ March	Formation of New Model Army; growing evidence of Scottish dislike of new developments strained the alliance; growing war-weariness in the country; Clubmen risings in the west; peace talks entered at Uxbridge; failed because of religious issues and mutual distrust.
June	Battle of Naseby; military and political disaster for the King
July	Goring (Royalist) defeated at Langport
September	Prince Rupert forced to surrender Bristol; Scottish Royalists defeated by the Covenanters
September/ October	Clubmen risings in Sussex and Wales

1646

April	The King left Oxford and surrendered to the Scots
June	Surrender of Oxford marked the virtual end of the war; Leveller demonstrations in London; Thomas Edwards published *Gangraena*, a bitter attack on radicalism
July	Peace terms offered to the King at Newcastle

1647

February	Scots handed King to Parliament and left England; Parliament voted for disbandment of the army
April/May	Army petitions and election of Agitators; regiments refused to disband on May 31
June	Seizure of the King by Cornet Joyce (June 4); Army Engagement – General Council set up (June 5) *Representation of the Army* published
July	Royalist mobs invaded Parliament; Independent MPs fled
August	Heads of the Proposals presented to the King (August 2); army entered London; conservative leaders fled and the Independents were restored to their seats
September	Army in winter quarters at Putney; Levellers suspicious of Grandees' negotiations with the King
October	Leveller John Wildman published the *Case of the Army*; Leveller plans, summarised in the *Agreement of the People*, debated by the Army Council at Putney
November	The King's escape brought the Putney debates to an end; Leveller mutiny at Ware easily crushed by Cromwell
December	The King signed an Engagement inviting the Scots to invade England

1648

January	Parliament voted 'No Further Addresses' to the King; Army Council disbanded; growing discontent and riots in Kent and Essex hardened into Royalist risings in April
April	Risings in Kent, Essex, Cornwall, Yorkshire and south Wales; easily dealt with except at Colchester (Essex) and in Wales
July	Scottish army led by Royalist Scots entered England
August	Cromwell completed defeat of Welsh rising and caught the Scots at Preston (August 17); conservative leaders returned to Parliament
September	Colchester forced to surrender to Fairfax; Second Civil War effectively over; parliamentary commissioners sent to the Isle of Wight to renew negotiations with the King
November	Army Remonstrance demanded the trial and punishment of the King
December	House of Commons voted the King's reply to their commissioners to be a basis for negotiation (December 5); Pride's Purge (December 6); purge approved by Cromwell on his return to London on December 7

1649

January   High Court of Justice set up to try the King (January 1); January 20: the King's trial opened; January 30:
                 King Charles I was executed at Whitehall

March   Abolition of the monarchy and House of Lords: England was declared to be a Commonwealth
                 (republic)

▼ Working on War and Revolution

As with earlier chapters, you should complete notes on the material
covered in this chapter.

Preparing Essays on the Execution of Charles I

The study guides following Chapters 1 to 4 have suggested ways of
defining causal factors as the basis of writing essays about causation,
and a conditional/contingent approach to considering the part that
they play in the causation process. It would be quite possible to use
these ideas in essays about the execution of Charles I. It could, for
example, be argued that the *personality of Charles I, his belief in divine
right kingship, his devotion to the Anglican Church and his past betrayals of
those whom he regarded as rebels* created conditions in which settlement
would be difficult if not impossible. These conditions worsened with
the quarrel of army and Parliament, which encouraged Charles to
believe that he could manipulate his enemies, and the *emergence of
radical groups* who appeared to be a threat to the Church in Scotland
as well as England. The result was that Charles was able to initiate a
second civil war, which combined with the *providential beliefs* of the
army and its leaders, to convince them that the King must be
brought to justice for his betrayal of man and God. What dictated
the timing of the process was the *attempt by conservatives to renew negotiations with Charles in December 1648, which triggered the army into purging
Parliament and enforcing the trial and execution of the King.*

Unlike the outbreak of civil war, however, the execution of the
King was not the result of a gradual build-up of problems over time.
Although conditional factors such as Charles's personality, radical
attitudes and the politicisation of the army had developed by mid-
1647, there was no intention to bring the King to trial and execution.
It was his action in starting a second war that convinced the army and
some MPs that he could not be trusted, and that he had rejected
God's will. In order to explain these ideas more fully, it may be useful
to adopt a different approach to essays of this kind, by considering
factors in terms of the relationship between ideas, actions and events.

The Civil War and the events associated with it brought about the emergence of new ideas and radical forces that had hardly existed in 1642. The execution of the King came about because his actions in this new situation made a settlement impossible, and a minority among his opponents was willing to take action against him. It is therefore possible to explain the *event* of the King's execution by looking at the *actions* that led up to it. To explain actions it is necessary to consider what they were intended to achieve, and what effects they had. This will often include unintended, or unforeseen effects, and it is therefore a useful way of explaining events that were not planned in advance, such as the execution of the King. In order to understand such intentions, and the impact that their related actions had, it is necessary to understand the attitudes and beliefs of those involved – the King's belief in divine right monarchy and the Anglican Church, the radical beliefs in favour of religious freedom, and beliefs about the role of Providence. It may therefore produce a better explanation of the execution to consider the relationship between the *event* of the King's execution, the *actions* of those who brought it about, and the *ideas* that shaped and influenced those actions.

This argument can be presented through a series of questions, and clarified by the flow chart in Figure 21. If you begin by considering the basic question of why Charles was executed in 1649, it is clear that his own actions played a part. Considering the King's actions after the first civil war, it is possible to ask:

▼ What actions did Charles take after his defeat in 1646?
▼ What was he trying to achieve by these actions?

These questions will lead you to examine *his attempt to play for time and manipulate his enemies in order to secure an advantageous settlement.* In turn you will need to ask:

▼ Why was he willing to act this way?
▼ Why did he think that he could succeed?

These questions require you to examine *Charles's personality and beliefs*, and those of the *majority of MPs*, whose fears Charles sought to exploit. You will need to consider *attitudes to kingship, the Church and the social hierarchy*, in order to explain why both Charles and the conservative MPs were unable to conceive of a settlement without him. It may also lead you to consider what they feared – *the radicals and their desire for religious freedom*. You will then need to ask:

▼ What beliefs influenced the army and the radicals?
▼ What actions did they take as a result of these beliefs?

You will then need to explain the *politicisation of the army and their reaction to the second civil war*. This will then enable you to show how the interaction of the personality and beliefs of Charles with the aims and convictions of the radical minority led to a confrontation in which the minority was willing and able to bring him to trial and execution. In this explanation, *the attempt by the conservatives to renew negotiations in December 1648, and Pride's Purge,* are much less important in themselves than the ideas and beliefs that shaped them.

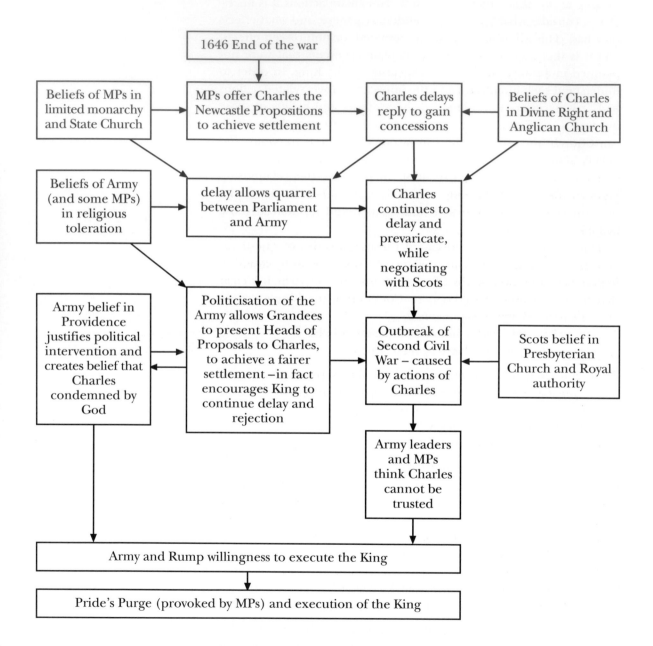

Figure 21 The execution of Charles I: actions, intentions and beliefs.

In the light of these arguments, you should now construct a plan for the essay question 'Why was Charles I executed in 1649?' When you have done this, consider the factors that you have defined, and use them to plan responses to the essays below. Then choose one of your plans, and write the essay.

1. To what extent was the death of Charles I the result of his own actions?

2. 'The key factor in the execution of Charles I was the political role of the army.' How far do you agree?

3. In 1642 Parliament took up arms to force the King to come to a settlement. Why, then, did a parliamentary minority bring him to trial and execution seven years later?

4. How far was the execution of Charles I a 'cruel necessity'?

5. To what extent should the execution of Charles I be regarded as a revolutionary act?

Further Reading

Books in the Access to History Series

Many of these issues are explained and considered in greater depth in A. Anderson, *The Civil Wars*. There are separate chapters on the victory of Parliament and on the emergence of the radicals. There is also a sample essay on the execution of Charles. For obvious reasons the arguments do not differ greatly from those introduced here, but the depth of explanation does.

General

The general textbooks cited in the Preface are also useful. Barry Coward's *Stuart England* is particularly useful in analysing key issues in a way that you can use once you have a clear idea of what happened. In Chapter 12 he explores the debate about the nature of the New Model Army and offers a coherent synthesis. In Chapter 13 he considers the issues involved in the execution of the King. In both cases, he offers some useful suggestions for further reading. For those who wish to explore radical ideas more fully, there are many useful works. It is probably better to look at radicalism in general at a later stage, after reading Chapter 6 and possibly Chapter 8, but you could certainly consider the Levellers in greater depth at this stage. As a starting-point, Howard Shaw *The Levellers*, Longman Seminar Studies 1973, remains useful, while the best analysis is probably provided by G.E. Aylmer, *The Levellers and the English Revolution*, Thames and Hudson 1973. For those with a liking for biography, Pauline Gregg's *Free-born John*, published by Dent in 1986, offers a sympathetic but not unbalanced portrait.

CHAPTER 6

REPUBLIC AND RESTORATION, 1649–60

KEY ISSUE

Why did the revolution of 1649 lead to a restoration of the monarchy in 1660?

POINTS TO CONSIDER

The short life of the Republic that was established in 1649 indicates the nature of the difficulties that it faced. Established by a military takeover, it was unable to rely on the support of more than a minority, and failed to widen its base sufficiently to survive. This has led some historians to argue that its failure was inevitable. In order to make your own judgements about this, you will need to examine the reasons for the failure of the different constitutional experiments that were introduced, and to decide whether their failure arose from a series of separate errors and problems, or from deep-seated and fundamental weaknesses that could not be overcome. You will then need to consider why they could not be overcome, and to decide whether their continued failure left no alternative but to restore monarchy in the shape of Charles II.

1 Introduction

The arrangements adopted to govern England in the aftermath of the King's execution in 1649 emphasise the fact that the **regicide** was hastily planned and carried out. Ireton had intended to dissolve Parliament and call new elections, but was persuaded that this would merely produce a Royalist majority, and agreed to purge Parliament instead. Thus government devolved by default to the MPs who remained thereafter, the butt-end of the Parliament, which came to be nicknamed the Rump. When the few remaining Lords refused to cooperate with regicide, the Rump declared itself to be the sole legislative authority in three resolutions passed on 4 January. After the King was executed, the same body elected a Council of State to take charge of government, while reserving legislative and supervisory powers to the Rump as a whole. Not until March 1649 were the monarchy and House of Lords abolished, and not until May was England declared a Commonwealth – a state governed by its people without a King.

The piecemeal process by which the new regime emerged, and the intense opposition faced in its early years, reveal certain key

REGICIDE

The murder of a king. Historians usually apply this to the men who actually sat in judgement on Charles and signed the warrant for his execution. Contemporary critics demonstrated a wider revulsion, directed at all those associated with the new regime; there were anti-English demonstrations in several parts of Europe, and in Spain and the Netherlands Royalist agents assassinated the respective English ambassadors.

features which helped to shape the events of the next decade. The first is the lack of prior planning that lay behind the revolutionary act of establishing the Commonwealth. Pride's Purge had been provoked by the determination of conservative MPs to restore a king who would not admit defeat. The army had taken the necessary action to prevent this and to ensure that its interests, particularly the desire for religious toleration, were taken into account. There was little time, or scope, however, to plan how to replace the institutions that were damaged or abolished, and the result was that supporters of the new regime often had very different visions of what that Commonwealth should be. While the Rump was concerned to ensure stability and calm conservative fears, the army and its radical supporters visualised a much greater social transformation to accompany the political changes.

This might not have mattered had it not been for the second feature – the fact that the regime could only command the support of a minority of the population. Within weeks of the execution it faced threats from Royalists abroad and Levellers at home, and the first two years of its existence were primarily occupied by a struggle for survival. While this process kept the army from interfering directly in politics, it also demonstrated that the regime could not survive without military support. The regimes of the **Interregnum** therefore faced a circle of problems. In order to widen support and ensure stability, they had to gain the confidence of the traditional ruling class, whose participation in local government and social leadership in the counties made them essential allies. Until this occurred, the army was necessary for security. The army, however, was expensive to maintain, and radical in politics. It therefore offended public opinion on both counts, and alienated potential supporters from the regime.

The events created by this situation are summarised in Table 2. What they reveal is a series of constitutional experiments applied in an increasingly desperate search for stability. By 1654 the Commonwealth had collapsed, to be replaced by a military Protectorate under the leadership of Oliver Cromwell. His ability to control the army while extending civilian support brought a measure of stability and the peaceful succession of Richard Cromwell in 1658. Richard, however, lacked his father's military background and army fears that he would abandon their interests led them to remove him from power in 1659 and attempt to revive the Commonwealth. The failure of this final experiment precipitated a slide into anarchy, from which the country was rescued when General George Monck engineered the return of monarchy in the restoration of Charles II.

At first sight this outcome can seem inevitable, but before accepting such a verdict, it is necessary to examine in greater detail the

INTERREGNUM

Literally meaning 'between reigns', is used to describe the period between 1649 and 1660, when England had no king. It therefore covers the period of both Commonwealth and Protectorate, and the anarchic year of 1659, which saw series of short-lived arrangements. Royalists, of course, did not recognise any such Interregnum – when Charles II returned in 1660 he claimed to be in the twelfth year of his reign, establishing the claim that he had become king at the moment of his father's death and merely been unable to exercise his power in person.

Table 2 The Constitutional Experiments of the Interregnum.

1	The Commonwealth

1649

March	Monarchy and House of Lords abolished
May	England declared to be a Commonwealth
August	The Pacification of Ireland began

1650

| June | Fairfax resigned as Lord General, and was replaced by Cromwell |
| August | Outbreak of the Third Civil War (between England and Scotland) |

1651

| September | Charles II defeated at Worcester |

1653

| April | Cromwell dissolved the Rump and the Council of State; Army Council of State appointed |
| July | Nominated assembly met, and declared itself a Parliament; dissolved itself in December |

2	The Protectorate

1653

| December | Cromwell established as Lord Protector under the Instrument of Government; government by a Single Person, Council of State, and a single-chamber Parliament |

1654

| September | First protectorate Parliament met |
| | MPs forced to sign a 'Recognition' of the Instrument; about 100 refused and were excluded |

1655

| January | First Protectorate Parliament dissolved |
| August | Establishment of eleven military districts and governors – the Major-Generals |

1656

| September | Second Protectorate Parliament met |

1657

January	Sindercombe Plot to assassinate Cromwell; ending of the Decimation Tax and the Major-Generals
February	Remonstrance (Humble Petition and Advice) introduced in Parliament
March	Humble Petition and Advice presented to Cromwell with the offer of the crown
April	Cromwell refused the crown
May	Cromwell accepted the revised Humble Petition and Advice, with a Lord Protector, Council and two-chamber Parliament; installed in June

1658

| February | Second Protectorate Parliament dissolved |
| September | Death of Cromwell: Richard Cromwell proclaimed Lord Protector |

1659

January	Third Protectorate Parliament met
April	Army Council began meeting again and forced Richard to dissolve Parliament
May	Richard Cromwell resigns as Lord Protector; Rump Parliament recalled

3	The Commonwealth

1659

| October | The army dissolved the Rump and set up an Army Committee of Safety |
| December | Rump restored after intervention by General Monck |

1660

February	Monck recalled the MPs excluded in 1648, restoring the Long Parliament on condition that it dissolved itself and called new elections
April	Convention Parliament assembled; voted for government by King, Lords and Commons
May	Charles Stuart returned as Charles II

forces ranged against the new Republic, and to determine whether any of the constitutional experiments were capable of overcoming them. By considering why each was adopted, and why it ultimately failed, it becomes possible to decide how far the causes of its failure were unique, and how far they reflected the same, or similar, fundamental weaknesses. This allows some conclusions to be established as to why the revolution of 1649 failed, but it does not entirely explain the return of the Stuart monarchy. It is therefore necessary to consider possible alternatives and to decide why the failure ended in the restoration of a monarchy, and why the monarch was Charles Stuart returning with his essential powers intact.

2 The Revolution and its Enemies

ISSUES
Who opposed the new regime in 1649?
How effectively were these enemies dealt with?

The execution of Charles I was greeted with shock and horror in both Britain and Europe. In Scotland Charles II was immediately proclaimed King, while the Irish rebels were still in arms and claimed allegiance to the Stuarts. The most immediate threats were closer to home. The groan that had echoed from the crowd as the axe fell symbolised the shock and outrage felt by many across the nation, but the first action came, ironically, from the republican radicals, the Levellers. At the time of Pride's Purge they had been sidetracked by Ireton into discussions of a new Agreement of the People, building up their expectations that any action against the King would be part of a wider settlement. In mid-December these negotiations failed over the extent of religious toleration to be established. The Levellers were left isolated and irrelevant while the army executed the King and placed the Rump of around seventy members in power.

a) The Leveller Challenge, 1649

Furious at being outmanoeuvred and denied influence at such a time, the Leveller leaders launched a bitter attack on Cromwell and Ireton, accusing them of ambition and deceit. More dangerously, they sought once more to use the army as a power base, encouraging the rank and file to petition against martial law now that the war was over. By March 1649 this had become an attempt to incite mutiny in the army, and it was undoubtedly this that motivated Cromwell to act against them. At his instigation, the Rump ordered the arrest of the leaders, and they were imprisoned in the Tower of London. In response they sought to exploit discontent among the regiments over arrears of pay and the prospect of service in Ireland, by calling for the restoration of the Agitators and the General Council. In April

ISSUE
Why were the Levellers so easily defeated?

the Baptist churches, hitherto their most reliable allies, publicly disassociated themselves from the movement.

In the same month, a minor mutiny over pay by troopers of Colonel Whalley's regiment in London led to the execution of one, Robert Lockyer, and a large demonstration at his funeral. May produced a brief mutiny at Salisbury among some of the men due for embarkation for Ireland, and a more serious outbreak at Oxford led by William Thompson, who called on other regiments in the area to join him in rebellion. At the same time, the prisoners in the Tower were putting the finishing touches to a third Agreement of the People, reverting to its most radical elements now that there was no virtue in compromise with the Grandees. On 14 May Cromwell and Fairfax caught up with the body of the mutineers at Burford and, taking them by surprise during the night, captured over three hundred, leaving the rest to disperse without horses or weapons. It is a measure of the Grandees' victory that only three mutineers were shot in a token reprisal. By the time the new Agreement saw the light of day, the movement that had created it was broken.

As in 1647, the ease with which Leveller influence was curtailed revealed how limited it was, although they retained the power to frighten many in authority. In October 1649 Lilburne was tried for treason, but acquitted amid popular celebration. He was exiled on the orders of the Rump, and when he sought to return, he was re-arrested despite his promises of good behaviour. From 1654 he was imprisoned, 'for the peace of the commonwealth', in Jersey where he seems to have found some personal fulfilment through conversion to the Quaker faith. The harsh treatment that he undoubtedly received is a testament to his talent as well as his continued defiance, but the Leveller threat ceased to be significant by the end of 1649. The fact was that the Levellers had no real support or organisation outside London, and always relied heavily on pamphlets and a literate readership to spread their ideas. The renewal of censorship by the Rump, while never completely successful, did much to curtail their impact, and the imprisonment of the leaders destroyed the incipient party organisation. After 1649 there were demands for radical reforms from within the army, and a radical threat to the existing hierarchy was posed by new religious groups such as the Ranters, Diggers and Quakers (see Figure 17 and pages 244–9), but overt political radicalism had effectively ceased. For the Rump and its successors, there were more serious problems to deal with.

ISSUE
How was the Republic established throughout Britain?

b) The Royalist Threat, 1649–51

Chief among these problems was the threat of Royalist invasion from Ireland or Scotland. The Irish rebellion, which had continued since

1641, was not a threat in itself, but the news of Charles's execution had united Irish Anglicans and Catholics, and enhanced the possibility of invasion by Charles II with foreign help. The defeat of the Levellers allowed Cromwell to land in Ireland in July, under pressure to achieve a rapid pacification because of the gathering threat from Scotland. This may partly explain the brutality with which he stormed Drogheda, to the north of Dublin, and slaughtered the garrison for their refusal to surrender. Many civilians died in the process. This was followed by a similar attack on Wexford. While Cromwell has been criticised by generations of historians for his actions, they were effective at the time. By the spring of 1650 he was able to return to Britain and counter the Scottish threat, leaving others to complete the pacification. Fewer historians have recorded the fact that this process was conducted with equal or greater brutality, involving the destruction of homes and crops, famine and slow starvation for the rural population.

Cromwell and Ireland, 1649

Cromwell's treatment of the garrisons at Drogheda and Wexford has become part of the political mythology of Anglo-Irish relations. While his behaviour was undoubtedly, and uncharacteristically, harsh, it was well within the rules of war used at the time, in which a garrison that had refused to surrender was at the mercy of the victors if it was subsequently taken by storm. The slaughter of civilians may well have occurred in the heat of the moment, or because of the anti-Catholic attitudes of the rank and file. Similar atrocities had been carried out by Lord Mountjoy in the reign of Elizabeth.

Nevertheless, it was unusual to apply the laws of battle so literally in England, and unusual in the career of Cromwell, who was normally anxious to avoid unnecessary loss of life. While the decisions may have been made in the heat of battle, he justified them in reporting his victories to Parliament and never expressed regret or suggested that the slaughter had gone further than he intended. There are a number of possible explanations for his behaviour. One is that he desired to make an impact and encourage other garrisons to surrender, in order to shorten the campaign. The tendency for English armies to become bogged down in Ireland was well known. A second is that he was angered by the loss of life among his own men as a result of the resistance. A third is that he was influenced by his anti-Catholic prejudice and by stories of the atrocities of 1641 – he certainly referred to this in explaining what had happened, although relief at the successful outcome may well have tinged the exultant tone of his letters. On balance it would appear that a combination of these factors caused him to behave in a way that he never repeated elsewhere.

Returning to England in the spring of 1650, Cromwell was dispatched by the Rump to Scotland in order to counter the threat of invasion from the north. Although the Scottish Covenanters and nobility had divided over the Engagement with Charles I in 1648,

Cromwell's victories are often quoted as evidence of English tyranny in Ireland, but their notoriety may rest on their importance in Anglo-Irish relations rather than the extent of his brutality. Did he behave more harshly than other English generals, or was it merely that his conquest was more successful and crucial in the destruction of Irish independence? How valid are the judgements of historians who criticise Cromwell's actions on moral grounds?

ISSUE
Why did Royalist sentiment remain a threat to the regime?

KEY DATES IN THE CONQUEST OF BRITAIN 1649–51

1649

May — Leveller mutineers defeated at Burford;

August — Cromwell in Ireland after the Irish Royalists under Ormonde deafeated at Rathmines by Michael Jones;

Sept/ Oct — Drogheda and Wexford captured and inhabitants massacred, other towns quickly surrendered;

they still possessed a formidable army under the leadership of David Leslie, which they now placed at the disposal of Charles II. Cromwell faced a difficult task, since Leslie had established a strong defensive barrier south of Edinburgh, and after months of frustration the English army was trapped in Dunbar, deprived of supplies and weakened by disease. A combination of impatience on the part of the Scots and a daring (and desperate) counter-assault by Cromwell led to his stunning victory on 3 September 1650, evidence for him of God's approval and blessing of the new order. When Charles turned to the west of Scotland and raised new forces for an attack on England itself, Cromwell moved to cut him off, and with greatly superior numbers destroyed the Royalist army at Worcester on 3 September 1651, the anniversary of Dunbar. With this 'crowning mercy' as he described it in dispatches, he had secured the new regime for the foreseeable future.

While Royalist armies could be dealt with, Royalist sentiment was another matter. If the political revolution of 1649 was to succeed in establishing a successful alternative to the Stuart monarchy, it would have to rely on more than military strength. The army could keep the regime in place, but it could not generate positive support. It was also a political liability. Eight years of war, high taxes, and the dislocation of trade had been followed by bad harvests in 1649. The economy was in desperate straits, and distress was widespread. To maintain an army on top of this was to burden both the regime and the taxpayer beyond reason. Secondly, the army's interference in politics was widely resented. Thirdly, the army was associated with radical groups and ideas that appeared to threaten stability at every level.

While the older 'Puritan' radicals such as the Baptists and Independents accepted the authority of the Bible as a restraint on individual freedom, a newer generation of radicals had repudiated even that. The argument that God spoke to the individual spirit directly had been interpreted to suggest that the voice of God within the individual was the supreme authority in religion. The execution of a reigning monarch suggested that anything was possible and while millenarian groups confidently awaited Christ's return to rule in person, others argued that He had already returned in the human heart and mind to justify complete individual freedom. The expression of this freedom varied. The Ranters repudiated conventional morality, declaring that since God made all things, all that was natural was part of God and sin existed only in the mind. The Diggers claimed communal use of the land, since the earth was made by God for all humanity to share. Whatever its form, this spirit was a direct threat to the existing hierarchy, and to all semblance of social stability.

The fears generated by such radical ideas served to enhance the image of monarchy as the guarantee of order and the normal process of law. The process had begun with Charles's claim that his trial was illegal, and represented arbitrary, military rule. His courage and dignity in the face of death had begun to restore respect for him, and for the monarchy that he represented. Royalist propaganda was already capitalising on this – the martyr King's supposed last thoughts, published as *Eikon Basilike* in 1649, went through thirty-six editions in the first year of publication. While sentiment and nostalgia increased its appeal, the attractions of monarchy were also based on political ideology and experience. These attitudes did not mean that the new order could not succeed, but it did make the task more difficult. The failure of Charles II to raise support when he entered England did not imply active support for the new Commonwealth, but war-weariness and reluctance to take risks. What the new regime had gained by 1651 was, at best, lukewarm acquiescence. While it was not impossible to win support, it would clearly take time, and would require successful alternatives to be put in place, offering stability as well as reform. This combination however, would prove difficult to find.

1650
May

Cromwell returned to England;

August

Cromwell sent north after resignation of Fairfax, to confront Scots and Charles II;

Sept 3rd

Scots defeated at Dunbar; Charles raised a second army from the western highlands and invaded England;

1651
Sept 3rd

Battle of Worcester – Charles heavily defeated by Cromwell;

1654
April

Union of England and Scotland under the protectorate.

Why was monarchy popular?

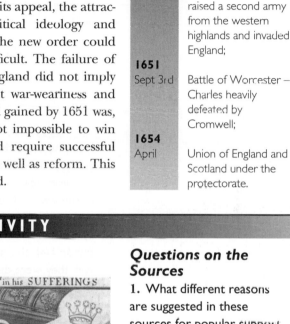

Source A Title page from *Eikon Basilike*, showing Charles as the martyr King.

Questions on the Sources

1. What different reasons are suggested in these sources for popular support for monarchy? [analysis]
2. What kind of monarchy is implied in the arguments set out here? [inference, cross-reference]
3. What evidence suggests that it was monarchy, and not Charles Stuart that was popular? [inference, cross-reference]
4. If it was monarchy rather than Charles I that was popular, how would you explain the success of *Eikon Basilike*? [interpretation in context]

The debates came on very high for setting up a King. All the lawyers ... were vehemently for this. They said no new government could be settled legally but by a King, who should pass bills for such a form as should be agreed on. Till then, all they did was like building upon sand ... [A]ll that had been done would be void of itself, as contrary to the law yet in being and not repealed ... And as no man's person was safe till that was done, so they said all the grants and sales [of land] that had been made were null and void.

Source B From Bishop Gilbert Burnet, *History of My Own Time*, 1723.

Kings here are the guides of the people, but the laws are their guides. They are above the people, but the laws are above them ... The lives, liberties and estates of the people are all in the keeping of the law ... The people of these nations were never out of love with the name of King, but have been with some of their persons, for their maladministration. King Edward II and King Richard II of England felt the smart of this truth. They were swayed with their will: they were deposed; but the son of the one and the cousin of the other was made King; so the person, and not the King, was destroyed. The office of the King standeth with the liberty of the people, else certainly it would not have been used so long here.

Source C From Sir Thomas Widdrington's speech to Cromwell in 1657, persuading him to accept the crown.

Kingship is not a Title, but an Office, so interwoven with the fundamental Laws of this Nation, that they cannot be executed or exercised without it ... The Law can tell when it [royal power] keeps within compass, and when it exceeds its limits. And the Law, knowing this, the People can know it also. And the people do love what they know ...

Source D From notes by Oliver Cromwell in 1657, summarising the arguments in favour of kingship.

3 The Failure of the Commonwealth

a) The Nature of the Rump

The piecemeal process by which the Commonwealth was set up was accompanied by the gradual return of MPs who had stayed away during the King's trial, but felt able to conform to the new order. By the spring of 1649 the number of MPs reached about 150, and the successes of the army and the gradual defeat of Royalist hopes encouraged more to make peace with the new regime. This also had the effect of increasing the more cautious and conservative elements of the Rump, at the expense of radical influence. This was probably less important, however, than the fact that little thought had been given to the nature of the government that should emerge from the revolution. The army had acted in defence of its interests against a conservative attempt to restore the powers of the monarchy and a coercive national Church. It was clear, therefore, that some kind of religious toleration would have to be established, and that there was an expectation of 'godly reformation' in government and society – but beyond this, little was defined.

The MPs who were expected to carry out this godly reformation found themselves beset by conflicting pressures. On the one hand the army, the radicals and other idealists demanded wholesale reform. The Council of Officers and their supporters favoured reform and refurbishment of the Church alongside a significant measure of religious freedom, simplification of the laws and greater social justice, such as an end to imprisonment for debt. The Baptist churches favoured the end of a national Church and the reliance of all ministers on voluntary contributions. The Independents favoured the retention of a reformed national Church with the payment of ministers by some means other than tithes. The more radical sects demanded complete religious freedom. Individual reformers like the scientist, Samuel Hartlib, and the Independent minister, Hugh Peter, proposed schemes for reform in education, medicine, the provision of work for the poor and guaranteed agricultural prices. Against a background of economic distress, these measures were appealing but were financially impossible.

On the other hand, most MPs were well aware of the need for control and the restoration of authority if confidence was to be restored, especially among the governing elite in the localities. While many of the greater gentry had withdrawn from commissions of the peace and county government, their replacements came mainly from the next in rank, who were part of the same hierarchy. Complaints of social unrest, the behaviour of radicals and the breakdown of parish administration led to county petitions demanding the restoration of

ISSUES
Was the failure of the Commonwealth inevitable? What were its fundamental weaknesses?

ISSUE
What difficulties stood in the way of reform?

order and the established Church. In addition, there were real obstacles in the way of reform. Law reform, for example, was a difficult and complex subject, which required careful consideration if the cure was not to be worse than the disease. The Rump was responsible for both the planning and debating of necessary legislation, and also the daily maintenance of government, a huge workload that parliaments had never previously undertaken. To add to the burdens, the army leaders also wanted to see progress made in constitutional reforms, to lay the foundations for a permanent new structure.

ISSUE
Why was the Rump increasingly unpopular?

b) The Failure of the Rump

There is, therefore, something to be said on behalf of the MPs who took on these burdens in the aftermath of the King's execution. Their task was undeniably difficult and complex. Nevertheless, a summary of the measures that they took reveals the conservative and authoritarian character of the regime, and explains its general unpopularity as well as the growing dissatisfaction of the army. Although the statutes compelling attendance at church were repealed, providing a measure of religious freedom, the **Blasphemy** and **Adultery** Acts of 1650 increased repression and launched an attack on the more radical sects. Measures were taken to improve the supply of good preaching ministers, especially in Wales, which was regarded as a 'dark corner' of the land, but no steps were taken to replace tithes or find a less oppressive means of supporting the ministry. Measures of economic regulation, especially the Navigation Acts, were passed to encourage the development of trade. A successful war against the Dutch helped to build up the navy and encourage expansion of overseas trade. In the long run these measures helped to lay the foundations of economic growth, but at the time they seemed merely to be furthering the interests of the merchants who were establishing an ever-growing influence in Parliament.

The appearance of self-interest increased with time. The Hales Commission was established to consider law reform in 1651, under pressure from the army after Worcester, but its report was set aside in February 1653. Whether or not the numerous lawyers in Parliament engineered this inaction, it suited their interests. Progress with electoral reform and new constitutional measures was also remarkably slow, nudged on only by the frequent prompting of the army and Cromwell. After Dunbar Sir Henry Vane suggested a plan for 'recruiting' new members, which would protect the seats of existing MPs and simply add new members for those which were vacant. After Worcester the House focused on arrangements to include members for Scotland and Ireland, and on the war with the Dutch. As the prospects of reform dwindled, so the irritation of the army rose. The

BLASPHEMY AND ADULTERY
Blasphemy means an insult to God, while adultery was interpreted as sexual immorality. Both laws were used to prosecute those whose behaviour offended the moral conventions of the time. Religious enthusiasm could lead to eccentric attitudes and a tendency to equate nakedness with purity led to actions and gestures that less enthusiastic souls found plainly shocking. Some early Quakers, for example, paraded naked through village streets carrying braziers of hot coals to symbolise the fires of hell. These laws allowed such actions to be punished without regard for the intentions and motives that lay behind them.

Rump's attitude indicated a willingness to cling to power, and the growing hostility with which MPs reacted to army pressure suggested that its views would have less and less influence. By the end of 1652 the Council of Officers were pressing General Cromwell to take action.

What finally goaded Cromwell into action is not entirely clear. On 20 April 1653 he entered the House of Commons with a military escort, delivered a tirade of criticism at the astonished members, and ordered them to leave. He later justified his action by claiming that they were planning to maintain themselves in power indefinitely, but there is evidence that they were at last preparing a bill for dissolution. Many historians have suggested that they were reviving Vane's idea for 'recruiting', but this seems unlikely. The best explanation seems to lie in a combination of the Rump's growing hostility to the army, and the character of Cromwell.

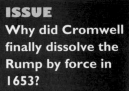

ISSUE
Why did Cromwell finally dissolve the Rump by force in 1653?

Figure 22 The Dissolution of the Rump. This contemporary engraving illustrates the general approval with which the dissolution of the Rump was greeted. The owl wearing glasses is intended to represent the blinkered and short-sighted stupidity of its members. Cromwell was probably speaking the truth when he later claimed that 'not a dog barked' at their removal.

Throughout 1652 Cromwell had tried to restrain the more radical sections of the army and maintain unity with the Rump to protect the common cause. As the winter of 1652–3 progressed, this became increasingly difficult. The Rump's unwillingness to consider meaningful reforms, the growing evidence that power itself encouraged self-seeking, and the growing resentment directed at army interference made it increasingly difficult to believe that anything could be achieved by such restraint. Cromwell was also aware that a system of government that united both legislative and executive powers in a single group of men was problematic in itself. Not only did it impose an impossible workload, it also made them impervious to any outside pressure. As so often, however, Cromwell was reluctant to act until he was sure of God's will – he sought guidance from Providence. Just as, in December 1648, he had hesitated until Pride's Purge provided the sign that God wished the King to be removed, he now waited for some providential event to show him the way forward.

The sign seems to have come in April, when the Rump finally considered a bill for its own dissolution. Cromwell knew that new elections on the existing franchise would produce a large number of conservative MPs. He therefore wanted some measures for electoral reform to be built in, and a Council of State that included both MPs and army officers to be appointed to govern in the interval and to supervise new elections. In April, however, he discovered that MPs planned to rush ahead with a bill that made no changes to the system and to appoint a committee of Rumpers to supervise elections and vet new MPs. There could be no clearer indication that the army would be allowed no part in proceedings, and that the new Parliament would be even more hostile to reform than this one. If Cromwell retained any hopes of godly reformation and freedom to search for truth, let alone legal and social reforms, they would be lost if this bill went ahead.

This explains the haste and anger with which he acted in April 1653. It also illustrates the problems created by the lack of solid support in the country. Having been forced to act, Cromwell was faced with the problem of finding a replacement that would serve the cause of reform and find some justification for its own power. As the Lord General, he was virtually the only senior official who could make any claim to legal power, and even that was doubtful. As the head of the army, God's chosen instrument, he no doubt felt morally justified in making such decisions, but the problem was to find an adequate alternative to the Rump. Not surprisingly, he turned to his officers for advice, and found two possibilities. Colonel John Lambert suggested a small executive council, an army Council of State, which would take over the King's functions alongside new parliaments. From the **Fifth Monarchist** Colonel Thomas Harrison came the suggestion of an Assembly of Saints, called from the best part of the nation, to plan a government fit to welcome the returning Christ! Cromwell chose the latter, although in a rather more practical form.

The key to understanding the contradictions of the Interregnum is to understand the contradictions of the man who now dominated it, Oliver Cromwell. The profile on pages 155–6 analyses the events that shaped his character, and it is the complexity of his character that has fascinated biographers and led to conflicting interpretations and judgements. On the one hand, Cromwell was a conservative member of the gentry, concerned to maintain social order, uphold

ISSUE
Why did Cromwell replace the Rump with a Nominated Assembly?

ISSUE
How did Cromwell's character and beliefs influence the course of events?

the existing social hierarchy and protect the interests of his class. He was never an original thinker in terms of political organisation, and relied on associates to provide the theoretical understanding behind the constitutional changes that he endorsed. In his own words, he was not 'wedded and glued' to particular forms of government, but was willing to consider any practical alternatives.

This explains why he was so hated by men like Lilburne and by the republicans who supported the Rump. He listened to their plans, sometimes tried them out, and was able to abandon them when they proved unworkable, leaving their authors feeling they had been used and betrayed. His own preference was for a 'government with something of the monarchical in it'. Like most gentlemen of his time, Cromwell believed that England was a 'mixed' monarchy, in which king, lords and commons all had some powers within the rule of law, and were able to act as a check on one another against any abuse of power. This preference had been strengthened by the problems arising from government by a single authority, such as the Rump, and would reappear in the establishment of the Protectorate at the end of 1653.

In the spring of 1653, however, the other side of Cromwell's character predominated. If his political thinking was conventional, his religious convictions were those of a radical. It is difficult to define his views in relation to the various sects of the time, but he was probably closest to the Independents, who supported the idea of a national Church with limited toleration for voluntary groups whose views were neither too outrageous nor dangerous to others. This broadly describes the kind of Church that he sought to create as Lord Protector. What is clear is that he was deeply committed to the work of godly reformation, and to the right of the godly to search for truth without unnecessary restraints. His whole career demonstrates his belief in Providence, and his desire to serve God and to act to further God's will. His notorious periods of hesitation – before the quarrel with Parliament in 1647, before the King's trial and execution in 1648–9, and before the dissolution of the Rump – arose from his desire to interpret the signs and understand God's will before acting. Once convinced, he acted with energy and determination. He did not share the extreme millenarian convictions of a man like Harrison, and had no intention of allowing the 'Saints' to tear down government. However, he was prepared to consider the possibility that the civil wars and execution of the King might indicate that the struggle for godly reformation was approaching its climax. In such circumstances, an assembly drawn from the godly part of the nation might be able to contribute to the work. The result was the calling, in July 1653, of the Nominated Assembly, later nicknamed the Barebones Parliament.

FIFTH MONARCHISTS

The Fifth Monarchists believed in an extreme form of the more widespread millenarian idea, that the world was dominated by a great struggle between God and the devil, the forces of good and evil. It would end with the final triumph of good and the return of Christ to rule on earth in person for a thousand years – the millenium. Many of these ideas were based on the biblical Book of Revelations, a mystical and often obscure description of visions and dreams, and there was considerable variation in the way they were interpreted. Some argued that there were four great earthly monarchies, which would be followed by the fifth monarchy, the rule of Christ. Enthusiasts identified the fourth monarchy as that which was brought to an end with the execution of Charles I, and expected that Christ's return was therefore imminent. The Fifth Monarchists argued that it was the duty of the 'saints' to tear down earthly government and prepare the way for Christ's return. Others took a less extreme view, arguing that God would act in His own way, while some even argued that the Kingdom of Christ would only ever exist in human hearts and minds.

CROMWELL'S MILITARY ADVISERS

Until 1651 Cromwell's closest associate and political adviser had been his son-in-law, Henry Ireton. The gap left by Ireton's death in that year was increasingly filled by the able Yorkshireman, John Lambert, whose family held substantial estates in the Craven area. Lambert was a republican by political conviction, influenced by the example of ancient Greece and Rome rather than religious views, and he was one of the few leading officers in the New Model who did not have strong Puritan convictions.

ISSUE

Why did the Nominated Assembly fail to achieve a settlement?

c) The Barebones Parliament

The nickname, created by Royalist propagandists to discredit the regime, has clouded historians' judgements of the assembly. This nickname was derived from the name of one member, Praise-God Barbon, a London leather-seller, and epitomised both the eccentric godliness and low social origins with which the assembly was to become associated. In fact, the army council had requested advice from local dignitaries before selecting those who were to attend, and, as Derek Hirst has pointed out, over one-third of the members were men of sufficient status to have been elected to any Parliament, and over two-thirds had been JPs for more than three years. Many were moderate and cautious reformers rather than fiery enthusiasts. However, they were often from the minor gentry rather than the greater families, some had links with the more flamboyant radical groups, and about a dozen out of the total of 144 were Fifth Monarchists, determined to destroy man-made government and the national Church, in order to usher in the rule of saints and the return of King Jesus.

These conflicting influences soon became apparent. To Cromwell's irritation, the Assembly began by declaring itself to be a Parliament, with all parliamentary privileges. This did not promise well for an assembly whose task was to create a new constitution. Nevertheless, the members soon warmed to their task, and in the five months of its existence, they passed over thirty acts, many of them eminently sensible and moderate. A new Council of State was established, with a good mix of members to represent both moderate and enthusiastic opinion. The work of the Hale Commission on law reform was taken up, producing some reform of the laws on debt, a civil marriage act, and a plan to abolish the notoriously slow and expensive Court of Chancery. Progress was made in uniting Scotland and Ireland with England and Wales, and in modifying lay control of Church livings. Here, however, the assembly began to tread on dangerous ground, since an attack on advowsons and tithes (see page 30) was seen by many as an attack on property itself. This strengthened the unease of the moderate members, who were concerned by the growing clamour of the Fifth Monarchists for the introduction of biblical laws, and by the changes that were taking place in local government. The summer of 1652 saw a series of purges in the commissions of the peace (JPs) that removed members of the gentry and replaced them with yeomen and shopkeepers. When the radicals succeeded on 10 December in pushing through a vote against tithes, the moderates decided to act before social order was seriously undermined. On 12 December they met early in the absence of the radicals, and voted to dissolve themselves, handing power back to Cromwell.

OLIVER CROMWELL (1599–1658)

Cromwell was born in Huntingdon, and educated at Huntingdon Free School and Sidney Sussex College, Cambridge. The grandson of a baronet, he was of the minor gentry, although at the lowest point in his fortunes he was forced to work as a yeoman farmer near St Ives in Huntingdonshire. Certainly his background was unremarkable – a generally Puritan upbringing and a period at a strongly Protestant college – but he demonstrated considerable strength of character at an early stage in life, when he quarrelled with the Huntingdon Corporation (for whom he had sat as MP in 1628) over their use of money left as a legacy to the borough. The Corporation were able to call on allies in the Privy Council to defeat him, and he was forced into a humiliating public apology. This seems to have caused him to sell his house and leave the town, and his purchase of a working farm suggests that he also suffered financial losses.

This may have been the period that he later described as God 'bringing him low' to teach him humility on the road to salvation. It was not unusual for Calvinists to see such personal difficulties as a test of their faith. Whatever the reason, Cromwell seems to have come close to a nervous breakdown at this point, from which he emerged with the unshakeable belief that he had been restored to health in order to serve God. The depth of his convictions is reflected in his lifelong habit of 'waiting on the Lord' when faced with difficult decisions. His providential beliefs led him to expect and await a sign from God to indicate how he should proceed in order to best serve God's purpose. Many Calvinists shared such views – what was exceptional about Cromwell, as the quote opposite suggests, was the nature of the decisions he had to make and the speed and energy with which he acted once he believed he knew what God required of him. The visible sign of his recovery was that he inherited from an uncle the position of Steward to the Cathedral of Ely. He moved to the town and lived in moderate

If thou wilt seek, seek to know the mind of God in all that chain of Providence, whereby God brought thee thither and that person [Charles I] to thee; how before and since, God has ordered him and affairs concerning him: and then tell me, whether there be not some glorious and high meaning in all this . . .

Source E From a letter written by Cromwell to his cousin, Robert Hammond when Hammond was Governor of the Isle of Wight and Gaoler to the King.

comfort there until in 1640 he became MP for Cambridge. This was a relatively prestigious position for a member of the minor gentry, but Cromwell was probably well-known in the area. He had publicly defended the right of fen-dwellers to be compensated for fen drainage schemes, which deprived them of customary sources of food and income, and he also had an extensive family network that included cousins such as John Hampden.

As an MP, Cromwell was closely associated with the opposition to Charles. He was very much a backbencher. What brought him to prominence was the outbreak of war. He always excelled when there was action to be taken, and in June 1642 he left London to secure Cambridge Castle for Parliament. He then raised a cavalry regiment for the Eastern Association army, and according to the diarist, Thomas May, played a major part in pressurising the gentry of the eastern counties to declare for Parliament. His energy and commitment led him to command of the cavalry under the Earl of Manchester. With no military experience before middle age, he proved astonishingly effective, mainly because of his character and common sense. His famous willingness to promote men on merit and his preference for a 'plain russet-coated captain' over the pretensions of the gentry were based on practical considerations and a concern for what would work best. Much of his strength lay in the men that he recruited and the discipline that he was able to instil, and his religious views played a part in both. While the idea that he created an army of saints has been shown to be too simplistic, there is little doubt that he encouraged recruitment of men who shared his Puritan outlook, and that he used their commitment to the cause to develop a disciplined force both on and off the battlefield. Unlike the dashing Prince Rupert, he taught his cavalry to regroup after a successful charge and return to the battlefield. This discipline proved crucial in the Parliamentarian victory at Marston Moor and in many of the other battles that followed.

Despite his reputation as a religious radical, there is little evidence to suggest that Cromwell deliberately sought to challenge authority. He believed in godly reformation, and sought to build a national Church and State that would support and enhance such work. What made him unusual among men of his background and station was his belief that an individual should be free to seek God in his own way, provided he was no danger to others, and that God revealed Himself through such individuals, regardless of education or social rank. Hence he protected separatists and challenged those in authority in order to enhance the search for truth, which he believed to be the main purpose of religion. In many ways unusually humane, he regarded the excesses and eccentricities of religious enthusiasts as misguided rather than wicked.

The turning-point in Cromwell's political career came with the army mutiny of 1647, when he allied himself with the soldiers in order to influence the political settlement. He seems to have hesitated at first, but came to believe that conservative provocations and the defiance of the army rank and file were part of God's purpose in shaping the settlement. The same providential thinking justified the army's intervention in politics. Although Fairfax remained as Lord General until 1650, it was Cromwell who was the army's political leader. Throughout 1647 he sought to create a compromise that would restore the King, protect Parliament, and secure a measure of religious toleration. The Heads of the Proposals would have created a flexible settlement and even included some Leveller demands for social and legal reforms. Thereafter, through changing circumstances and by different strategies, Cromwell continued to pursue these aims. Although he accepted the necessity of executing Charles and the abolition of the monarchy, his overall purpose remained remarkably consistent – to balance freedom and authority in pursuit of the godly reformation. In order to achieve this he allied in turn with republicans, millenarians, army officers, lawyers and constitutional monarchists. An outstanding military leader, a political pragmatist, and a religious zealot who distrusted dogmatic authority and disliked persecution, he spent the remaining years of his life trying to establish a compromise and reconcile aims that were probably irreconcilable except in his own mind.

I confess I never looked to see such a day as this ... when Christ should be so owned as He is, at this day, and in this work ... I say you are called with a high call. And why should we be afraid to say or think, that this may be the day to usher in the things that God has promised ... Indeed I do think something is at the door; we are at the threshold.

Source F From Cromwell's speech at the opening of the Barebones Parliament.

There is no doubt about Cromwell's disappointment regarding the Barebones Parliament, but he was pragmatic enough to recognise failure, and to realise that it arose from the same issue that had destroyed the Rump Parliament – the difficulty of balancing the desire for reform with the need for stability. Where the Rump had proceeded too slowly, the radicals of the nominated assembly had moved too fast. He therefore turned to the alternative suggested by Lambert, of an executive council to rule with the help of parliaments. The Rump and Barebones parliaments had demonstrated the problems caused by a single central authority which chose to ignore other opinions. Cromwell and Lambert now sought to restore the principle of mixed government in the hope of achieving a blend of reform and stability. On 16 December 1653 the Commonwealth was ended when Cromwell was appointed Lord Protector, to rule with the help of a Council of State and parliaments elected every three years on a reformed franchise.

The Instrument of Government, 1653

England's first written constitution was also Britain's first formal constitution, since Scotland and Ireland were to be included. It provided for a single person to rule as executive, with powers that were limited and defined. Parliaments of 460 MPs were to be elected every three years. Voters were required to own £200 of personal property. This maintained a property qualification but removed the need to own land. Seats were distributed on the basis of taxation, and parliaments were to sit for a minimum of five months. Royalists were to be excluded from the first four parliaments. They had control of legislation, although the Protector could issue ordinances when Parliament was not in session, and he could veto (forbid) attempts to change the constitution itself. There was to be a state Church, but with freedom of worship for all except Catholics and Prelatists (supporters of bishops). As a constitution, the Instrument had obvious weaknesses, notably the failure to provide for future amendment or for adjudication in case of disputes. Nevertheless, in the words of Derek Hirst, it 'did wrestle with the central problems of the over-mighty prince and an over-mighty Parliament, and given mutual tolerance and adequate funding, it might have worked'.

What political and religious principles were implied by these arrangements?
What social groups and classes would be influential in this system?

ISSUE
Did the Protectorate represent a step back towards monarchy?

4 The Protectorate and its Problems, 1654–7

a) The Nature of the New Government

The return to government by a single person, combined with hindsight (that it was followed by a second, more conservative Protectorate and by a restoration of monarchy in 1660) has encouraged some historians to see the Protectorate as an essentially conservative regime leading inexorably back to monarchy. While this is understandable, there is considerable evidence to suggest that Cromwell, at least, did not view it in this light. He continued to dress in plain

Figure 23 The Emblem of England's Distraction, 1658. Although this engraving relates to the later years of Cromwell's rule, it reveals the basis of his power and the image that he sought to present.

What does the engraving suggest about:
– the sources of Cromwell's power?
– the aims of his government?
– the justification of his rule?
How does this compare with the images of Charles I presented on pages 75 and 147?
Is Cromwell depicted here as a King, or as a Protector?

clothes and to pursue a simple personal lifestyle. He adopted some of the trappings of royalty by restoring the palace of Whitehall and some of its treasures, and signing his documents 'Oliver P' in mimicry of traditional royal signatures. This, however, seems to have been intended to encourage outward respect for the regime, especially among foreign visitors and ambassadors. It is hardly surprising that, in constructing this new regime, he and his associates should draw on their own political experience and utilise the best elements of institutions with which they were familiar.

Cromwell's aims were, in his own words, the 'healing and settling' of the nation. While he employed civilian advisers and sought to bring the established gentry back into local government, he also listened to the advice of soldiers like John Lambert, and pursued his vision of reform. In creating space for conservatives and monarchists, he was seeking to broaden the base of support and provide stability, rather than abandoning his cause. Unfortunately, many of his old comrades were unable to see it in this light, and their restlessness, if not outright opposition, made his task considerably more difficult. Nevertheless, it is clear that for him the Protectorate represented a new approach to the business of providing balanced government, and to his key purpose of establishing reform while also maintaining an acceptable level of authority and stability. His difficulty lay in the fact that for many of his contemporaries, these aims were essentially incompatible. In addition, while he and Lambert might not see the Protectorate as a stepping-stone to monarchy, there were others who might try to make it just that.

b) The Progress of Reform

The months before the calling of the first Protectorate Parliament offered the best opportunity for reform. Cromwell quickly appointed Matthew Hale, author of the report on law reform, as a judge and followed this up with a Chancery Ordinance that simplified procedures and reduced fees. Unfortunately, the Council of State felt that it was necessary to entrust reform to the senior lawyers and judges, who ensured that any changes were both cautious and slow. The common law judges introduced some further regulation in December 1654, but thereafter little was done. Similarly, attempts to open up economic opportunities by reducing the power of merchant guilds and borough corporations received little support. The Council included too many traditionalists and vested interests to make significant change in this area, so that old methods of organisation persisted. In 1657 the new trade of framework knitting was organised into a guild, and the monopoly granted to the East India Company was restored in return for a loan to the government.

ISSUE
Why was reform so difficult to achieve?

CROMWELL'S CIVILIAN ADVISERS

Cromwell's civilian advisers were disliked by the army, with some good reason. Sir Charles Wolseley was among the moderate MPs who engineered the downfall of the Barebones Parliament, while Sir Antony Ashley Cooper had fought for the King in 1642. Lord Broghill held an Irish peerage and was the brother of Robert Boyle, the Oxford scientist. They sought to reduce army influence but, despite army suspicions, they were not a coherent group. In 1656–7 when Parliament debated the possibility of offering Cromwell the crown, Cooper was one of the republicans excluded from Parliament, while Broghill was a key supporter of the scheme. Essentially, they were pragmatists, whose main purpose was to restore moderate, civilian government.

ISSUE

How did Cromwell reform the Church?

The nature and activities of these separatist groups are examined in greater detail in Chapter 8.

This also points to a further obstacle in the way of reform measures – the government's serious financial problems. The Rump had confiscated lands from the Church and the monarchy, but this had been swallowed up by the costs of the army and the Dutch War. Although Cromwell quickly brought the war to an end, he embarked in 1655 on a war with Spain. There were a number of reasons for this. Lacking the money to pay off the fleet used against the Dutch, he hoped to use it against Spain in the West Indies, and make the war pay for itself by seizing Spanish treasure ships and colonies. It also encouraged closer relations with Spain's enemy, France, depriving Charles II of possible French aid. Religious considerations played a part in his calculations – Spain had always been a more actively Catholic power than France. In the event, however, his Western Design to capture Hispaniola proved a costly failure, and the seizure of Jamaica was little consolation. While Cromwell's foreign policy brought a measure of prestige, his financial problems continued to hamper the work of reform.

However, Cromwell's first priority was the Church. Although the upheavals of war had led to some ministers being ejected, or voluntarily leaving their parishes, many had simply continued to carry out their duties according to their own preferences. The result was a wide variation of services and ceremonies, supported by voluntary associations such as the Presbyterian group headed by Richard Baxter in Worcestershire. Cromwell's approach was to encourage such efforts and allow variation within a framework of acceptable doctrine. In March a Committee of Triers was established with responsibility for examining the qualities and beliefs of the parish clergy, confirming the livings of those who were acceptable, and appointing new ministers to vacant parishes. The committee sought ministers who were educated and capable of preaching, and who accepted the fundamentals of Christianity; neither their personal beliefs about salvation nor their preferences for particular ceremonies were considered. In August, the government added a Committee of Ejectors whose function was to remove the inadequate and the scandalous, but again, the decision was based on their quality as ministers rather than on their denominational preferences.

What Cromwell sought to establish was a broad, flexible and tolerant Church, which would contribute to the godly reformation through education and upholding moral standards. At the same time, as a believer in the search for truth, he allowed freedom to those who wished to meet in voluntary gatherings outside the establishment, provided that their doctrines were neither blasphemous nor dangerous. The dangerous category included both Catholics and Arminians, while the blasphemy laws curtailed the activities of some of the wilder sects. Nevertheless, the system allowed for a broad spectrum of belief, and even those who stood beyond it were often tolerated in practice, provided they were discreet. Both Catholics and the Anglican groups who continued to use the Prayer Book were often able to worship undisturbed, and Cromwell's personal sympathy with those who followed their conscience was revealed in his attitude to the Quaker, James Nayler, in 1656. When Nayler reenacted Christ's entry into Jerusalem at the gates of Bristol, and was accused of blasphemy, some MPs called for the death sentence. As Parliament debated Nayler's fate, Cromwell intervened to argue that he was foolish rather than wicked, and to challenge Parliament's right to inflict punishment on anyone. His intervention may have saved Nayler's life, but he was unable to prevent Parliament's order being carried out that Nayler should be flogged, bored through the tongue as a blasphemer, and committed to prison.

The Nayler case illustrates the problem that undermined Cromwell's efforts in this area – how to reconcile freedom with order, and how to calm the fears of the conservatives who saw the collapse of social discipline all around them. Within the established Church, ministers were faced with the problem of enforcing parish order and standards of behaviour on a populace who had the freedom to ignore them. Their only sanction was to exclude the sinful from communion, which had little effect on those who chose not to attend. Faced with widespread ignorance among a people who lived short, brutal lives, the educational schemes of government and individuals alike failed for lack of money and resources. The new University of Durham, an attempt to enlighten the **'dark' regions** of the north, was a short-lived exception. Despite heroic efforts by individual ministers, the reformation of the ungodly could make little progress without both financial support and legal compulsion.

Meanwhile, the radical sects exercised their right to worship outside the Church. For Conservatives this was, in itself, a threat to order and hierarchy. Many voluntary groups acted with discipline and moderation. The 1650s saw the Baptist and Congregationalist Churches take shape, establishing national and regional associations, and issuing formal statements of doctrine. It was by no means unusual for Independents (Congregationalists) to serve as parish ministers, while also conducting meetings of a voluntary 'gathered' church in their homes or other premises. Alongside this, however, the activities of the more eccentric sects reinforced the fears of those in authority. By 1654 there was little sign of Ranter activity, and the Diggers had long been dispersed, but they had been replaced by a new and more dynamic threat, the Quakers. Their eccentric manners and challenge to authority, their attacks on clerical privilege and social injustice, and above all their success in attracting converts seemed to threaten further revolution. While Cromwell might

ISSUE
In what ways did religious toleration undermine stablity?

'DARK' REGIONS
The 'dark' regions of the north of England were a matter of concern, because they were badly served by the Church. In Yorkshire and the Pennine region, across to Lancaster, Cumberland and Westmorland, the hilly nature of the country meant that population was thinly scattered and that parishes were therefore very large and often poor. Educational provision was also thin, and it was difficult to attract graduates as either ministers or teachers. The problem was highlighted by the strength of the Quakers in the area; the many chapels of rest situated in outlying villages provided meeting-places for separate congregations and migrant preachers.

take pride in his godly reformation, the majority of the population, and especially the gentry in the localities saw it as seriously undermining authority in Church and State.

The Quaker movement

The Quaker movement was founded in the north between 1650 and 1652 when George Fox began a series of journeys through Yorkshire, Lancashire and Cumbria to preach the doctrine of salvation through the inner light. He found fertile ground for his message in the groups of 'seekers' already established in the area, and the movement quickly took shape. By 1654 they were ready to launch a great 'mission to the south'. Some sixty First Publishers of Truth, including the charismatic Fox and James Nayler, set out to convert the world to an understanding of the light within, the voice of God in the human heart, which was the only authority needed in religion. Nicknamed Quakers because of their ecstatic trembling and passionate celebration of God's mercy, they entered churches and harangued ministers for their greed in taking payment for preaching, and refused to acknowledge their 'betters' by removing hats and addressing them as 'sir'. Not only did they demand the abolition of tithes and complete religious toleration, they condemned the wealthy and powerful to their faces, for their oppressions and lack of concern for the poor.

Most worrying for those in authority, the Quakers' message held a wide popular appeal, and their mission was spectacularly successful. It was by no means unusual for their preachers to draw large crowds, and to publicly 'convert' tens and even hundreds of people at a time. It is not surprising that anxious justices complained of this new plague from the north, devouring the land like locusts! By 1656 when Nayler's theatrics at Bristol brought such fears to a head, Fox was beginning to establish a national framework for the movement, now called the Society of Friends. By 1660 there were probably 60,000 Quakers in England, linked by their travelling preachers and by annual meetings of representatives from all parts of the country. After the Restoration this embryonic organisation was shattered by the onslaught of persecution, and many of the First Publishers died in prison. Fox, however, survived to create a new and more lasting system of local and regional meetings, which became the basis of a worldwide church.

ISSUE
What divisions brought about the failure of the Instrument of Government?

c) The Failure of the Instrument of Government

The result was that Cromwell's hopes of 'healing and settling' proved no more successful than the regimes that he had replaced. In August 1654 a Parliament was called, as required by the Instrument of Government, to ratify the new constitution. Instead, MPs attacked the very authority by which they had been summoned, and set out to alter the constitution. Initially, republican MPs such as Haselrig and Thomas Scot, who had been members of the Rump and had never forgiven Cromwell for its dissolution, led the attack. Skilled in parliamentary tactics, they were able to hold up business and deny the government both ratification of the Instrument and financial support. In September Cromwell responded by excluding MPs who refused to sign a 'recognition' of the constitution, and about a hundred republicans withdrew. The remainder, however, turned their attention to the radicals and the army who protected them. They voted against a new tax assessment, and for the reduction of the army to 30,000 men. By January 1655, it was clear that Cromwell would get no help from this assembly, and he dissolved it as soon as the Instrument allowed.

The first year of the Protectorate had therefore revealed the continuing problem of a fundamental division between civilian/conservative supporters and the army/radical interest, which had undermined the Rump and Barebones parliaments. In 1655 this threatened to destroy the regime. The winter of 1654–5 saw unrest in the army from Fifth Monarchists and republicans, followed in the spring by a Royalist uprising in Wiltshire, led by John Penruddock. The rising generated little support, and was easily contained, but it did raise concern about security and highlight the dangers of division. More seriously, the failure of Parliament to ratify the Instrument threatened the legal and constitutional basis of the regime. Throughout the spring and early summer the government's right to collect taxes was challenged in the courts, driving Cromwell to replace five judges who were likely to find against him. In May the case of George Cony, a merchant who had refused to pay customs duties, provoked Cromwell to imprison not only Cony, but also his entire legal counsel without trial.

His reaction to the Cony Case explains why the regime survived the crisis. Whatever his concern for legality, Cromwell was quite capable of decisive action, and with an army at his back he had no intention of surrendering control. In the summer of 1655 he reduced the monthly Assessment (tax), cut the soldiers' pay and brought army numbers down to 40,000 men. To ensure that security was not compromised, he divided the country into eleven districts and established a new local militia in each, to be raised and controlled by a Major-General who would also supervise local government. Their work would be financed by a Decimation Tax – a 10 per cent levy on Royalist estates. In the words of Derek Hirst, 'The ensuing rule of the Major-Generals combined police work and tax-gathering with moral reform in a way that shaped the legend of the Cromwellian years as the triumph of blue-nosed puritanism'.

d) The Rule of the Major-Generals

The rule of the Major-Generals was portrayed by Royalist propaganda (and some historians) as a military dictatorship manned by social inferiors and killjoys. Like most generalisations, this claim contains some truth. Their methods of control could be somewhat arbi-

---

THREATS TO THE PROTECTORATE

1654 Cromwell forced to purge Fifth Monarchist officers after failure of Barebones Parliament;

1654 –5 secret meetings between ex-Levellers and Royalist agents;

1655 Penruddock's rising in Wiltshire;

1657 January: Plot by Leveller, Miles Sindercombe, to assassinate Cromwell discovered;
April: Attempt to seize power led by Fifth Monarchist, Thomas Venner in London.

THE CONY CASE

Cromwell's treatment of George Cony and his lawyers has echoes of James I's 'impositions' and Charles's struggles over Tunnage and Poundage. It may be of significance, however, that Cony was a religious radical, and his legal counsel had royalist links. It was not unusual for the enemies of the regime to cooperate in this way – a number of plots against Cromwell were organised by royalist agents with ex-Levellers.

ISSUE
Was the rule of the Major-Generals a military tyranny?

trary. In the West Country, Major-General Desborough took bonds for good behaviour from over 5,000 suspected dissidents. Many borough corporations were forcibly purged of suspected 'Royalists', and in Hythe, Kent, Major-General Kelsey surrounded the Town Hall with troops in order to ensure that his orders were carried out. In Lancashire Major-General Worsley was particularly active in the suppression of alehouses, closing 215 in one part of the county, while he shut almost 200 in the city of Chester. The regime was deeply unpopular with the gentry, who resented their loss of control over local government and the restrictions imposed on them.

Nevertheless, the picture is more varied and complex than their complaints would suggest. The social origins of the Major-Generals differed greatly. Worsley was of obscure origins, but Goffe was the son of a clergyman, Haynes was a member of the gentry, and Whalley was a cousin of Cromwell. It is undoubtedly true that they were generally not of the greater gentry, but neither were they as obscure and unfit as their enemies suggested. Many provided careful and conscientious administration. The records show a marked increase in both the levying and expenditure of the poor rate, and the provision of almshouses. It is certainly possible that some of the resentment felt by the ruling elite arose from the fact that they were paying more for the benefit of the poor. Complaints about the suppression of traditional sports such as cock-fighting and horse-racing tend to exaggerate the extent to which the killjoy element was in control. The main reason for banning such activities was to prevent them being used as a cover for political action. In addition, there was great variation in the energy and efficiency demonstrated by the new regime. In the north-west, where there was a relatively isolated Puritan community surrounded by conservatives, they supported Worsley and enabled him to be particularly effective. In Hampshire and Sussex, William Goffe had little impact.

Nevertheless, it is clear that the experiment of the Major-Generals was widely resented. The strongest evidence of this came in 1656, when the government's financial needs led to elections for a new Parliament. The Major-Generals seem to have believed that they could manipulate elections to produce support, but they were quickly disillusioned. Local communities proved united against military control and radical influence. In Kent, Major-General Kelsey could not gain one of the eleven seats available, and Baptist candidates were threatened with lynching in Middlesex. Their efforts were further undermined by lack of support from Cromwell himself, who seemed to disapprove of interfering in elections. He was, however, quite willing to prevent hostile MPs from taking their seats, and used the Instrument's requirement for MPs to be of godly character in order to exclude about a hundred republicans and Royalists. The result was a pragmatic assembly, willing to get on with business, while deeply hostile to army and radical influence. After three months of dealing with private bills and business, this House of Commons formally offered the crown to Oliver Cromwell!

5 King Oliver?

ISSUE
Why did Parliament offer Cromwell the crown in 1657?

This was not the first time that a King Oliver had been suggested as a solution to the country's problems, although it was the first time that the suggestion had been made in Parliament. It was a logical response to the desires of the ruling class for a return to monarchy and civilian government. As king, Cromwell would retain control of the armed forces, but he would operate within a recognised framework of law and custom acceptable to the nation as a whole. While it was clear that the nation preferred monarchy, there was nothing to suggest that the majority were determined that the incumbent should be a Stuart. There were many who remained suspicious of the character and Catholic associations of Charles and his sons, while others feared that a second Charles might wish to punish those who had opposed the first. The rule of the Major-Generals had sharpened fears of military dictatorship, while the James Nayler incident highlighted the dangers of radical beliefs. If Cromwell's position could be given constitutional validity, it might yet offer a real prospect of stable government and lasting reconciliation.

Moreover, Cromwell's own actions in the autumn and winter of 1656–7 raised the possibility that he might accept the crown. To his providential thinking, the continued failures of the 'good old cause' might suggest that its adherents had lost God's approval. He was well aware of how arbitrary some of his government's actions had been, and if these could not be justified as furthering God's purpose, they could not be continued. In December, when Desborough proposed that Parliament should approve the Decimation Tax and confirm the position of the Major-Generals, Cromwell failed to support him, and the tax was voted down. This refusal to defend the Major-Generals might well indicate that Cromwell had lost faith in the army as the instrument of God. It was also clear that Cromwell was disturbed by the arbitrary treatment of James Nayler and his own inability to restrain Parliament. Kingship, with the return of a second chamber in the House of Lords and a clearer definition of his own powers of intervention, might well prevent such incidents in future.

The trigger to action came in January 1657 when the discovery of a plot to assassinate Cromwell led by the Leveller, Miles Sindercombe, highlighted the lack of any accepted successor. By emphasising Cromwell's mortality, the plot raised the question of what would happen when he died. The Instrument of Government made no effective provision, and the possibility of conflict between different factions of the army, or renewed civil war between the army and Royalist forces, was very real. A monarchy would solve the problem, since Cromwell had two healthy sons. It would also provide protection for his family, a powerful inducement for him to accept the crown. On 23 February 1657, the London Alderman, Sir Christopher Packe introduced a motion in Parliament to the effect that Cromwell be offered the crown, with a restored House of Lords consisting of his nominees, to sit alongside the Commons. To the fury of republicans and army officers, the proposal was debated for some weeks and finally offered to the Protector in March, as the Humble Petition and Advice.

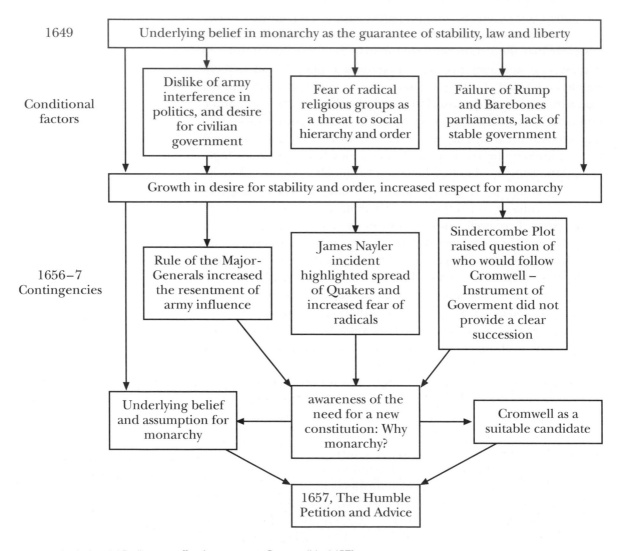

Figure 24 Why did Parliament offer the crown to Cromwell in 1657?

The new proposals would have established an effective constitutional monarchy, with a two-chamber Parliament, clear limits on royal power, the great officers of state approved by Parliament, and a reduction of the army as well as new restrictions on religious toleration. While some Royalists were enthusiastic, believing this to be first step towards a Stuart restoration, others were dismayed. In the words of Clarendon, in exile with Charles Stuart:

> The more sober persons of the King's party ... believed that ... much of that affection that appeared under the notion of allegiance to the King was more directed to the monarchy than to the person, and if Cromwell were once made King, and so the government ran again in the old channel ... he would receive abundant reparation of strength by the access of those who preferred monarchy, and which probably would reconcile most men of estates to an absolute acquiescence.

All that was required, was for Cromwell to accept. Instead, he agonised. On 7 March he had received a petition, signed by 100 army officers, opposing the notion of restoring the monarchy. He pointed out to them that a settlement was needed, that arbitrary proceedings must come to an end. Privately, he consulted his closest associates, and sought to persuade them that the plan offered the best solution to their problems, but was clearly disturbed by their continued opposition. In April he met with Parliament's commissioners to explain why he still hesitated. Finally, in May 1657, he rejected the title of king, but accepted a revised Petition in which the title was changed to that of Lord Protector for life, with the right to nominate his successor. He was crowned with many of the trappings of royalty in June 1657.

Like most compromises, the second Protectorate satisfied few of those involved. Many of the officers remained suspicious of the new regime, and John Lambert resigned from the Council of State. Lord Broghill and some of the architects of the original scheme withdrew

ACTIVITY

Why did Cromwell refuse the crown in 1657?

The republican MP, Edmund Ludlow, claimed that Cromwell's rejection of the crown was forced on him by the opposition of the army. In his view, the entire army, including Cromwell's closest associates, Fleetwood and Desborough, was deeply opposed to the idea. Faced with this united opposition, and in fear for his own safety, Cromwell gave in and rejected the crown. Ludlow's dislike of Cromwell is clear in the tone of his writing. He is therefore not a reliable witness – but this does not mean that his account is incorrect. Use the questions and the sources to evaluate his explanation and develop your own.

Questions on Sources G to J

1. What evidence supports Ludlow's claims?

2. What evidence conflicts with Ludlow's account?

3. What alternative explanations for Cromwell's refusal of the crown are put forward?

4. Which of the authors do you consider to be offering the most reliable evidence?

5. In the light of Sources H and I, how do you think that Cromwell would feel about the opposition of the army?

6. In the light of Sources H and I, how do you think he might interpret the opposition that he faced?

7. Using all the evidence in the context of your own knowledge, construct your own explanation of why Cromwell rejected the offer of the crown in 1657.

I suppose you have heard of the address made by one hundred Officers to his Highness yesterday sevennight that his Highness would not hearken to the title [of King] because it was not pleasing to his army, and was a matter of scandal to the people of God, of great rejoicing to the enemy; that it was hazardous to his own person, and of great danger to the three nations; such an assumption making way for Charles Stuart to come in again.

Source G From the diary of Thomas Burton, 7 March 1657.

Truly, the Providence of God hath laid aside this title of King, providentially ... and that not by a sudden humour or passion ... It hath been by issue of ten or twelve years Civil War, wherein much blood hath been shed ... And God hath seemed Providential ... not only in striking at the family, but [also] at the name ... I will not seek to set up that which Providence hath destroyed, and laid in the dust: I would not build Jericho again.

Source H From a speech made by Cromwell to the House of Commons, 13 April 1657, explaining his doubts about the offer of the crown.

Yesterday his Highness gave answer to the committee ... That for his part he values not one name more than another ... but in respect many godly men that have hazarded their lives in this cause are dissatisfied with it, and Providence having with the old family eradicated the old title, he thinks it his duty to beg of the Parliament not to put upon those good men [that] which they cannot swallow ... I believe his Highness is jealous there may be some distemper in the Army.

Source I From a letter written by the MP John Bridge to Henry Cromwell in Ireland, 13 April 1657.

Source J From Clarendon, *History of the Rebellion.*

Lambert, who was the second man of the army, and many other officers of account and interest, opposed this [offer] with great bitterness and indignation ... That which put an end to the present debate was ... that some of his own family ... as Desborough, Fleetwood, Whalley and others, as passionately contradicted the motion as any of the other officers.

He was not terrified with the opposition that Lambert gave him ... nor did he much consider those other officers of the army who in the House concurred with Lambert ... But he trembled at the obstinacy of those who he knew loved him.

in disgust. The new House of Lords was established, with many of Cromwell's supporters transferred to it, and the excluded republicans were allowed to take their seats in the Commons. Since they had lost neither their hostility to the regime nor their skill in using parliamentary procedures to delay business, the second session of Parliament ended in chaos and frustration for the Protector. In February 1658 he finally dissolved it, but it is likely that financial pressures would have forced him to call another had he lived.

Ironically, the summer of 1658 saw a number of loyal addresses sent from the counties to the Protector – a year earlier they might have persuaded him to override army concerns and accept the crown. It was widely rumoured that a new Parliament would repeat the offer, and that this time Cromwell might accept. The opportunity never arose, for by September 1658, Cromwell was dead, worn out by time (he was 59 years old) and effort. He died on 3 September, the anniversary of his victories at Dunbar and Worcester. In the last week of his life he nominated his elder son, Richard, to succeed him. Although Richard, a country squire of moderate Presbyterian views, was greeted with some enthusiasm by the ruling elite, his lack of political experience and inability to control the army led to his resignation in May 1659. With his demise, the regime turned full circle as the Rump of 1649 returned to power and proclaimed the restoration of the Commonwealth.

a) The Failure of the Protectorate

Richard's failure highlights once more the fatal weakness of all the regimes of the Interregnum – the need to serve two political masters. The propertied classes throughout the country craved stability and order, and the army demanded religious freedom and some measure of reform. No ruler could survive for long without the support of both, but what pleased one would inevitably alienate the other. In that sense, the army was a liability to any regime – yet conservative attitudes and preference for monarchy in the country meant that no republican regime could survive without it. In 1655–6 Cromwell had come close to military dictatorship in order to preserve the cause of godly reformation. In Richard's case, the very qualities that enabled him to win popularity in the country and work well with Parliament reinforced the fears of a suspicious army and drove it into opposition. A stronger, or more politically determined, character might have resisted their pressure, and Richard's resignation does highlight the importance of Oliver Cromwell as an individual. His religious convictions and army links made him uniquely able to seek a wider basis of support without entirely losing the confidence of the officers. From time to time he faced conspiracy or resistance from particular factions, such as Harrison and the millenarians (see

> **ISSUES**
> Why did the Protectorate fail? Was its failure inevitable?

RICHARD CROMWELL AND THE COLLAPSE OF THE PROTECTORATE

-*Profile*-

Richard Cromwell was born in 1626, and served in the Parliamentarian army during the Civil War. He sat as an MP in both parliaments of the Protectorate, but held no office until 1657, when he became a member of the Council of State and of the new House of Lords. While he was able and intelligent, and undeserving of the Royalist nickname of 'Tumbledown Dick', there is no doubt that his experience of government was as limited as his ambition. He tried to do his duty, but he had little desire for power.

Richard's failure to maintain his own position and the security of the Protectorate has been variously attributed: to his own weakness and inexperience, to the inability of the surviving Grandees, Fleetwood and Desborough, to control the junior officers, to the propaganda of the old republican MPs, and to the seriousness of the problems that he inherited from his father.

The events listed below suggest that all of these factors played a part, but above all, his failure reflects the resurgence of that basic division between army/republican and civilian/conservative supporters of the regime, which only Oliver Cromwell and his unique affinities with both groups had been able to contain.

1658

September	Richard Cromwell proclaimed Protector.
October	Richard appointed Fleetwood as General of the army, but retained his own authority as Commander-in-Chief.

1659

January	Parliament assembled; accepted Richard's authority, and indicated a willingness to vote supplies; also began to discuss the reduction of the army and the establishment of a local militia.
January to April	Republican MPs in contact with junior officers; demands for the re-establishment of the Army Council of officers to discuss military grievances.
April	Fleetwood persuaded Richard to agree to the restoration of the Army Council; officers met, and four days later, petitioned Richard to dissolve Parliament. On 22 April, Fleetwood informed Richard that he could not guarantee the loyalty of the army if Parliament was not dissolved. Richard agreed to end the Parliament, declaring that 'I will not have a drop of blood spilt for the preservation of my greatness, which is a burden to me'.
May	On 7 May the army leaders recalled the Rump Parliament. Richard agreed to retire on receipt of a pension and payment of his debts. He endured exile and poverty after 1660, but returned in 1680 living at Cheshunt until his death in 1712.

page 163), but for the most part the essential bonds of comradeship and shared dangers, built up over two civil wars and years of struggle, held firm.

This raises the question of whether the Protectorate could have survived or evolved into a constitutional monarchy that would have preserved some elements of the revolution of 1649. By 1657 there was growing support for monarchy, although not necessarily for the Stuarts, and it seems unlikely that the Protectorate could have survived in the long term. It survived at the time because Cromwell's loyalty to the army and his belief in providence were ultimately stronger than his desire to create stability. It is therefore useful to consider what might have happened had he accepted the crown. This is not idle speculation – by considering some other feasible outcomes, it may be possible to make some judgements as to how far failure was inevitable, and to assess the importance of his decision.

Had Cromwell accepted the crown in 1657, it is likely that he would have faced some kind of army revolt. According to Clarendon, 'he was informed and gave credit to it, that there were a number of men who bound themselves by oath to kill him within so many hours after he should accept that title'. While Clarendon's informants may not have been reliable, the possibility of some kind of radical or army plot seems strong. Nevertheless, there is little reason to believe that it would have been successful or widely supported. At every point of crisis since 1647, army discipline had held and by 1657 successive plots and purges of the most radical officers had increased the professional element against the political. Although leading officers like Desborough and Fleetwood threatened to resign if Cromwell accepted the crown, it is inconceivable that they would have supported a physical attack on him. Lambert, who had been widely regarded as Cromwell's successor, resigned in protest at the new constitution – his departure raised little reaction. The evidence suggests that any resistance would have lacked leadership and organisation, and that Cromwell's power would have survived.

However, this depended on a fund of loyalty and shared experience with the army that only Cromwell possessed. Although Richard's popularity suggests that he could have succeeded his father and consolidated the regime, only Oliver could control the army to establish it. The final irony, therefore, is that the trust and loyalty that would have enabled him to do so was also the main reason why he decided against it. To judge whether he would have continued to refuse had he lived longer is to speculate too far, but it is clear that when he rejected the crown in 1657, he rejected the best opportunity for a peaceful transition to a limited monarchy. It can therefore be argued that the Protectorate could not have survived in the long term, but that it could have evolved into a new monarchy rather than collapsing as yet another failure.

6　Anarchy and Order, 1659–60

ISSUES
Why did the army fail in its attempt to preserve the 'good old cause'?
Why did it lead to the restoration of Charles Stuart?

**KEY DATES:
DRIFT TO
ANARCHY**

1659

May Army leaders restored the Rump; Rump purged Army and local government of supporters of the Protectorate;

July – August Booth's rising in Cheshire temporarily united Rump and Army and was easily suppressed;

Sept Army petitioned for reform;

October Rump rebuked Petitioners and voted to dismiss 9 leading officers; Army stopped Rump meeting (13th); Army set up Committee of Safety; Monck declared for Rump (22nd);

Dec Rump restored again.

The actions of the army and republicans in 1659 reveal how politically bankrupt the revolutionaries had become. Having forced Richard to resign, the army officers could think of nothing better than to restore the Rump. This was not surprising, since the republican MPs and ex-Rumpers like Haselrig had played a significant part in stirring up army fears against Richard. What is more remarkable is that, having been restored to power by the military, the Rump should so quickly turn on their allies and demonstrate how little they had learned. Determined to assert the superiority of civilian authority, they began to purge the army of moderates whom Cromwell had encouraged, and to promote republicans. A reorganisation of the army was planned, with the establishment of a local militia to complement the professionals. Meanwhile, a similar purge of moderates in local government and the appointment of radicals and even Quakers to office raised fears in the country and led to calls for a free Parliament. In August rebellion broke out in Cheshire, led by the Presbyterian Parliamentarian, Sir George Booth. While this demonstrated the fragmentation of Parliament's ex-supporters, it also briefly united the Rump and army while the rebellion was suppressed. Thereafter, however, the Rump pressed ahead with its plans, and when the army protested and petitioned for reforms in October, voted to dismiss nine leading officers including both Fleetwood and Desborough. In effect, it had signed its own death warrant.

On 13 October the Parliament buildings were once more surrounded by troopers, and the Rump was denied entry. A Committee of Safety was established by the Council of Officers to maintain some form of government while alternatives were considered. Quite simply, there were none. While the country slipped into political anarchy and rumours of a Quaker rising spread, Haselrig appealed for support, and General George Monck, commander of the army in Scotland declared his support for the Rump and civilian government. As he gathered his troops and crossed the river Tweed into England, the Committee of Safety authorised Lambert to raise a force in Yorkshire to resist him. Army morale, however, had at last broken. Forced into open military dictatorship, demoralised by successive failures and devoid of ideas, Lambert's men simply melted away as Monck approached. The providential beliefs that had drawn political justification from military success now destroyed confidence in their cause. As Monck continued south at the invitation of the Rump, now restored once more, he was inundated with petitions from the county associations for a free Parliament and the return of monarchy. For the first time, a genuine groundswell of enthusiasm for the Stuarts had begun, and would shape the events of the ensuing months. Although it was Monck who controlled the restoration of monarchy and the final collapse of revolution, it was the pressure from a population desperate for stability that ensured that restoration would be both rapid and without prior conditions. In the final analysis, the revolution of 1649 and the 'good old cause' that inspired it had collapsed under the weight of its own failures.

The collapse of army morale removed the last barrier in the way of a restoration, but did nothing to determine the terms on which it would take place. The groundswell of support for monarchy may have convinced Monck that it was the only solution and that it must take place quickly, but this did not preclude some attempt to negotiate terms that would establish some of the constitutional changes for which the wars had been fought. The fact that Charles II returned with no specific commitments to fulfil was the work of two men – Monck himself, and Edward Hyde, soon to be Lord Clarendon.

If Monck retained any loyalty to the restored Rump when he arrived in London, its members quickly destroyed it by ordering him to suppress demonstrations against them, and by querying the validity of his commission from Cromwell. Since his declared intention in intervening had been the desire to end military government, he was hardly likely to relish using his army to maintain such an unpopular minority in power. He responded in February 1660 by recalling the members who had been excluded in 1648, on condition that they voted to dissolve this Long Parliament and call free elections. Given the public mood, there was no doubt that the elections would produce a majority in favour of a Stuart restoration – the remaining question was, on what terms? When Parliament assembled in April 1660, Monck presented them with a declaration, issued by Charles Stuart from the Dutch port of Breda (where he had moved on Monck's advice). The **Declaration of Breda** promised harmony and reconciliation, no punishment for actions during the war and Interregnum except against those who had signed the King's death warrant, and declared that a settlement of outstanding issues would be worked out in partnership with Parliament.

The declaration, drawn up by Hyde on Monck's advice, was an immensely skilful document. Since it promised all that Parliament could have asked, it made preconditions for the Restoration impossible. At the same time, however, it made no specific commitments to which the King would have to adhere. The result was that on 5 May Parliament voted that government was by King, Lords and Commons, and on 25 May, Charles landed at Dover to a tumultuous welcome. Significantly, he claimed that he was taking up his throne 'in the twelfth year of his reign'. Whatever MPs might intend, divine right monarchy had returned.

ISSUE
Why was Charles restored without preconditions?

DECLARATION OF BREDA
Carefully planned to remove suspicion of the Stuarts, as well as its promised cooperation, it sought to distance Charles from the Catholic associations that had caused his father such difficulty. For this reason it was issued from Breda in Protestant Holland, rather than from Catholic France where Charles had been living until Monck advised him to move.

GENERAL MONCK, ARCHITECT OF THE RESTORATION

-*Profile*-

Monck's intervention on behalf of the Rump split the army. His recall of the excluded members provided the majority needed to dissolve Parliament. He advised Charles to leave Catholic France for Protestant Holland in order to weaken the rumours that he was a Catholic and helped Charles and Hyde to construct the Declaration of Breda. Two things remain unclear – when did he decide not only to restore civilian government but to restore the monarchy, and why did he ensure that it happened so quickly as to prevent prior conditions from being laid down?

Monck was first and foremost a professional soldier. Born in 1608, he served in the army throughout the 1620s and 1630s, and fought for the King in the early months of the Civil War. This does not necessarily mean that he was a political Royalist – he was already in the King's service. Taken prisoner in 1644, he was imprisoned in the Tower for two years. After the Civil War he was persuaded to take the Covenant and serve Parliament in Ireland until Cromwell arrived in 1649. He then accompanied Cromwell to Scotland, and was left as commander-in-chief of the army in Scotland in 1651. He served both Oliver and Richard Cromwell.

'I am engaged ... to assert the liberty and authority of Parliament, to see my country freed from that intolerable slavery of a sword government', Monck, 1660.

There is, therefore, no reason to doubt his belief in civilian government, but he is also known to have had Royalist connections, and may already have intended to restore the King. If he did not, then the obvious unpopularity of the Rump as he moved south might well have convinced him. The actions of the Rump on his arrival, and their willingness to use force to maintain themselves were probably the final touch required. What remains uncertain, however, is whether he deliberately prevented preconditions from being imposed on Charles. The likelihood is that he was mainly concerned to ensure a smooth transition, and that delay might have proved disruptive. In that case, the political advantage that Charles gained from the nature of his return can probably be attributed to the skills of Hyde, his friend and adviser.

1659

October	Army replaced the Rump with a Committee of Safety: Monck declared his support for the Rump.
November	Lambert failed in an attempt to raise forces.
December	Anti-army riots began in London. Monck moved his army to the border with England: the Navy declared for the Rump. 26th Fleetwood recalled the Rump.

1660

1 January	Monck's army marched into England. Arrived February. His journey south marked by demonstrations and petitions in favour of free elections.
9–11 February	Monck ordered to take action against anti-Rump demonstrations in London.
21 February	Excluded members returned to Parliament.
March	Lambert imprisoned in the Tower of London. The Long Parliament dissolved itself.
25 April	New Parliament assembled: known as the Convention Parliament because not called by a King.
1 May	Declaration of Breda presented to Parliament.
5 May	Parliament voted government to be by King, Lords and Commons.
25 May	Charles II landed at Dover.

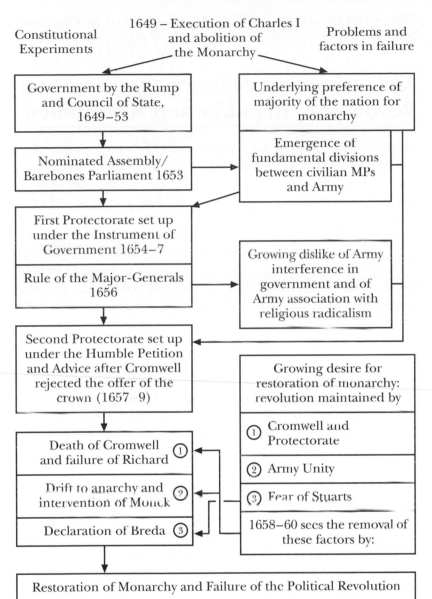

Constitutional Experiments

1649 – Execution of Charles I and abolition of the Monarchy

Problems and factors in failure

Government by the Rump and Council of State, 1649–53

Underlying preference of majority of the nation for monarchy

Nominated Assembly/ Barebones Parliament 1653

Emergence of fundamental divisions between civilian MPs and Army

First Protectorate set up under the Instrument of Government 1654–7

Rule of the Major-Generals 1656

Growing dislike of Army interference in government and of Army association with religious radicalism

Second Protectorate set up under the Humble Petition and Advice after Cromwell rejected the offer of the crown (1657–9)

Growing desire for restoration of monarchy: revolution maintained by

Death of Cromwell and failure of Richard ①

① Cromwell and Protectorate

Drift to anarchy and intervention of Monck ②

② Army Unity

Declaration of Breda ③

③ Fear of Stuarts

1658–60 secs the removal of these factors by:

Restoration of Monarchy and Failure of the Political Revolution

Summary of the failure of the political revolution

▼ Working on Revolution, Republic and Restoration

As with earlier chapters, you should complete linear notes on the material in this chapter before attempting any exercises or extended writing on this topic. You should, by now, be quite used to organising these, using the section headings, sub-headings and issue boxes to help you. You can then begin to address the exercises below.

Answering Source-based Questions on Revolution, Republic and Restoration

Chapters 2 to 6 provided a number of source exercises that were designed to enable you to build up the skills required for handling sources. It would be useful to try to apply these to the kind of questions that you may meet in examinations. Many exams provide one or more sources as a stimulus, and ask you to use your skills and knowledge of the period to interpret them and use them for investigation of particular issues. The exercise below provides an example of this kind of question. As you consider your answers, take note of the mark allocation, which indicates the level and length of answer required for each part – it is an important element of exam technique to divide your time appropriately and give the greatest space and time to the most highly rewarded questions.

> Upon Richard's leaving the stage, the commonwealth was again set up: and the Parliament which Cromwell had broke was brought together: but the army and they fell into new disputes: so they were broke again by the army: and upon that the nation was like to fall into great convulsions. The enthusiasts became very fierce, and talked of nothing but the destroying of all the records and the law, which, they said, had been made by a succession of tyrants and papists: so they resolved to model all anew by a levelling and a spiritual government of the saints . . . and it made many conclude, it was necessary to call home the King, so that matters might fall again into their old channel. Lambert became the man on whom the army depended most. Upon his forcing the Parliament great applications were made to Monck to declare for the Parliament, but under this the declaring for the King was generally understood. Yet he kept himself under such a reserve, that he declared all the while in the most solemn manner for a commonwealth, and against a single person, in particular against the King; so that none had any ground from him to believe he had any design that way. Some have thought that he intended to try, if it was possible, to set up for himself: others rather believed that he had no settled design any way, and resolved to do as occasion should be offered to him.

Source K From *An Account of the Restoration* by Bishop Gilbert Burnet, written in 1723.

▼ QUESTIONS ON THE SOURCE

1. Who was referred to in the phrases 'the Parliament that Cromwell had broke'? **[2 marks]**

2. Explain what events are described in the first sentence of the source. **[4 marks]**

3. What was meant by the phrase 'a levelling and spiritual government of the saints'? **[2 marks]**

4. Explain the nature of the 'enthusiasts' who would support such a government. **[4 marks]**

5. What reasons does Burnet suggest for the popular desire to see a restoration at this time? **[3 marks]**

6. What possible motives does he suggest for Monck's intervention? **[4 marks]**

7. Use your knowledge of the situation in 1659–60, and of Monck's character, to evaluate which is more convincing. **[6 marks]**

8. Given that Burnet is writing more than 60 years after the events that he describes, how reliable do you consider his evidence to be? **[10 marks]**

9. Using the evidence in this source and your own knowledge of the period, explain whether the Restoration should be seen as the cause, or the result, of the failure of the political revolution of 1649. **[15marks]**

Points to note about questions

Questions 1–4 You will often find questions of this type at the beginning of a source-based exercise. They require you to use your background knowledge to identify and explain certain points within a source. They do not usually carry many marks because they are 'closed' questions, relying on knowledge rather than judgement, but they do help you to get into the source.

Questions 5–8 These questions require you to analyse, interpret and evaluate the source. They require a range of skills and judgement to be applied and explained, and therefore carry more marks. Question 5 requires a measure of inference, question 6 refers to two motives. Question 7 requires you to relate your own knowledge to the evidence, and since evaluation is a more complex skill, carries more marks than those preceding it. Question 8 is still more demanding. You need to consider how Burnet might have got his information, whether his relative detachment from the period would make him more, or less, reliable, and to use your own knowledge to make some judgement about how accurate he is.

Question 9 The most difficult question, and therefore worth most. First, you must make sure that you understand it. The Restoration brought the Republic to an end and destroyed any hope of new experiments – it can therefore be seen as the cause of its ultimate failure. On the other hand, Burnet suggests that it was the collapse into anarchy that led to calls for the return of the King – in which case the revolution had already failed and its failure caused people to turn back to monarchy. The question requires you to synthesise the source with your own knowledge in order to weigh up both arguments and select one, or elements of both as the best way of explaining what happened in 1659–60.

Writing Essays on the Failure of the Political Revolution and the Causes of the Restoration

The main focus of Chapter 6 has been to consider why the revolution of 1649 failed to introduce lasting changes in the nature of government in England, and why it resulted in the restoration of the Stuarts. Although these issues are linked, they are not exactly the same, and by considering the differences between them as well as the similarities, it is possible to explore the issues more fully and address a number of possible essay questions.

The revolutionaries experienced failure from shortly after 1649 – the failure of the Rump, Barebones Parliament, and two Protectorates provided clear evidence that they had not succeeded in establishing stable government, but it was not until the Stuart Restoration took place that failure was complete, or clear-cut. Questions about the failure of the revolution may therefore be phrased similarly to questions about the Restoration; the difference is that the former are asking about *a* restoration, while the latter are concerned with *the* Restoration. In the first case it is the fact that a restoration occurred, not the details of timing and conditions, that is crucial, because it shows that the revolution had failed. In the second case, the nature of the Restoration, its date and the lack of preconditions need to be fully explained, because the question is focused on why that restoration occurred, at that time and in that way.

The difference is important, because it affects the significance of the different factors and the part that they played in the causal process. For example, *the intervention of Monck* was crucial in bringing about the Restoration, in 1660 and without preconditions. However, even if Monck had not existed, *the lack of viable alternatives, the collapse of army morale, and the desperate need for stable government* would probably have brought about a restoration of monarchy at some stage, because the revolution had failed. Therefore Monck's contribution would need to be considered in detail to explain *the* Restoration, but could be passed over quickly, as a final trigger factor in explaining *a* restoration.

This approach is essentially drawing on the idea of conditional and contingent factors that you have already explored. You can define these by drawing on the diagrams provided in the chapter to construct your own flow chart, showing how the causes of *a* Restoration provide the conditional factors for *the* Restoration.

You can now begin to look at some specific questions and use the flow chart to plan a response and outline a possible essay. If questions appear to ask about the Restoration, you must first decide on what is the focus of each question, i.e. a Restoration, or the Restoration. Then consider what factors you would need to include, and what part they would play. You can also consider which factors seem to be most important, and will therefore need to be considered fully. One way of doing this is to decide which factors were essential or *necessary* to the explanation, by considering whether the results would have still occurred if they had not existed. This is not speculation – you know the factor did exist and your explanation must be based on the fact that it did. It is simply a way of measuring its importance by temporarily removing it and using the result to argue how important it was in what did happen. Another way is to decide whether some factors depended on others. For example, *Cromwell's death* sparked off the *collapse of the Protectorate, the slide into anarchy and the collapse of army morale.* This suggests that his death was an important trigger to a restoration. However, if you consider why his death had this effect, it is because of his ability to hold together the *conflicting interests of Parliament and army* – only Cromwell was capable of overcoming the *fundamental divisions among supporters of the regime.* Therefore, the most important factor in the failure of the revolution was this fundamental weakness, which undermined all the constitutional experiments of the Interregnum.

All this is straightforward if the question clearly asks 'why', but examiners sometimes phrase questions differently. Some questions, for example, ask about the *effects* of a particular event or factor or its significance – this is still essentially concerned with why certain things happened and what part different factors played. It may be that a particular factor has several effects, and they must be assessed alongside the role of other factors. You still have to consider the focus of the question, and your basic flow chart, or causal outline, still applies – but you may have to turn it around by beginning with one factor and then comparing the part played by others.

With these ideas in mind, you should now consider the questions below, and outline a response, using a summary or flow chart to set out your answer and plan an essay.

1. Why was Charles II restored to the throne in 1660, when his father had been executed only eleven years before?

2. How far does an explanation of the failure of the Protectorate also explain the restoration of the monarchy in 1660?

3. What was the effect of the religious and political radicalism that emerged between 1642 and 1660?

4. Why did the execution of Charles I result in the restoration of Charles II?

5. 'Without the New Model Army, the execution of Charles I would not have taken place; and neither would the restoration of Charles II.' How far do you agree?

6. How significant was Cromwell's rejection of the crown in 1657?

7. Why did the revolution of 1649 fail to transform English government and society?

Further Reading

Books in the Access to History Series

You will find the relevant volume of the Access to History series, *The Interregnum* by Michael Lynch very helpful. It explores the issues raised in this chapter, and widens the field of study to include issues such as foreign policy which cannot be included here.

General

In addition to the general works recommended in the introductory reading list, you should look for the work of Austin Woolrych. His Lancaster Pamphlet (1983) entitled *England Without a King* provides a very accessible starting-point, while his more detailed study *From Commonwealth to Protectorate* (OUP 1983) offers greater depth. You should also try to read some of the works of Ronald Hutton on this period: *The Restoration: a Political and Religious History, 1658–67* was produced by OUP in 1985, while *The British Republic* was published by Macmillan in 1990. Both are helpful, as are the many other articles and essays that he has produced. For further material on the radicals, B. Reay, *The Quakers and the English Revolution* (Temple Smith 1985) and Bernard Capp, *The Fifth Monarchy Men* (Faber 1972) are both of particular interest, but the best starting points are Frances Dow, *Radicalism in the English Revolution* (Blackwell 1989) and J.F. McGregor and B. Reay (eds) *Radical Religion in the English Revolution* (OUP 1984). Both offer relatively short and accessible explanations of the ideas, attitudes and significance of the main radical groups. Finally, one of the many biographies of Oliver Cromwell is a must – several are recommended in the introductory reading list on page xiv.

THE STUART MONARCHY, 1660–1714

1 Introduction: The Significance of Events and the Nature of Change

The first part of this book dealt with the so-called English Revolution, and considered how and why it took place. The focus of our questions was therefore the process of cause and effect, and events were judged to be significant, or not, in terms of how they affected the people and situations of the time. This is an essential part of understanding the past, but it is not the only approach to consider. The series of events and their results over a period of time create changes, and an equally important part of historical study is to explain the nature of these changes, and the significance of particular events in creating them. In order to see changes and development clearly, it is necessary for historians to stand back and take a wider view of the situation, which may involve considering a longer span of time, or may require other aspects of life and society to be brought into consideration. The second part of this book attempts to consider these wider contexts.

The years following the Restoration of 1660 saw the establishment of a constitutional monarchy in Britain, in which the cooperation of King and Parliament enabled reforms in administration and finance, which, in turn, allowed Britain to develop as a great power. Although this system was not fully developed until the mid-eighteenth century, the essential components were established and accepted by 1714, when James Stuart, the nearest relative of the Queen, was set aside as monarch in favour of a distant Hanoverian cousin. This denial of hereditary divine right as the basis for monarchy completed a process that, according to some historians, began on the scaffold at Whitehall in January 1649. Other historians have challenged this view, arguing that the Restoration of 1660 reversed the effects of 1649, and that the development of constitutional monarchy involved a process of slow change across the seventeenth century. Not only did the rise of parliamentary power begin well before 1640, but there were Royalist **reactions** in 1660–65 and 1681–7, which could still have introduced absolute monarchy, and the Tory reaction of Queen Anne's reign could still have re-established the Stuarts.

If this argument is accepted, then the 'English Revolution' was, at most, one of a number of events that brought change, and may even have helped to delay it. Hence the emergence of constitutional monarchy should be seen in terms of *evolution* rather than *revolution*. This view is strengthened if the context is widened to consider the social, economic and intellectual changes that took place in this period. The nature of change in these aspects of life tends to be gradual, and can only be traced over a significant period of time. Understanding historical change therefore requires different techniques from those already used in studying cause and effect. It is necessary to trace the course of events over a longer period of time, in order to assess their long-term significance, and to compare their effects in different areas of society and government. One way of analysing the nature of the English Revolution is to evaluate its significance in these terms. This may well involve discovering that change occurred at different rates in different areas, and evaluating the combined effect in the development of society and government as a whole. This and the ensuing chapters are intended to enable you to begin this process.

ROYALIST AND TORY REACTIONS

Royalist and Tory reactions tended to follow periods when the monarchy came under attack, or had been seriously weakened in some way. In addition to those referred to in the text, there were two Jacobite rebellions in 1715 and 1745, aimed at restoring the Stuarts. The term Jacobite means a supporter of James Stuart. Most of these events are described in more detail below – the key point here is that they illustrate lingering conservative attitudes and challenge any assumption that change is irreversible.

ISSUES
What was restored at the Restoration?
What was settled by the settlement?

2 The Restoration Settlement, 1660–65

Because the Declaration of Breda prevented Parliament from opening negotiations that might have laid down terms for the monarch's return, the restoration of the Stuarts in 1660 was effectively unconditional. This meant that the details of settlement had to be worked out after the King's return, and by parliaments that reflected the public mood. For this reason, the Restoration settlement fell into two parts, the first emphasising reconciliation as intended by the **Convention Parliament** of 1660, the second focusing on revenge desired by the **Cavalier Parliament** of 1661. As a result, the settlement settled little, and certainly not the problems that had been responsible for war and revolution in the first place.

The details of the settlement are set out in Table 3 on page 185. The key features of 1660 included a financial settlement that provided the King with revenue from taxation, in return for the abolition of his feudal and prerogative taxing powers. Hence taxes such as Ship Money, or the forced loans of the 1620s could not be reintroduced. In addition, the prerogative courts, abolished in 1641, were not restored. The chief beneficiaries of these changes were the gentry, whose estates were now free of feudal obligations, and the wealthy merchants who would benefit from a free market in land. The same groups gained from the Navigation Act of 1660, which confirmed and extended controls over trade and the colonies to the benefit of English merchants at the expense of Irish and Scottish traders as well as the Dutch.

In 1661 the new Parliament took a different approach. Cavalier enthusiasm for the King led them to restore his control over the militia in 1661–2, and to replace the **Triennial Act** of 1641 with a weaker version in 1664. While the King's freedom of action was therefore increased, society was to be more tightly controlled with the restoration of censorship in the Licensing Act of 1662. Above all, however, the change of Parliament brought a change in the religious settlement. Although the Church and the bishops were restored in 1660, the details of the settlement were to be left to a conference of ministers, called to meet at the Savoy Palace in London in April 1661. The King had signalled his sympathy with a broad and flexible Church by appointing Presbyterians as well as Anglicans to posts at Court and in the royal chapel, and the leading Presbyterian, Richard Baxter, had been offered a bishopric. As a result, Presbyterian hopes of a broad, comprehensive Church were high.

They were soon disabused. In April 1661 they found themselves negotiating with an assertive and obstructive High Church party, led by Gilbert Sheldon, who was appointed Bishop of London in 1660 and became Archbishop of Canterbury in 1663 (following the career pattern set by Laud!). Sheldon and his supporters were determined to restore much of the Laudian structure in the Church, and ignored the concerns of the Presbyterians regarding popish ceremonies and the powers exercised by bishops. Their attitude was reinforced by the

THE CONVENTION AND CAVALIER PARLIAMENTS

The Convention Parliament was elected before the King's return in 1660, and was heavily influenced by the Presbyterian Royalists who wanted to see moderate settlements in Church and State. Charles appeared to share their attitude, especially regarding a broad and tolerant Church. By 1661, however, a failed rebellion led by the Fifth Monarchist, Thomas Venner, had soured the atmosphere. This added to quarrels over the nature of the restored Church and a land settlement that did not satisfy the old Royalists, to produce a Cavalier majority in the elections of 1661. The resulting Cavalier Parliament, described as 'more Royalist than the King' sat for eighteen years and shaped Restoration politics.

TRIENNIAL ACT

Both Triennial Acts declared that Parliament was to be in session every three years at least. However, the Act of 1664 made no provision to call MPs if the King failed to do so, whereas the Act of 1641 had made arrangements for new elections to take place even without the King's agreement. Hence in practice, the 1664 Act was likely to be ineffective, and when Charles chose not to call a parliament from 1681 to 1685, nothing could be done.

meeting of the Cavalier Parliament in May, and by the tactical errors of the Presbyterians in allowing the discussions to become bogged down in detail. In November the Parliament showed its willingness to persecute by passing the Corporation Act, which insisted that only those who took Anglican communion could be elected to municipal corporations and effectively drove old Puritans and Parliamentarians from a traditional source of power. The result was an Act of Uniformity in May 1662, which made it impossible for most Presbyterians to remain within the Church, and forced them to join their more genuinely separatist brethren – the Baptists, Congregationalists and Quakers – as **nonconformists** or Protestant **dissenters**. About 1,800 ministers, roughly 25 per cent of the parish clergy, were unable to conform.

NON-CONFORMISTS AND DISSENTERS

Terms used to describe those who felt unable to attend Church regularly, or to take Anglican Communion, and preferred to worship in separate, often private meetings. The terms covered a number of denominational groups, but not Catholics, who also refused to attend Church.

Municipal Corporations

Municipal Corporations (often led by a Mayor and Aldermen) governed the 200 or so towns and boroughs that held a royal charter. Their powers varied, but usually included regulation of trade and administration of local law courts. In addition, many had the right to elect two MPs to Parliament, and nineteen of the larger towns and ports, styled 'county' boroughs, were almost completely self-governing under the King's authority. The strength of Puritan belief among the merchants and middling sort had made the boroughs strongholds of opposition to Charles I, and they continued to influence the shape of Parliaments. The Corporation Act was therefore an attack on Puritans and Puritan political influence.

Having created a substantial body of dissenters by defining the Anglican Church in such narrow terms, the High Church party and its parliamentary allies then set about driving them out of existence by persecution. A harsh Quaker Act had already been passed in early 1662. In June the King sought to soften the effects of the Act of Uniformity, by suspending its operation for three months; he was forced by parliamentary pressure to withdraw his promise. In 1663, Sheldon became Archbishop of Canterbury, and in 1664 he obtained a Conventicle Act that made it illegal for more than five persons not of the same household to meet for religious worship. When it expired in 1668, Sheldon complained at the spread of such meetings, and had it renewed in 1670. In 1665, meanwhile, the Five Mile Act made it illegal for nonconformist ministers to come within five miles of any city or borough, or a parish where they had served.

Table 3 The Restoration Settlement, 1660–65.

Date	King, Church & Parliament	Political Parties	Government – Finance, Admin & Foreign Policy
1660	Monarchy and Church of England (with bishops) restored; Act of Indemnity and Oblivion; only regicides and 9 others excepted. Convention Parliament dissolved.		Abolition of Feudal Tenures ended the monarch's right to feudal taxes e.g. forced loans Failure to restore the Prerogative Courts and prerogative taxes e.g. Ship Money. King compensated with annual revenue from taxation (mainly customs & excise) of £1,200,000.
1661 January April	Venner's Rising (5th Monarchist) renewed fears of radical dissenters. Conference to discuss Church reform began at Savoy.		
May	Assembly of Cavalier Parliament secured Anglican control and encouraged the High Church party. Failure of Savoy conference.	Division in the conference between High Church party led by Sheldon (Archbishop of Canterbury 1663) and the 'latitudinarians' who favoured a broad, comprehensive Church.	Charles doubled the size of the Privy Council to 120, in order to accommodate different factions. This was unwieldy and encouraged the use of smaller sub-groups and councils, which later developed into Cabinet government.
November	Corporation Act excluded those who did not take communion in the Church of England from local government. Quaker Act – subjected Quakers to severe penalties.		
1662	Licensing Act – reintroduced censorship of press. Act of Uniformity – defined the Church in a narrow Anglican form – many parish ministers driven into non-conformity.	Although majority in the Cavalier Parliament were 'more royalist than the King', a minority continued to favour toleration for dissenters and a broader, more flexible Church, e.g. Anthony Ashley Cooper (Earl of Shaftesbury) who was a Privy councillor 1667–72 and encouraged the 1672 Declaration of Indulgence. To some extent they were encouraged by the King who sought toleration for dissent in order to extend it to Catholics.	Hearth Tax voted to increase royal income. Dunkirk sold to Louis XIV – end of any English possessions in France.
1664	King issued a Declaration of Indulgence but Parliament forced its withdrawal. Conventicle Act passed in England. Triennial Act of 1641 replaced with a weaker version.		
1665	Five Mile Act – forbade ex-clergy or unlicensed preachers to live within 5 miles of a parish where they had served, or of any town or city.		

The Quaker Act

Quakers were forbidden by their religion to swear oaths of any kind. The Quaker Act empowered judges to present them with the Oath of Allegiance to the King and to imprison them if they refused it. Many Quakers were imprisoned by this device, regardless of whether they were found guilty of the original charge against them. Even when they offered to make a declaration of their loyalty, the courts tended to insist on the literal interpretation of the law. In some cases there may have been a genuine misunderstanding of the Quakers' reasons for refusing the oath, but more often it was a deliberate ploy to keep them in prison.

CLARENDON CODE

Named after the King's chief adviser in this period. Edward Hyde, Earl of Clarendon. A staunch supporter of the Church, he bore some responsibility for the persecution laws, but they were not especially his creation. Having served both Charles II and his father with loyalty and distinction, Clarendon's political touch seemed to desert him in the years after the Restoration. Although he opposed the war against the Dutch that Charles entered in 1665, its inefficient management gave his enemies their opportunity; he was impeached in 1667 and sentenced to permanent exile.

These Acts, which made up the so-called **Clarendon Code** (see pages 245, 248–9) initiated an attack on Puritan dissenters of all kinds, and an attempt to persecute them into oblivion. Although it failed, for a variety of reasons, it symbolises the desire for revenge that characterised the early years of the Cavalier Parliament. In this context, the Parliament not only failed to solve the old problems in government, but also created some new ones. They surrendered powers to the King that would help to renew tension between King and Parliament and enhanced the possibility of further absolutist behaviour. In addition, by forcing many moderate Puritans into nonconformity, they did much to ensure that nonconformity would survive. Although Baptists and Congregationalists would have chosen to separate from any state Church, they were relatively few in number. The Quakers were more numerous, but open to harsh persecution of a kind that almost destroyed them. Dissent survived because of the dedication of dissenters who were numerous enough to hold together, and because of sympathy and support from sections of the gentry and borough corporations. It was often the Presbyterian dissenters who had, and maintained, such connections. While it cannot be said that persecution would have succeeded in different circumstances, a broad, flexible and welcoming Church would have made it much more feasible. On balance, the bitterness of the Cavaliers weakened the powers of Parliament, and made certain social and religious divisions permanent.

3 The Development of Constitutional Monarchy, 1665–1714

a) King, Church and Parliament

By failing to deal with the problems that had led to war and revolution, the Restoration settlement left the future shape of the monarchy open, to be worked out in practice between the King and his partners in government. The events of 1640–60 had brought few permanent changes to the theoretical basis of government but attitudes and expectations had been considerably affected by the trial and execution of a king, and eleven years of republican rule. By claiming that 1660 was the twelfth year of his reign, Charles II made it clear that he regarded himself as monarch by hereditary divine right. In practice, however, he had been recalled by Parliament. Parliament had provided him with an independent income from taxation. In practice, it was never sufficient. Similarly, it was the King's undoubted right to make war and peace – in practice, however, war required parliamentary finance. In theory, the King had to call Parliament every three years. In practice, when he achieved financial independence through a pension from Louis XIV of France, he ignored the provision. In theory, the King was the head of the Church. In practice, he was unable to establish toleration without the support of Parliament, and his attempts to do so were frustrated by MPs' prejudices.

These contradictions indicate that the effects of the Civil Wars and Interregnum on the later development of the monarchy were complex and difficult to assess. It would appear that the powers of both monarch and Parliament were strengthened in some ways and undermined in others. The development of the monarchy was therefore shaped by the way that this complex legacy was handled in the conditions of post-Restoration Britain, and this is open to varying interpretations. What is clear, however, is that the unsolved problems quickly re-emerged, and that chief among them were the old issues of religion and the balance of power. The bitter mood of the 1660s created a programme of persecution in Church and Parliament that the King did not share. The Protestant dissenters bore the brunt of Royalist revenge, and the King's attempts to soften the impact of the law were to no avail. One reason for this, however, was that his intentions involved a hidden agenda, of sympathy for Catholicism, and by 1670, a number of his actions had betrayed this to parliamentary observers.

ISSUES
Was Charles a secret Catholic?
Was he an effective King?

i) Religion and Politics under Charles II

The King's foreign policy was decidedly pro-French and anti-Dutch. The anti-Dutch element was justified by rivalries over trade, and the Anglo-Dutch war of 1665–7 undoubtedly arose through competition for overseas trade and possessions. The war was badly conducted, and this combined with the psychological effects of the plague and fire in London in 1665–6 to undermine the government's support. In 1668, however, the King's brother James, Duke of York, publicly announced that he had become a Catholic. Two years later, in 1670, Charles signed the Treaty of Dover, which committed England to a further Dutch war in support of France. The secret clause, that Charles would announce his conversion to Catholicism at an appropriate time, remained undetected, but this combination of events was enough to fuel growing suspicions. It was as well that MPs were also unaware that the French subsidy, which accompanied the treaty, was a step towards the kind of financial independence that might allow Charles to ignore the wishes of parliaments.

In this context, the King's second attempt to establish religious toleration, in the Declaration of Indulgence of 1672, took on a more sinister aspect. By this time the anti-Puritan hysteria that had shaped the Clarendon Code and portrayed Protestant dissenters as dangerous radicals had begun to subside. The fading of the memory of war and upheaval, growing disenchantment with the restored government, and the reality of persecuting otherwise peaceable neighbours for their religious beliefs, all contributed to a greater willingness among a section of the governing class to consider some form of toleration. The Declaration of Indulgence, however, included Catholics, which was one reason for Parliament's opposition. In addition, it was based on the argument that the King's **dispensing power** was not simply a device to protect individuals from injustice, but could be applied to whole groups and classes of people on the basis of his wishes. Even those who favoured toleration would regard this as a dangerous precedent.

The Indulgence lasted for a year, and contributed enormously to the survival of Protestant dissent (see pages 248–9) but by 1673 the King's financial needs forced him to recall Parliament. In 1672 he had suspended repayments to his creditors in the Stop of the Exchequer, and faced with a new Dutch war, he had little choice but to ask for parliamentary grants. These were forthcoming, but at the price of withdrawing the Indulgence. An attempt to replace it with parliamentary toleration for Protestants passed the Commons in March, but was blocked in the Lords by the combined opposition of the King and the bishops. Charles could not, however, prevent the passing of a Test Act, which forced holders of public office to deny the key Catholic doctrine of Transubstantiation (see page 69). The

DISPENSING POWER
The power of a king to dispense with the normal operation of the law was, and is, widely accepted. However well laws are framed, there will be cases where the letter of the law does not work equitably (fairly), and the power of a head of state to intervene in such cases is a useful corrective. Charles's attempt to apply this to religious toleration, however, would have greatly expanded his powers in this area, and could easily have lead to later abuse if it were allowed to succeed.

Lord Treasurer, Lord Clifford, and the Duke of York, the Lord Admiral, were among those forced to resign their posts.

Unlike his father, Charles was an astute politician, and in his own words, 'wished never to go on his travels again'. He therefore recognised the need for retreat, and abandoned his pro-Catholic policies, turning instead to an alliance with the Church party. This was forged by the new Treasurer, Thomas Osborne, Earl of Danby. Throughout the 1670s Danby sought to build up support in Parliament by combining a pro-Dutch (Protestant) foreign policy with defence of the Anglican Church at home through renewed persecution of Catholics and dissenters. His efforts produced a marriage between the Dutch prince, William of Orange and the King's niece, Mary, in 1677, but Charles accepted these policies out of necessity rather than conviction, and Danby was therefore unable to destroy lingering suspicions of the King's true intent. These, and his efforts to manage Parliament through bribery and gifts of office, produced a potential opposition, gathered around the Earl of Shaftesbury, Anthony Ashley Cooper. Its purpose was to secure a Protestant alliance between Anglican and dissenter, by establishing toleration for the latter through Parliament, and to use its strength to contain Catholic influence at Court.

Anthony Ashley Cooper, Earl of Shaftesbury

Ashley Cooper had fought for the King during the first civil war, and later served in Cromwell's governments – an indication of his political flexibility. This does not necessarily mean that he was unprincipled; he had served Charles II as Chancellor of the Exchequer from 1667, and supported his policy of toleration. In this he was consistent, and his emergence as an opposition leader came about when Charles abandoned the policy in the interests of his own power and his Catholic allies. He was undoubtedly ambitious, and his exploitation of the Popish Plot in 1678–81 proved his willingness to use unscrupulous methods in pursuit of his genuine fear that the accession of the Catholic James would threaten both religion and liberty. He paid the price when he was forced into exile in 1682, dying two months later in January 1683.

These divisions came to a head in 1678–9, with the emergence of the so-called Popish Plot and the ensuing Exclusion Crisis. In August 1678 Titus Oates approached the London magistrate, Sir Edmund Berry Godfrey, with a story of a plot organised by the Jesuits and the French, to murder Charles II and replace him on the throne with his

THE POPISH PLOT

-*Profile*-

The illustration below, based on contemporary prints sold as a broadsheet, or sometimes as playing cards, shows why the Plot created such fears. The combination of Catholicism with French and Irish contacts, the role of the Jesuits and the murder of a King provided classic ingredients that were almost bound to create panic in seventeenth-century England. It is most likely that Oates initially sought to make trouble for the Jesuits and money for himself as an informer, and that the coincidental murder of Justice Godfrey, combined with the actual intrigues of French agents at Court, gave his claims a spurious credibility and spurred him to further flights of imagination.

Q What actual historical events are woven into the story of the Popish Plot portrayed here? Does this mean that the Plot could have been genuine?

Figure 25 The Popish plot.

Catholic brother James. The story lacked credibility and the character of Oates still more – he had been a pupil at a Jesuit school in St
Omer until expelled. Shortly afterwards, however, Godfrey was found
mysteriously murdered, and the plot began to seem more believable.
When letters written by Edward Coleman, a former employee of the
Duke of York, revealed links with Jesuit and French agents, both Parliament and public accepted the existence of the Plot. For the next
year Oates was able to denounce whom he chose, until his imagination began to carry him too far and doubts emerged. By then,
however, the rumours had created a full-scale political crisis when
the opposition in Parliament attempted to pass a law to exclude
James from the throne.

Whether or not Shaftesbury and his associates believed the details
of the Plot, they had good reason to fear the accession of James. For
the previous decade the King had sought to manipulate Parliament
and public opinion in the interests of Catholics, and James had made
no secret of his faith. It was inevitable that, if he became King, he
would adopt pro-Catholic policies and might well be prepared to
impose them by force. The association of Catholicism with absolute
monarchy, already well established in the 1630s (see pages 76–7),
was strengthened by the contemporary example of Louis XIV. He
had not only secured absolute power, but was embarking on a persecution of Protestants that would culminate in revoking their guaran-
tees of toleration and driving them out of France as refugees in 1685.
There was no reason to believe that James would behave differently,
and as the childless Charles II and his wife grew older, every reason
to fear that this nightmare would become reality.

In 1678 the opposition attempted to impeach Danby, using evidence provided by the French ambassador that he had accepted subsidies from France. In January 1679 Charles tried to save him by
dissolving the Cavalier Parliament, but new elections only produced
a majority of opposition MPs, and the impeachment was successfully
carried through. These MPs were by now known as **Whigs** – an
unflattering nickname derived from the Covenanters' rebellion in
Scotland. In reply, the Whigs labelled their High Church enemies
Tories, a reference to Irish Catholic bandits. They then forced
Charles to accept a new Privy Council, chosen by Parliament, and followed this in May with a bill to exclude James from the throne and
replace him with Charles's illegitimate son, the Duke of Monmouth.
The Commons passed the bill, but faced with such an open invasion
of pragmatism over divine right, Charles dissolved Parliament before
it could go to the Lords. In October 1680, when a new House of
Commons passed a similar bill, it was defeated in the Lords after
heavy pressure from the King.

WHIGS AND TORIES

The development of party labels such as Whig and Tory marks a new stage in Parliamentary politics, because they relate to defined groups with clear, and permanent, philosophical differences. While political factions had always been defined by ideas about policy as well as personal relationships, and while personal relationships would continue to influence party development, the names given to these parties reflected their basic attitudes towards government, monarchy and religion. Hence their differences were general and fundamental, rather than relating to specific issues of policy such as how to conduct a particular war, and were beginning to represent different political traditions derived from the events of 1640–60.

ISSUE

What was the
significance of the
Exclusion Crisis?

ii) Crisis and Reaction, 1679–85

The Exclusion Crisis (so-called because of the attempts by Parliament to exclude James from the succession to the throne) revealed a number of things, including the political skills of Charles II. He showed a determination and resolve in defence of monarchy that contrasted with his apparent indolence in other matters. However willing to avoid confrontation and compromise with Parliament on many issues, he showed that in defence of the principles of divine right, he was not only determined, but also tactically aware. He had prevented Whig triumph by using his powers of delay, and by 1680, the anti-popish hysteria that had influenced MPs towards Whig policies was subsiding. By 1681 some thirty-five Catholics had been tried and executed, or fled into exile, but Oates was running out of credible victims. While the Parliament of 1680 busied itself with attempts to remove the legal restrictions on Protestant dissenters (which never received royal assent) Charles entered secret negotiations with Louis XIV for new subsidies. Hence, when he summoned a new Parliament to Oxford in 1681, thereby removing them from Whig-dominated London, he was financially independent. When the Whigs passed yet another Exclusion Bill he dissolved Parliament and ordered the arrest of Shaftesbury for treason. Acquitted by a Whig jury, Shaftesbury found himself facing new charges and was forced into exile in November 1682. In desperation, a group of old Cromwellian soldiers concocted a plot to kill Charles at Rye House in April 1683 and to replace him with Monmouth. The plot failed, and was used as an excuse to destroy the remaining Whig leaders. Some of them had undoubtedly known of the plot, others such as Lord William Russell were convicted on doubtful evidence because of their political role.

The Rye House Plot completed the King's victory by discrediting the Whigs, and introduced a Royalist backlash that allowed Charles to dispense with Parliament for the rest of his reign, in direct contravention of the Triennial Act. In the meantime, he began a programme of recalling and remodelling borough charters, in order to extend government control of elections and the choice of parliamentary candidates. By vesting the power to vote in a small group of aldermen, who could be hand-picked as Tories, or subjected to government pressure, it was possible to ensure the election of more compliant parliaments in future. The process took time, and was incomplete when Charles died in 1685, but it was continued by James, who succeeded his brother without opposition. When Monmouth raised a desperate rebellion in Dorset in June 1685, he received little support from the ruling classes, and was easily defeated. The rebellion was followed by mass executions among his often-illiterate followers, known as the Bloody Assizes from the unusual brutality displayed by the Lord Chief Justice, Judge Jeffreys.

THE POPISH PLOT AND THE EXCLUSION CRISIS

1678 Titus Oates revealed so-called Popish Plot to Sir Edmund Berry Godfrey, who was murdered shortly after; Second Test Act and attempted impeachment of Danby; Charles dissolved Cavalier Parliament;

1679 first Exclusion Parliament and Bill;

1680 second Exclusion Parliament and Bill;

1681 third Exclusion Bill defeated in Oxford Parliament; Shaftesbury brought to trial and acquitted;

1682 Shaftesbury driven into exile;

1683 Rye House Plot and destruction of Whigs.

The extent of this victory has led some historians to label the 1680s a 'second Stuart despotism' and to argue that it proves how little real power parliaments had acquired as a result of the Civil Wars and Interregnum. The strength of James's position at his accession seems to support this argument. He received a generous financial settlement that gave him some independence of Parliament, and the lack of support for Monmouth indicates both respect for the King's hereditary rights and fear of further upheaval. The policy of remodelling borough charters that Charles had initiated offered a real possibility of obtaining a compliant Parliament if continued for long enough. If that was achieved, there would be no need to dispense with Parliament and the extra powers that it provided.

However, it should not be assumed that the mid-century crisis had made no significant difference. What the Exclusion Crisis had also revealed was a willingness among some MPs to deny the principles of divine right and insist on a monarch who would govern in accordance with the safety of the people – the principle used to justify the execution of Charles I. In practice, the Whigs had overplayed their hand, but they had been defeated only by an astute and determined King over a period of three years. On balance, the crisis reveals that civil war and the execution of the monarch had left a double-edged legacy. On the one hand, the King could call on a fund of loyalty and a fear of the upheaval that civil war would bring. On the other hand, it had left an awareness that kings were replaceable, and a theoretical justification for replacing them. For the moment the fear of upheaval prevailed, but such a legacy needed careful handling; and ominously, when James faced an apparently compliant Parliament in 1685, he was provoked into dissolving it because MPs refused to grant toleration to Catholics.

> **ISSUE**
> Could the Tory reaction have led to absolute monarchy?

> The theory of a social contract and the safety of the people as the primary purpose of government is summarised on page 195. It reflects the arguments used in 1649, and published again after 1689.

b) The Collapse of Royal Power, 1685–8

Within three years the strong position in which Charles had left the monarchy had disintegrated, and a second Stuart monarch was removed from the throne by force, and with results that affected the nature of the monarchy itself. The reasons for this can be summed up by the character and beliefs of James II, but the importance of his individual qualities should not obscure the underlying issue – that he was deposed because he represented a threat to the Protestant religion and the rule of law. It was James's personal characteristics that led him to act arbitrarily and the depth of his faith that caused him to put his throne at risk. Nevertheless, the resistance with which he was faced arose from that fear of Catholic absolutism that had divided kings from parliaments throughout the century, and created problems that had never been fully resolved.

> **ISSUES**
> Why did James face invasion and revolution by 1688? How important was James as an individual in the development of the monarchy?

KEY DATES: FALL OF JAMES II

1685 Monmouth's Rebellion followed by the Bloody Assizes; Dissolution of Parliament;

1686 *Godden* v. *Hales* case;

1687 attack on the Church: Declaration of Indulgence; Ecclesiastical Commission; Magdelen College scandal;

1688 attack continued: second Declaration of Indulgence to be read in churches; trial of 7 bishops who refused; bishops acquitted; James's son born.

THE WARMING-PAN PRINCE

This was the nickname applied to James's new son by those who claimed that he was not James's son at all. The King's failure to produce an heir for fifteen years after his second marriage led to rumours that the Queen's pregnancy had been a sham, and that the new baby had been smuggled into the palace in a warming-pan. This was a large covered pan, used to hold hot coals for warming a bed. There is no evidence to support the story, but it reflects both the surprise and concern that James should produce a male heir to take precedence over his Protestant daughters.

Faced with the refusal of Parliament to provide religious freedom and legal equality for Catholics, James set about establishing their rights by royal prerogative. In 1686 he issued personal dispensations to allow Catholics to become army officers, and pressurised the judges in the case of *Godden* v. *Hales* to declare that he could issue such dispensations as and when he thought necessary. In 1687 he extended this by issuing a new Declaration of Indulgence, granting freedom of worship to both Catholic and Protestant dissenters. It is quite possible that James was genuine in his desire for toleration – his friendship with the Quaker, William Penn, is evidence of his respect for the views of others. It is also quite possible that he had no secret design to establish Catholic superiority, that all he sought was equality. However, in the context of events in France and the persecution of continental Protestants, it was unlikely that this would be believed. Moreover, his autocratic methods reinforced fears that he threatened Parliament and the rule of law. Borough charters were remodelled, and Catholics were appointed as magistrates. An Ecclesiastical Commission was set up to act as a Court for Church affairs, with power to make and unmake appointments and property settlements. Technically, this was illegal after the abolition of the Court of High Commission in 1641. In 1687 James used it to expel the Fellows of Magdalen College, Oxford, and replace them with Catholics. For James this may only have been a matter of creating equality and redistributing privilege; for others it was an attack on the Church, the Protestant religion, and the security of law and property, in a blunt confrontation that Charles II would never have attempted.

The result was predictable, even if the form and outcome were not. In 1688 James renewed the Declaration of Indulgence, and ordered that it be read from the pulpit in every parish. This was pushing the loyalty of the Church too far, and seven bishops refused to obey the order. They were arrested, charged with sedition, tried and acquitted amid public celebration. Two days later James's young, second wife, Mary of Modena, gave birth to a son. This was the final straw. Until this point those who detested and feared James's policies had been held back by the equal, or greater, fear of renewed civil war and by the knowledge that James was an old man with two Protestant daughters to succeed him. Essentially, they could afford to wait. Now, however, they faced the prospect of a Catholic heir, who would take precedence over his sisters. If James was to be the first of a long line of Catholic monarchs, then the prospects for Parliament and Protestantism were bleak.

In the summer of 1688 an invitation was sent to Holland to invite William of Orange, the husband of James's daughter, Mary, to rescue English religion and liberty. This was not an invitation to take the throne, although that is how it turned out. In many ways, an invitation to invade a foreign country cannot have been greatly appealing to William, but two circumstances encouraged him to accept. The first is that the invitation came from a wide cross-section of political leaders. The names of Russell and Sidney represented Whig traditions, the Earls of Devonshire and Danby (whose impeachment had been rescinded in 1685) were well-known Tories, and Bishop Compton represented the established Church. Such names were a sign of how many factions James had alienated, and of the potential support for William. The second factor was that invasion offered the only way of securing the help of England for a Dutch republic that was threatened with extinction by James's friend and ally, Louis XIV of France. It was for this reason that the rulers of the republic agreed to finance and equip an army for William, and it was a factor that would have considerable influence on the future development of the monarchy in Britain.

After a series of delays occasioned by bad weather, William landed with a small Dutch army at Torbay in Devon in November 1688. Even at this stage the outcome of events was uncertain. James had an effective army at his disposal, and might well have rallied support against a foreign invasion. Instead he hesitated, and while he hesitated, his supporters deserted him. Finally, as William approached London in December, James panicked and fled into exile. So convenient was this outcome that, when he was recaptured on his first attempt and returned to London, an opportunity was provided for him to escape once more. By leaving the throne vacant, James allowed his opponents to claim that he had abdicated, and to invite William and Mary, his Protestant heir, to take his place. There is a good deal of evidence to suggest that his tame surrender to revolution was encouraged, if not determined, by the memory of what had happened to his father forty years earlier.

c) Revolution and Settlement, 1688–1714

i) A Glorious Revolution?

As the Profile on page 196 shows, the so-called Revolution of 1688 did not introduce government by Parliament. Many of the monarch's powers remained intact, although they were more clearly subject to the rule of law. King William proved an independent and determined ruler, inclined to govern through his chosen advisers and reluctant to consult Parliament on many issues. This was particularly true of foreign policy and the **continental war**, which was his major preoccupation. As a result, further restrictions were placed on royal power in the years that followed the Revolution. The Mutiny Act of 1689, which settled army discipline for only one year at a time, helped to ensure regular sessions of Parliament, but the Triennial

ISSUES
How great a risk was William's invasion? Why did he undertake it?

A THEORY FOR REVOLUTION

Men being... by nature all free, equal and independent, no one can be ... subjected to the political power of another without his own consent, which is done by agreeing with other men to join and unite into a community for their comfortable, safe and peaceable living ... [agreeing that power] is to be exercised by such alone as shall be appointed to it amongst them; and by such rules as the community, or those authorised by them to that purpose, shall agree on ... And so, whoever has the legislative or supreme power of any commonwealth is bound to govern by established standing laws, made known to the people, and not by arbitrary decrees ... And all this is to be directed to no other end but the peace, safety and public good of the people.

Source A From *Two Treaties on Government* by John Locke, 1690.

THE GLORIOUS REVOLUTION AND THE SETTLEMENT OF 1688–9

-Profile-

Key points in revolution and settlement

▼ James was declared to have abdicated by leaving the kingdom, and the throne was declared vacant. This preserved an appearance of legal succession.

▼ William and Mary were offered a joint throne, because William had made it clear that he would not become his wife's 'gentleman usher'. This was an infringement of the hereditary principle.

▼ In February 1689, before their coronation, William and Mary were asked to agree to a list of demands set out by Parliament as a Declaration of Rights. Some of these were incorporated in the Bill of Rights, others in later Acts such as the Toleration Act and the Triennial Act of 1694; others were never implemented.

▼ The Bill of Rights and the Toleration Act were both compromise measures, accepted by both Whig and Tory majorities in order to achieve a quick settlement and avoid renewed disorder.

▼ In 1690 the monarchs were voted the income from the excise duty for life, but that from customs duties for only four years. Unlike that of 1660, this financial settlement was deliberately made inadequate, in order to ensure dependence on Parliament.

Questions

1. What changes did the Revolution of 1688–9 make in the role and power of the monarch?

2. How did the Revolution change the role and power of the Church?

3. How far did the Revolution and settlement imply changes in the attitude to monarchy?

4. In what ways was the settlement of 1688–9 influenced by the events of 1640–60?

Main points of the Bill of Rights, 1689

1. The King's powers to suspend the law or dispense individuals from its effects were declared unconstitutional.

2. No taxes were to be raised without the consent of Parliament.

3. There was to be no standing army.

4. There were to be no Ecclesiastical Commissions.

5. Elections were to be free from interference, and MPs were to have freedom of debate.

6. No Catholic was to inherit the throne; nor could the King marry a Catholic.

Main points about the Toleration Act, 1689

1. There was to be freedom of worship for all Protestants, excepting only the Unitarians (who denied the doctrine of the Holy Trinity and that Jesus was God).

2. The Test and Corporation Acts remained in place, depriving dissenters of civil and political rights.

3. Attempts to extend toleration by reforming the Church of England through a Comprehension Bill were undermined by the Scottish abolition of bishops and anti-dissenter feeling in the Church.

Source A on page 195 expressed the Whig view of monarchy and justified the removal of James. The Whigs had wanted to depose him openly, but accepted the fiction of an abdication to ensure Tory support.

Act of 1694 went further and ensured general elections at least every three years.

This had a marked effect on the development of political parties, and also prevented the King from holding onto a compliant Parliament as Charles II had done from 1661 to 1679. Party politics developed further when the Licensing Act lapsed in 1695, allowing a free press to debate political issues. Combined with regular elections, this helped to make government more genuinely representative of public opinion, or at least of the electorate. In 1701 the Act of Settlement laid down the Protestant succession, ignoring the Catholic son of James II and transferring the throne to the Hanoverian descendants of James I (through his daughter Elizabeth and the Elector Palatine, see page 40). Not only did this further weaken any concept of divine right and hereditary monarchy, but it was also accompanied by restrictions on the monarch's right to travel abroad or employ foreign advisers without the consent of Parliament.

As with so many aspects of the post-1688 settlement, these acts in Parliament were a reaction to immediate concerns and pressures rather than a coherent restructuring of the monarchy. Nevertheless, the ability and willingness of Parliament to take such steps, and the cooperation of William in the process, signifies a new balance of power between them. There is no doubt that William's preoccupation with the war against Louis XIV made this easier to achieve. He would undoubtedly have been more resistant to parliamentary encroachments had he not been frequently absent, and dependent on Parliament for money to finance the war. In fact, these years saw a significant development of the power of government and its control of resources (see pages 200–2) which made the monarchy more powerful than ever before, but it is also clear that this power was conditional upon the monarch's cooperation with Parliament. Parliamentary monarchy unlocked resources that divine right monarchs could only dream of.

In political terms, therefore, the Revolution of 1688–9 did bring about substantial change. The combined effects of James having been forced to 'abdicate' by the threat of armed rebellion, the significant new limits placed on royal power, the theoretical justification proposed by Locke and the ensuing dominance of a Whig party that shared many of his ideas, were to tip the balance in favour of parliamentary government decisively. Just as the Parliament of 1640–42 had sought to dismantle the machinery of the Personal Rule, so that of 1688–9 removed the powers that Charles II and James had applied in the 'second Stuart absolutism' of 1681–8. The arguments put forward by Locke bore a strong resemblance to those used to justify the King's execution in 1649, and developed by John Milton in his defence of the Commonwealth, *The Tenure of Kings and*

ISSUES
How revolutionary was the Glorious Revolution?
Was it a repetition or a continuation of the English Revolution of 1640–60?

CONTINENTAL WAR

William's actions, both in accepting the invitation to invade England and in shaping foreign policy thereafter, were heavily influenced by his desire to secure England as an ally in an ongoing war against Louis XIV. As a Catholic who detested Protestants, an absolute monarch who hated republics, and a French king who wished to expand his lands and powers, Louis had set out to destroy the Dutch state and take control of the Low Countries (modern Holland and Belgium). In a series of wars beginning in 1672 he had come close to success, but from 1688 William was able to widen the war into a European struggle that lasted until 1697 and was renewed between 1702 and 1714.

Magistrates. This suggests that the 'revolutionaries' of 1688–9 owed a direct debt to those of 1642–9, but if this was the case, they learned more than one lesson from earlier events. Their ideas and objectives were similar to those who had opposed Charles I, but their emphasis on a quick and orderly solution was the direct result of earlier failures. They were prepared to limit the revolutionary elements of the settlement in order to avoid upheaval and avert the possibility of another civil war.

ii) A Tolerant Establishment?

There is a similar complexity to the religious settlement. While the establishment of religious toleration for Protestants was a significant step forward, and brought about a major change in the role and powers of the Church, it did not create religious peace. Some dissenters were dissatisfied with their continued exclusion from political rights and powers, after the failure of the Comprehension Bill in 1690, but many were able to find a way around this through the practice of **Occasional Conformity**.

For some the practice reflected a genuine desire to be reunited with the mainstream of Protestant worship, and it was encouraged in this spirit by the **latitudinarian** bishops who were appointed after 1689. Others, however, made more cynical use of a convenient loophole in the law, and this contributed to the growing bitterness of Anglicans and Tories at the reduced power and status of the Church.

Initially these resentments created divisions within the Church. In 1689 about 400 members of the Church, including a number of bishops, refused the Oath of Allegiance to William and Mary on the grounds that they had not been released from their earlier oath to James. William replaced them with latitudinarians who sought to encourage compromise, but in November a meeting of Convocation revealed a depth of bitterness that destroyed hopes of reconciliation, as ministers called for measures against dissent. While the Whigs remained politically dominant, there was little chance of this, but the cry of 'the Church in danger' became a Tory rallying-cry and bitterness continued to grow.

In 1702, when Anne became Queen, her High Church sympathies encouraged Tory MPs to introduce a Bill to prevent Occasional Conformity, designed both to isolate dissenters and weaken the Whigs. When the Lords rejected the Bill, an attempt was made to attach it to the Land Tax Bill of 1704, much to the Queen's irritation. The dispute continued to simmer until 1710, when it brought the fall of the government. The Whigs had attempted to prosecute Henry Sacheverell, whose vitriolic attacks on dissenters in the pulpit and press had inflamed public opinion. His acquittal provoked popular demonstrations and the elections of 1710 produced a huge Tory

---

ISSUE
Did the Revolution solve religious problems?

OCCASIONAL CONFORMITY

The practice developed by some Protestant dissenters of attending Church a few times a year and taking communion occasionally. This allowed them to avoid the restrictions of the Test and Corporation Acts and hold public office. It was not new in 1689. In the early years of the Clarendon Code it reflected the uncertainty of some moderate dissenters about where their loyalties lay, but it infuriated the opponents of dissent because those who retained office by this method often used it to protect other dissenters from persecution.

majority. In 1711 an Act was passed to prevent Occasional Conformity, followed in 1714 by a Schism Act, which prevented dissenters from establishing their own schools. In that year, however, the accession of George I and the Jacobite sympathies displayed by extreme Tories brought the Whigs back to power, and both Acts were repealed.

In religious affairs more than in politics, therefore, the settlement of 1688–9 represented the victory of one competing tradition over another, and religious issues continued to be the subject of confrontation rather than negotiation. The ensuing struggle can be seen as the attempt of the Anglican party to fight a rearguard action against dissenter demands for equality, to preserve the traditional place of the Church at the centre of government. For this reason, the matter became a defining issue for the development of political parties, because the role of the Church as a national institution, controlling ideas and upholding the traditional hierarchy, was an essential part of Tory thinking. Just as the defence of the Anglican Church, for both social and political reasons, had influenced conservative supporters who rallied to the King in 1642, so the cry of 'the Church in danger' expressed the fears of those who sought to uphold traditional relationships in the years after 1688. They had been forced by the arbitrary actions of James II to join with the Whigs in opposition to his plans, but they were determined to limit the effects.

In the same way, the Church lost far more than the monarchy by the settlement of 1688–9. Its power and importance rested on a belief that Church and State should coincide, and that political loyalty was dependent on religious uniformity. The ideas behind this are explored more fully in Chapter 8, but there were also clear practical results. In the partnership of Church and King the Church received wealth and protection in return for teaching obedience to authority as a duty to God. If attendance at Church could not be enforced, then the Church was unable to fulfil this function effectively. By establishing **religious pluralism** and freedom of choice, the settlement of 1688–9 began a long process by which the ability of the Church to influence popular attitudes began to decline, and so, as a result, did its political power and significance. It is also clear that from 1689, the process was irreversible. Tory attacks on dissenters were aimed at restricting their freedom and influence, perhaps in the hope that they would wither and die, but never at reversing the grant of toleration. Religious divisions and prejudice would linger in society, but the Church as an institution and religion as a political issue became increasingly irrelevant after 1689, and the bitterness engendered between 1689 and 1714 indicates that this was what its supporters feared.

LATITUDINARIANS

Moderate Anglicans who sought to create a broad, flexible Church that could encompass a variety of opinions. They reflected an approach to religious unity that had been developing before 1640, and was greatly strengthened by the experience of upheaval thereafter. They had been outmanoeuvred by the High Church party in 1660–62, but had continued to argue for moderation and were well placed to support, and benefit from, William's desire for Protestant unity.

ISSUE

How did the settlement influence the development of political parties?

RELIGIOUS PLURALISM

Refers to the fact that the national Church had lost its monopoly, and people were able to exercise choice in religion. Separatist churches had existed since before 1640, and had been defined by the Clarendon Code, which made them illegal. The difference from 1689 onwards was that their existence and right to exist were recognised and accepted by law.

ACTIVITY

The questions below are designed to help you assess the effects of the Civil Wars and Interregnum on the longer-term development of King, Church and Parliament. They should allow you to organise and record information about various aspects of government and to consider the importance of immediate influences and those inherited from the earlier crisis.

▼ How far did the Restoration settlement address the problems that caused the Civil War? (You should consider finance, the powers of King and Parliament, fear of Catholicism and the nature and organisation of the Church.)

▼ Why did some problems re-emerge?

▼ What did the Exclusion Crisis reveal about: the attitudes and beliefs of King and MPs, and the relative powers of Crown and Parliament?

▼ How important were the actions and personalities of individual monarchs in the outcome of events between 1681 and 1688?

▼ Could absolute monarchy have been established in England in the 1680s? Does this mean that it was likely, or merely possible?

▼ How far were the problems faced in 1688 the same as those faced in 1660, or in 1640?

▼ How far was the Revolution of 1688–9 a result of the Restoration settlement of 1660?

▼ How far did the settlement of 1688–9 ensure that England became:
(a) a Protestant monarchy, (b) a parliamentary monarchy, (c) religiously tolerant?

▼ What evidence from the events of 1660–88 suggests that the Civil Wars and Interregnum had (a) strengthened the powers of Parliament at the expense of the Crown, and (b) enhanced the importance and security of the monarchy?

ISSUES

How and why did government finance and administration change as a result of the events of 1688–9? How important was the war in Europe?

d) The Financial Revolution and its Significance

i) The Nature of Financial Reform

The events of 1688–9 also paved the way for huge administrative and financial changes, which have been labelled a financial revolution. Historians such as Barry Coward have argued that it was these changes, rather than the political conflicts of King and Parliament that created constitutional monarchy and rendered the change irreversible. The key factor involved was England's entry into a major European war, and her sustained intervention on a hitherto unknown scale. English armies fought on land in Belgium, Germany and later in Spain. In 1689 the army numbered roughly 10,000 men, rising to over 76,000 (on average) in the first stage of war between 1689 and 1697, and over 92,000 between 1702 and 1713. In addition, the war involved important naval campaigns, conducted by a navy of over 40,000 sailors.

Not surprisingly, the costs were enormous by English standards. It is estimated that the war cost around £5.5 million a year between 1689 and 1697, and around £7 million a year from 1702 to 1713. By comparison, Charles II and James II had received a total income from taxation (in addition to revenue from Crown lands and fines) of around £1 million a year. After a series of money-raising schemes (including a state lottery) were tried out between 1689 and 1693, it became clear that a thorough restructuring of government finances was essential. In 1690 William had agreed to the Public Accounts Act, which established a Public Accounts Commission to examine government income and expenditure. Such public accountability opened the way for a new approach to royal expenses and much greater access to national resources in the form of taxation. The Excise Tax was extended to a wide range of goods, customs duties were increased, and in 1692–3 a Land Tax was introduced, levying four shillings in the pound (20p) on income from land. Thereafter it became a regular tax, voted annually by Parliament, although not always levied at such a high rate. By 1710 the Crown was in receipt of over £5 million a year from taxation, of which roughly a quarter came from customs and excise, and over 30 per cent from the land tax.

In addition to revolutionising the income from taxation, the 1690s saw a new approach to government borrowing. Monarchs had always borrowed money, in anticipation of revenue, from private creditors such as the great merchants and merchant companies of London. Since they were not always able to repay their loans on time, this could lead to embarrassing refusals of further credit and paralysis of government such as that suffered by Charles I in 1640. In 1672 Charles II was forced to suspend repayments in the Stop of the Exchequer. He was only rescued by Parliament after promising to withdraw the Declaration of Indulgence. In both cases, Parliament was able to use financial weakness as a means of forcing an untrustworthy King to accept parliamentary demands. But by 1693 the King and Parliament had common aims and, despite occasional friction, a new level of trust.

In 1693, therefore, William was permitted to raise a loan of £1 million by the Million Loan Act, which guaranteed repayments out of parliamentary taxation. The following year saw the introduction of an effective system of government borrowing through the establishment of a Bank of England. In return for a further loan of £1.2 million, the creditors were permitted to set up the bank to provide banking services and to arrange future government borrowing. The debt was to be underwritten (i.e. payment of creditors guaranteed) by Parliament, so that it was no longer the royal debt, but the responsibility of the nation – the National Debt, to be covered and managed by future taxation. So successful was the plan in allowing government access to national wealth and resources, that it remains the basis of government finance today. To complete the transition from personal to government finance, the Civil List was

KEY DATES: FINANCIAL REVOLUTION

1689 William took England into the war of the League of Augsburg against France;

1690 Parliament voted a financial settlement on the monarchy for four years only; William agreed to a Commission of Public Accounts;

1692 Land Tax introduced;

1693 Million Loan Act;

1694 Bank of England established to manage the National Debt;

1698 Government and royal finances separated by introduction of Civil List.

introduced in 1698 to provide for the monarch's personal and household expenses as a separate item, clearly distinguishable from the costs of government. The system of personal gifts and courtier administration that had so undermined attempts at financial reform and encouraged corruption in the reign of James I (see pages 36–9) had finally been reformed and replaced.

(see pages 36–9)

ISSUE
Did the financial revolution create constitutional monarchy?

ii) The Effects of Financial Reform

More than any other single factor, these financial reforms introduced a new era of constitutional government, a parliamentary monarchy in which the Parliament was a regular and necessary part of the administration, rather than an occasional law-making or fund-raising body. While the Triennial Act of 1694 had ensured regular elections, it was the administration of finance, the need for regular taxation and setting of appropriate rates that ensured frequent sessions and effectively deprived the monarch of his power to dissolve Parliament as and when he wished. In addition, the need to work closely with Parliament affected the monarch's freedom of choice regarding advisers and policies. In theory still free to choose whomever he wished to advise and govern, and to decide on peace, war and foreign policy without restriction, William found that in practice he needed advisers who could **manage Parliament** and ensure support.

This also encouraged the development of a cabinet of ministers to carry out these tasks. The tendency to establish small committees of advisers to take responsibility for aspects of government had been encouraged by Charles II, who expanded the Privy Council to 70 members in order to accommodate a range of factions. Since this made the Council too unwieldy to supervise government, he had developed the tendency to select small groups for particular purposes. In the 1690s, however, the need to manage parliaments on a regular basis, combined with the King's frequent absence from the country while conducting the war, led to the selection of a small group of parliamentary advisers to carry out the tasks of government on his behalf. The death of Queen Mary in 1694 made this cabinet even more essential and established a pattern that Queen Anne was to continue.

The management of Parliament further encouraged the growth of political party organisation, both during and after elections. Although the office of Prime Minister did not develop until the reign of George I, Anne relied on particular 'managers' to plan government strategy and ensure parliamentary majorities on her behalf. Her three key advisers, Sidney Godolphin, John Churchill and Robert Harley, were not associated exclusively with either Whigs or Tories, but tended to work with one or other because they could be

MANAGING PARLIAMENT

Government ministers had always been expected to make arrangements to ensure that the government's decisions were supported and accepted in Parliament, so that any necessary laws could be passed or extra money granted. Managing Parliament had usually involved building support among particular factions, but before 1640 this had been on a short-term basis related to a limited government programme. The increasing role of Parliament, the demands of war and the growth of political parties had transformed the aim of parliamentary managers into the provision of a permanent majority in the House of Commons.

relied upon to support chosen policies. Godolphin and Churchill drew mainly from Whig support, while Harley, like the Queen herself, tended to favour the Tories. Like her predecessors, Anne retained and used her extensive personal powers, but the cumulative effect of the new financial structure, the increased importance of Parliament and the evolution of political parties was to take a decisive step on a path from personal to parliamentary monarchy and government.

iii) The Evolution of Parliamentary Government

These new financial and political structures support the contention that the key cause of the development of parliamentary government in England was not political revolution, either in 1649 or 1688, but the outbreak of war against Louis XIV and the struggle to prevent **French hegemony** in Europe. There is no doubt of the immediate importance of the war in shaping the new settlement, and it was almost certainly the major factor in ensuring that William accepted it. William was no more willing than his predecessors to see the powers of monarchy reduced. He had accepted the limitations imposed on him in 1688 because his priority was to remove the French-supporting James II and ensure that England entered a war on which the survival of the Dutch republic and nation depended. Thereafter, he showed a desire to act independently. This led to further constitutional restrictions on royal freedoms in the 1701 Act of Settlement. Nevertheless, when faced with the need to finance and maintain his crusade against Louis, he accepted the financial revolution and its effects as the necessary price. For William, it was a question of priorities.

However, there are a number of arguments that cast doubt on these claims. The new structures that had been put in place also reflected major changes in the attitudes of Parliament – the willingness and ability of MPs to take on new responsibilities and extend Parliament's role – and the war alone is not sufficient explanation for that. A comparison with earlier parliaments can illustrate the changing attitudes of MPs regarding the importance and purpose of their control of finance. In 1610 Salisbury's Great Contract had failed because MPs were aware that financial problems were one of the few factors that enabled them to influence, if not control, royal decisions. In the 1620s, parliaments had refused to finance the wars of Charles I without some means of rendering advisers like Buckingham accountable for their mistakes. In both instances, control of finance was seen as a political weapon, enabling Parliament to restrict the powers of the monarch. In the 1690s the Bill of Rights, the Public Accounts Commission, and the confidence of Whig MPs that William shared at least their basic aims, provided the necessary

ISSUE
How and why did parliamentary government develop?

FRENCH HEGEMONY
The term hegemony describes a situation in which one country is so powerful compared to its neighbours that its dominant position is recognised and accepted as a fact of life in the relationship between the different states in the area. By the late seventeenth century the France of Louis XIV had defeated the Spanish and Austrian Habsburgs, and was in a position to dominate European trade and diplomacy. The struggle to contain France became the major aim of British foreign policy, and is often claimed to have established the principle that no single power should be allowed to achieve such status, which later drew Britain into similar conflict with the France of Napoleon and the Germany of Kaiser Wilhelm II.

accountability and trust that was required for a cooperative approach.

Furthermore, the years between the wars of Charles I and Buckingham and those of William had provided MPs with considerable experience of government and administration which led to greater awareness of the problems and requirements involved. The experience of governing and managing a war between 1642 and 1646, and of taking over royal responsibilities thereafter, did much to educate parliaments in these matters. The development of parliamentary committees to carry out executive functions foreshadowed the emergence of cabinet government. The Land Tax of the 1690s had a forerunner in the weekly and monthly assessments levied during the Civil War, which were devised by Parliament to pay for it. The willingness of the Convention Parliament of 1660, and the first Parliament of James II in 1685, to establish viable government finances indicates the effects of this experience in changing parliamentary attitudes. This did not necessarily guarantee co-operation for the future. James II had abused the generous financial settlement that he received in 1685, and MPs showed themselves willing to restrict William's discretion in both 1689 and thereafter. As the summary on pages 205–7 suggests, both monarchy and parliaments devised new strategies to exercise their power, and Queen Anne's use of royal patronage and parliamentary 'managers' indicated that the crown was as capable as parliaments of learning new tricks. The establishment of parliamentary government between 1689 and 1714 occurred because of a combination of factors, both long and short term. The immediate cause was the need to conduct a war against France, the common enemy of both William and his subjects. This provided the motive for co-operation, and dictated the strategies required. Nevertheless, it is unlikely that these strategies would have been as easily adopted or as effective had not parliaments learned from experience across the century. What is equally significant for the development of constitutional monarchy, is that both parliaments and monarchs continued to learn and develop the techniques required for government in an evolving situation.

Summary of Development, 1665–1714

Date	King, Church & Parliament	Political Parties	Government – Finance, Administration & Foreign Policy
1665			Second Anglo-Dutch War broke out over trade rivalry and possession of colonies. Some victories, but badly organised and led to Dutch raid on the Thames Estuary in 1667. Stalemate peace concluded at Breda in 1667.
1668	James, Duke of York declared his conversion to Catholicism.		Treaty of Dover with France, in which Charles secretly agreed to declare himself a Catholic at an appropriate time, in return for French subsidies.
1670	Conventicle Act renewed.		
1672–3	Issue of royal Declaration of Indulgence – allowed licences to dissenters to set up separate congregations. Lasted for a year before Parliament forced its withdrawal and did much to ensure the survival of dissent.		1672 Stop of the Exchequer – King's failure to pay debts caused City bankruptcies. Charles adopted pro-French foreign policy which included renewed war with Dutch 1672–4.
	Faced with failure, Charles abandoned his attempts to establish toleration and began to rely on a new chief adviser, the Earl of Danby, who sought to manage Parliament through pensions, rewards and Anglican High Church policies →	emergence of two parliamentary factions. (1) High Church and Cavalier, led by Darby and nicknamed 'Tories' 2) Low Church, tolerationist, pro-Dissent, anti-Catholic, led by Earl of Shaftesbury and nicknamed 'Whigs'.	
1673	Test Act excluded all those who could not prove that they had taken Anglican communion from public office – prescribed an Oath of Allegiance and Supremacy and a declaration against the (Catholic) belief of Transubstantiation. James, Duke of York and Earl of Clifford forced to resign offices.		1674 Treaty of Westminster brought mutual acceptance of existing colonial possessions, giving the Dutch the advantage in the Pacific but England possession of North American seaboard colonies as well as Barbados, Bermuda and Jamaica. Danby tried to introduce a more pro-Dutch policy. Only succeeded briefly in 1677, but this was enough to arrange the marriage of Mary, daughter of the Duke of York, to William of Orange, Stadtholder of the Netherlands.
1677	Marriage of Mary to William of Orange.		
1678	Titus Oates revealed 'Popish Plot' to justice Godfrey, who was later murdered. Anti-Catholic hysteria led to Danby's impeachment and dissolution of Cavalier Parliament. Second Test Act.		Louis XIV's expansionist policies bring concern at French acquisition of Rhineland territories and threat to Luxembourg.
1679	First Exclusion Parliament, dominated by Shaftesbury and the Whigs.		
1679–81	Exclusion Crisis saw three attempts by the Whigs to exclude James from the throne, before Charles was able to rally Church and Tory support.		
1682–3	Tory backlash saw defeat of Whigs, exile and death of Shaftesbury and the Rye House Plot, with the trial and execution of Whig leaders.		

Date	King, Church & Parliament	Political Parties	Government – Finance, Administration & Foreign Policy
1681–5	No Parliament called and policy of remoulding borough charters to ensure royal control by packing corporations with Tories – threat of absolutism through control of (not abolition of) parliaments.		
1685	Death of Charles II, accession of James II. Parliament summoned and dissolved for refusing to grant toleration to Catholics.		Louis XIV revoked Edict of Nantes – French Protestants persecuted and exiled. Generous financial settlement voted, allowing James to achieve a measure of independence from parliamentary grants.
1686	*Godden v. Hales* case confirmed James's right to dispense with laws. Ecclesiastical Commission set up to examine rights of Church and universities.		James appointed Catholics to positions in army and government, on the basis of his dispensing powers.
1687	James issued his first Declaration of Indulgence. Seized Magdalen College, Oxford for a Catholic seminary.		1687–8 further expansion by Louis XIV creates League of Augsburg against him and renewed war 1688. James' support of Louis makes Dutch leaders ready to see him removed.
1689	Catholic Bishops appointed; Second Declaration of Indulgence to be published in churches; refusal led to trial of Seven Bishops (June). Birth of a son to James led seven leading political figures, Whig and Tory, to invite William of Orange to come to England. William landed with army in Nov. 1688; James fled in December.		
1688–9	The Glorious Revolution removes James from the throne and replaces him with William and Mary.		
1689	Bill of Rights accepted by William and Mary, lays down new limits on the monarch and forbids monarch to be Catholic. Toleration Act provides freedom of worship for Protestant dissenters, but Test and Corporation Acts stand, limiting their civil and political rights. Latitudinarian influence in the church greatly increased by appointments to replace non-jurors → divisions in Church. William's first parliament replaces the Convention Parliament. Comprehensive bill aimed at broadening Church failed because of extremists in Church and Scotland.	About 400 High Church and Tory 'non-jurors 'refuse the Oath of Allegiance to William and Mary. Convocation meets in November and demands anti-dissenter measures.	William leads England into the Grand Alliance with European powers for war against France – continued until Treaty of Ryswick 1697.
1690		Party lines clearly drawn with revived Whigs supporting war with France. William naturally inclined towards Tories, but non-jurors and Jacobite sympathies force him to rely on Whigs.	Parliament votes financial settlement, giving monarchs excise tax for life but customs for only 4 years. This, with Mutiny Act of 1689 only securing Army discipline for one year at a time, ensures frequent parliaments.

Date	King, Church & Parliament	Political Parties	Government – Finance, Administration & Foreign Policy
1690	John Locke's publication of 'Two Treatises on Government' justifies the revolution on the basis of a social contract between people and government. Emphasises the representative role of Parliament and undermines the idea of divine right. Provides theoretical basis for parliamentary monarchy and Whig political theory. → These ideas were not accepted by William, but his need for support and his preoccupation with the French war led him to cooperate with parliament and the Whigs and led to a financial and administrative revolution.		William's absences in war encouraged the development of Cabinet government, at first to aid Mary, then, after 1694 to run the government in the King's absence. Costs of war and William's cooperation with Parliament e.g. accepting a Commission of Public Accounts in 1690. →
1694	Triennial Act – provides for General Election every three years – this, with the lapsing of the Licensing Act in 1695 leads to freedom of the press and intensifies party rivalry – Whigs and Tories both establish party newspapers and the rivalry results in 'rage of party' in Anne's reign.		1694 Bank of England and National Debt established.
1694	Death of Mary.		
1696	Fenwick Plot – to assassinate William.		
1698	Civil List Act.		1698 Civil List Act separates household and government expenses. William signs partition treaties to prevent France gaining control of Spain on death of Carlos II.
1700	Death of Duke of Gloucester, only surviving son of Anne, raises concerns over the Protestant Succession.		
1701	Act of Settlement ensured that after Anne's death the throne would pass to Hanoverian cousins – opportunity also taken to place further restrictions on royal power e.g. monarchs needed parliamentary permission to travel abroad or employ foreign advisers.		
1702	Death of William – Accession of Queen Anne.	Anne favoured Tories but their attacks on the war force her to use Whig ministers, especially those associated with the Duke of Marlborough, victorious general (Blenheim 1704, Ramillies 1706, Malplaquet 1709) Tories attempt to weaken Whigs by Occasional Conformity Bill directed against dissenters.	
1704	Tories attempted to include moves against dissenters in the Land Tax Bill. An irritated Queen appoints Whig ministers but costs of war and growing accusations of Whig profiteering begin to undermine the influence of Godolphin and Marlborough.		
1705–6	Regency Acts allow for a Cabinet council and Parliament to remain in session for six months after the death of a monarch to ensure a smooth succession – gives Parliament separate existence.	Renewal of Tory attacks on dissenters raises cry of 'the Church in danger' – leads to the prosecution and acquittal of Dr Sacheverall.	
1710	Issue of Sacheverall trial enables Tories to bring about the fall of the Whig administration – replaced by the Tory, Harley, after an overwhelming Tory election victory in 1710. New power used to attack dissenters in Occasional Conformity Act 1711 and Schism Act 1714 but extremism of some High Tories led by Henry St John, Viscount Bolingbroke, leads to Jacobite intrigues, fall of Tories and repeal of both acts at the accession of George I.		Marlborough dismissed by Tories and peace negotiations begin with France → Treaty of Utrecht 1713 – secures French recognition of Hanoverian kings and colonial gains for Britain which lay the basis of British empire.
1714	Accession of George I.		

4 Conclusion – The Significance of the English Revolution

The series of upheavals that occurred between 1640 and 1714 cast doubt upon the idea of a single English revolution. The term can be defended if we define the revolution by its most radical act – the execution of Charles I in 1649. Not only does this best fit the term 'revolution', since it involved the public trial and execution of an anointed King (justified in the name of his people), but it was also an entirely English act, opposed by the King's subjects in Scotland and Ireland, and imposed on them by an English army. In this narrow sense, therefore, it is possible to argue that there was an English Revolution in the seventeenth century. What is more in doubt, and remains hotly debated, is the importance of the 'revolution' and its associated developments in the evolution of monarchy and government in Britain. (The interaction between events in England and those in the rest of Britain is explained more fully in Chapter 8.)

The events outlined in this chapter suggest that the debate will continue, because the effects of the revolutionary period were both complex and contradictory. For this reason it is impossible to produce a single assessment of its significance – the significance of the revolutionary period varies according to the aspect of government and society that is under consideration, and the weight that different historians give to the different aspects. On the one hand divine right monarchy was successfully challenged, on the other hand it was restored in 1660. The balance of power between King and Parliament in the period that followed reflects both elements, and the friction between them in this later period shaped the constitutional monarchy that finally emerged. In contrast, the position of the Church was permanently weakened, while the effectiveness of government and administration was greatly enhanced. To assess the significance of the revolution by considering its effects, it is necessary to examine these effects in different areas of government and society and evaluate the importance of the contradictions that result, before drawing final conclusions.

There is, however, another aspect to the idea of significance and the nature of revolution; the effects of a so-called revolution may well offer a new perspective and further insights into the nature of its causes. One of the main arguments between different schools of historians has focused on how far the English Revolution arose from serious structural problems that made a conflict between King and Parliament the likely outcome at some point, and how far it arose from individual errors and short-term difficulties. It is widely agreed that the intentions of those who took up arms in 1642 were not revolutionary, and that the revolution of 1649 came from groups and forces that were released by the impact of war rather than the problems that led up to it. This fact, and the obvious failure of that revolution, has encouraged the idea that the Civil Wars represented little more than a quarrel within the ruling elite, which allowed the revolution to happen by mistake. In this case it would seem likely that, once the ruling elite had closed ranks in 1660, the causes of their quarrel would be resolved and there would be no further upheavals.

The events of the period from 1660 to 1714 tend to challenge this argument. In 1688 a second revolution took place. It was far more carefully controlled than the events of 1640–49, and it has been called 'neither Glorious nor a Revolution', but its impact has led some historians to regard it as more decisive than the revolution of 1649. What is most important, however, is that the revolution of 1688 arose from the same problems that caused the upheavals of 1640–60 – the conflicts between the needs of government and the rule of law, between royal prerogative and parliamentary privilege, and the deep-seated fear of Catholic absolutism that pervaded the thinking of most seventeenth-century Englishmen. It could be argued that the revolution of 1649 failed to solve these problems and created a backlash that restored the monarchy without addressing them effectively. They therefore re-emerged in the years that followed, causing a second phase of revolution in 1688, which laid the foundations for constitutional monarchy in Britain.

This does not mean that the outcome was inevitable, or that it was made so by the English Revolution of 1640–60. What it does suggest, however, is that the English monarchy in the seventeenth century was facing major problems that would have to be resolved if it was to remain secure. The actions of individual monarchs could influence the way in which it was resolved, and did help to bring about revolution in the process. Whether we consider there to have been one revolution or two, and how far the first made the second inevitable is a matter for historical judgement and debate. What is clear, however, is that the revolution(s) arose from significant underlying issues and ideologies, that political stability could not be achieved until they were effectively addressed, and that the process would inevitably involve a major transformation of British politics and society.

▼ Working on The Stuart Monarchy

Making notes and collecting information

The summaries of developments on pages 185 and 205–7 provide you with an outline of what happened in this period. The material in the chapter does not offer a detailed examination of events, except those which are relevant to the chosen themes, but it does provide a basic explanation of the main political developments. You can therefore use the questions and headings within each section to construct units for linear notes, and add to them through further reading if you require greater depth and detail.

Assessing the significance of the English Revolution

The summaries provided in this chapter cover a number of areas or themes related to monarchy, Church and parliament, political parties and structure of government. In order to assess the significance of the English Revolution, you could construct a brief thematic account of the developments in each area, using three key questions.

▼ What changes and developments took place between 1660 and 1714?

▼ What events brought about these changes?

▼ How far did they originate in events and ideas that were associated with the English Revolution of 1640–60?

You will probably find that your answers differ in relation to the different themes. To make your own decisions about the significance of the English Revolution, you must weigh up the different elements, consider any interactions between them, and summarise the overall effects. You might wish to consider the possibility within this, that even if the effects in each theme do not amount to 'revolution' the cumulative impact across government and society might be said to do so.

Answering Source-based Questions on the Stuart Monarchy

As a second example of the kind of document questions that can occur in examinations, use your knowledge of the period to assess the validity and implications of the Marquess of Halifax's view of the character of Charles II.

One great objection made to him was the concealing himself, and disguising his thoughts. In this there ought to be a latitude given; it is a defect not to have it at all, and a fault to have it too much ... Princes dissemble with too many not to have it discovered; no wonder then that he carried it so far that it was discovered. Men compared notes and got evidence, so that those whose morality would give them leave took it for an excuse of serving him ill ... When he thought fit to be angry he had a very peevish memory, there was hardly a blot that escaped him. He lived with his ministers as he did with his mistresses; he used them, but he was not in love with them. He showed his judgement in this, that he cannot properly be said ever to have had a Favourite, though some might look so at a distance. The present use he might have of them made him throw favours upon them which might lead the lookers on into that mistake; but he tied himself no more to them than they did to him, which implied a sufficient liberty on either side... That some of his Ministers seemed to have a superiority did not spring from his resignation to them, but to his ease. He chose rather to be eclipsed than to be troubled.

If he sometimes let a servant fall, let it be examined whether he did not weigh so much on his master as to give him fair excuse. That yieldingness, whatever foundations it might lay to the disadvantage of posterity, was a specific to preserve us in peace for his own time ... Ruin saw this, and therefore removed him first to make way for further overturnings.

Although written by Halifax in the early 1690s, *A Character of Charles II* was not published until 1750. Halifax was known as the 'Trimmer' because of his attempts to establish a compromise during the Exclusion Crisis by 'trimming' or moderating his political views.

Source B From *A Character of Charles II* by the Marquess of Halifax.

▼ QUESTIONS ON THE SOURCE

1. What strengths and weaknesses did Halifax attribute to Charles II?
[**4 marks**] (analysis)
2. Does the language and tone of the document suggest any hostility or bias? Give examples to support your answer. [**5 marks**] (inference, reliability)
3. What political events of the period 1660–90 might Halifax be referring to in the final paragraph? [**5 marks**] (interpretation in context)
4. In what ways can events before 1660 help to explain (a) the character and behaviour of Charles, and (b) the reaction shown by Halifax?
[**5 marks each**] (interpretation in context)
5. Using your knowledge of the period, explain how far this is an accurate assessment of the character of Charles II, and whether or not he should be regarded as a successful monarch. [**16 marks**] (synthesis and evaluation)

Extended Writing and Essay Questions on the Development of the British Monarchy, 1660–1714

Essays that focus on change and development can be phrased and presented in a number of ways. One way is to consider the *effects* of certain events, such as the Restoration settlement or the revolution of 1688–9. Essays of this kind can be approached using an adaptation of the way that you have learned to deal with causation, using the idea of effects in place of factors and explaining their interaction in a similar way to causes. The spider diagram set out in Figure 26 lists the main effects of the Restoration settlement. As it stands, it makes no distinction between direct and indirect effects, but if you group the different effects on this basis, it will provide an explanation of how they interacted. For example, consider a standard essay question such as: 'In what ways did the circumstances in which the monarchy was restored in 1660 affect the future development of monarchy and Parliament?' This can be broken down into three key questions:

▼ How did the circumstances of the Restoration (i.e. without precondi-tions and limitations) affect the nature of the settlement?

▼ What effects did this have on the relationship between King, Church and Parliament in the years that followed?

▼ How did this help to bring about a further crisis and revolution in 1688–9?

The first question can be answered by listing and explaining the parts of the Restoration settlement set out below, the second by explaining the direct effects, and the third by explaining how they combined and interacted to create indirect, or second order effects.

1. Use Figure 26 to plan an essay response to the question above.

2. Construct a similar diagram to summarise the effects of the Glori-ous Revolution, and use it to plan and write a response to the question: 'How did the Glorious Revolution of 1688–9 bring about the development of constitutional monarchy in Britain?'

This approach is useful in dealing with essays that consider relatively short, or medium-term developments, but as effects are considered over a longer time span, the interaction becomes more complex and difficult to explain. What you are effectively doing is to explain change over time by establishing a chain of cause and effect. As you address questions that deal with a longer time span, perhaps of 100 years or more, you will need to pay less attention to cause and effect, and con-centrate initially on establishing 'what happened' in terms of the course of events. However, this is not simply a matter of writing a narrative. In

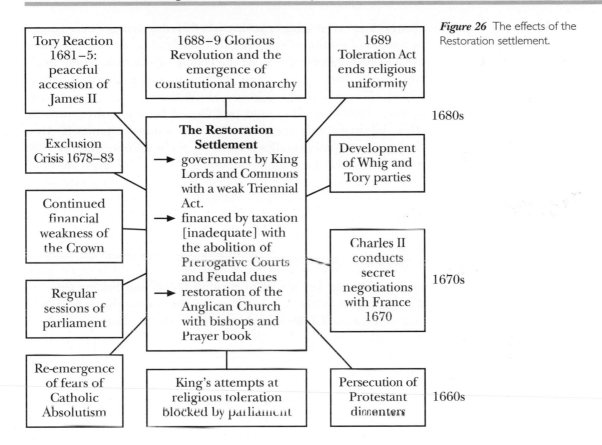

Figure 26 The effects of the Restoration settlement.

Tory Reaction 1681–5: peaceful accession of James II

1688–9 Glorious Revolution and the emergence of constitutional monarchy

1689 Toleration Act ends religious uniformity

1680s

Exclusion Crisis 1678–83

The Restoration Settlement
→ government by King Lords and Commons with a weak Triennial Act.
→ financed by taxation [inadequate] with the abolition of Prerogative Courts and Feudal dues
→ restoration of the Anglican Church with bishops and Prayer book

Development of Whig and Tory parties

Continued financial weakness of the Crown

Charles II conducts secret negotiations with France 1670

1670s

Regular sessions of parliament

Re-emergence of fears of Catholic Absolutism

King's attempts at religious toleration blocked by parliament

Persecution of Protestant dissenters

1660s

order to cover 100 years or anything like it, you will have to be selective about what events you include – you will need to pick a theme that allows you to leave out some events and establish links between those that you include, even if there is some time between them.

This offers an alternative approach to explaining change and development, using the idea of themes, trends and turning points. The theme that you use can often be defined by the question that you are asked. For example, if you are asked to explain the changing relationship between king and Parliament across the seventeenth century, you know that you have to pick out events that influenced this relationship and brought changes. You can use the same theme to deal with any question that deals with the development of parliament, the development of constitutional monarchy or the evolution of government. You could therefore prepare for questions of this kind by defining a number of such themes and tracing the events that you would need to include.

However, explaining change may well involve something more. You will need to look at the pace of change, and the relative significance of events within it. One of the best ways of doing this is to try and identify trends and turning points within your description of change. You can do this by asking whether the changes were caused by a series of events, of roughly equal importance, or by a particular event (a turning point) that set the changes in motion. These issues can often be highlighted in two part questions that appear in examinations. For example, a question about the changes in monarchy between 1660 and 1714 could be followed by alternatives, such as: 'How important were the personality and actions of James II? How far were developments influenced by events in Europe? Did the 1688 Revolution make the outcome inevitable?' These questions are quite easy to organise by tracing the course of events and then explaining and comparing the part played by different factors as the question suggests. You should be aware that you need to do more than explain the role of the specified factor – its importance is always related to other factors and you need to compare them.

When you have practised this approach, you will become quite used to defining key events or turning points and linking them to the trends that follow. You will then be able to use the approach to deal with thematic questions about change that do not give you help by offering two or three parts to guide you. For example, use the material in Chapter 7 and the ideas here to plan the two essays that follow, and write one of them.

1. (a) In what ways did the powers of parliament change between 1660 and 1714?
   (b) How did this weaken the powers of the monarch?
   (c) Did the powers of the monarch increase in any way as the result of the new relationship?
2. 'In 1660 the restored monarch remained the senior partner in government'. Explain how far this relationship changed between 1660 and 1714.

Further Reading

Books in the Access to History Series

Reading the relevant volume of the Access to History series *Charles II and James II* by Nicholas Fellowes would be the best way to build up your knowledge of the period from 1660 to 1689. It examines the issues addressed here in greater depth. There is no equivalent for the period from 1689–1714. However, there are useful chapters covering this period in *The Years of Turmoil*, ed. R. Wilkinson, published by Hodder and Stoughton in 1999.

General

Once you have established a clear understanding of the course of events and the issues that they raised, you could usefully move on to Barry Coward's *Stuart England*. While it lacks the narrative spine that you might need initially, it is excellent for analysis of key issues once you know what to look for. A great deal of very useful and interesting material has been produced by different historians of the later seventeenth century, especially J.R. Jones, W. Speck and K.II.D. Haley, but their work is spread through numerous volumes, articles and essays. The key issues examined in *Stuart England* are followed by further reading recommendations that will help you find your way through the range of material available, and would therefore be a sensible starting point for further study. For those seeking to adopt a more thematic approach to the period, Barry Williams, *Elusive Settlement* (Nelson 1984) is particularly useful in tracing the search for a settlement and the stages of development that were involved. In addition, a number of the more long-term developmental issues are considered in R. Ellis, *People, Power and Politics: a development study* (Modules 1 and 2), published by Stanley Thornes for the Cambridge History Project in 1992.

THE TRANSFORMATION OF BRITAIN

KEY ISSUE

What part did the English Revolution of 1640–60 play in the transformation of Britain?

POINTS TO CONSIDER

This study of the English Revolution and its longer-term significance has focused on government, and to a great extent, government in England. These developments took place, however, in a wider context of economy, society and belief, and in the geographical context of Britain as a whole. In order to assess the importance of any event, or sequence of events, we therefore need to consider them in this wider context, and to relate their effects to the more long-term developments that had already been taking place. It is clear that the seventeenth century saw a transformation of the economy and society across Britain, and the emergence of a single United Kingdom based on Anglo-Scottish Union and the continued subjugation of Ireland. What we now need to consider is whether these changes were the result of revolutionary upheaval, or evolutionary developments.

ISSUE

Why did the Anglo-Scottish Union desired by James I in 1603 finally take place in 1707?

1 The Making of the United Kingdom

The crucial stage in the making of a United Kingdom in Britain came in the aftermath of the 1688 Revolution. Between 1688 and 1690 the new monarchy was imposed on Scotland and Ireland and in 1707 the Act of Union brought England and Scotland together in a single kingdom. Although the Act of Union with Ireland did not take place until 1800, the events following the Glorious Revolution of 1688 completed the subjugation of Irish Catholics to English and Scottish Protestants. The integration of the British kingdoms had been developing over the century, but it reached completion at the same time as the new order became established in England and the immediate cause was the need to protect the settlement of 1688–9 by extending it to cover Britain as a whole.

a) The Settlement of Britain, 1688–9

The events of the 'Glorious Revolution' in England encouraged attempts to assert the separate identity of the Celtic kingdoms. The Patriot Parliament in Ireland passed a number of anti-English laws intended to secure a measure of independence. The effort was initially encouraged by the invasion of James II at the head of a French army, but his defeat by William at the battle of the Boyne in 1690 reasserted English power. Thereafter William repealed the anti-English laws and replaced them with a series of Penal Laws, which were designed to secure Protestant control and deprive the Catholics of property and power. This **Protestant Ascendancy** was to remain the main method of controlling Ireland for a century.

In Scotland the pattern of events was similar. In 1689 the Scottish Convention Parliament demanded the repeal of the 1669 Act of Supremacy, the abolition of bishops and of the Lords of the Articles, who controlled Scottish parliaments on behalf of the Crown. William seemed inclined to resist until, in July 1690, a force of Jacobite highlanders supporting the return of James II was victorious at Killiecrankie. Faced with the need to ensure support in the Presbyterian Lowlands, William accepted the demands of the Covenanters, who defeated the Jacobites in August to secure his throne. Thereafter the Highland clans were ordered to demonstrate their loyalty by a formal submission, and when the MacDonalds proved slow to do so, an example was made of them. In the infamous Glencoe massacre of 1692, a party of Campbells, their traditional clan enemies, visited Glencoe. They were welcomed as guests by the unsuspecting MacDonalds. They rewarded this hospitality by murdering their hosts, justifying their action as the execution of traitors.

ISSUE
Why was it necessary to impose the settlement of 1688–9 on Ireland and Scotland?

THE PROTESTANT ASCENDANCY
The social and political system set up by William to enable Irish Protestants to act as a controlling elite in Ireland. The Penal Laws prevented the Catholic Irish from owning land, entering the professions, or exercising political power. Hence the Protestant minority were able to gain a position of power and privilege that depended on England, and caused them to identify with English interests. They were therefore able and willing to control Ireland for the benefit of England and themselves.

Jacobites and Covenanters

Jacobite is the term used to describe those who supported the return of the Stuart monarchy of James II. It is derived from the Latin word for James – Jacobus. The term Covenanters refers to the supporters of the Scottish Kirk, the Presbyterian Church of Scotland, and refers back to the rebels of 1637 who rose against Charles I in defence of their Presbyterian system. Since Jacobite support was concentrated in the conservative, Gaelic and Catholic Highlands, while the Covenanters were associated with the Lowland areas of Lothian, the borders and Ayrshire, the political division of Scotland coincided with the underlying religious and cultural patterns defined in Chapter 1, pages 5,13,14.

The events of 1689–90 and the Glencoe massacre illustrate the three key elements in the relationship between the different peoples of the British kingdoms:

▼ From the English point of view, strategic logic made it necessary to control the outlying kingdoms, and the attempted Jacobite rebellions and invasions reinforced the lesson that the settlement in England would only be secure if it was also imposed on Scotland and Ireland.

▼ In Scotland and Ireland a distinctive cultural identity created a desire to escape English control and a perception of English behaviour as arrogance.

▼ In both countries there were religious divisions that cut across national boundaries and undermined national identity, allowing the English to find allies with whom to share power.

Ultimately, it was this alliance with Protestant residents that allowed the English to control Ireland and create a union with Scotland. To understand this process, it is necessary to study the relationship between the three kingdoms across the Stuart century.

b) The Evolution of Three Kingdoms

The religious divisions in Scotland dated back to the Scottish reformation of 1560, and reflected a deeper cultural divide between the Gaelic-speaking north and west, the Highlands, and the more anglicised Lowlands of the south and east. While the Presbyterian Kirk had established itself in the latter, the Highlands continued to be dominated by a semi-feudal clan system that allowed the clan chiefs to control and manipulate the religious and political loyalties of their largely illiterate followers. This culture was unsympathetic to Protestant ideas, as was the closely related culture of the Gaelic Irish. The more populous lowlands were able to dominate Scotland politically, but the existence of a conservative and largely Catholic Highland population was to play a significant part in shaping the relationship between the English and Scottish Kingdoms.

In Ireland the divisions had been created by government policy. Most of the **Old English settlers** had remained Catholic after the English Reformation, and Protestant settlers had been deliberately introduced by Elizabeth to strengthen English control. From 1607 James I had adopted a Plantation scheme, whereby English and Scottish Protestants were granted land in Ireland, especially in Ulster, as an inducement to settle there. The result was a complex racial and religious mix, with Old English and Irish Catholics living under the control of an Anglican Church alongside English Anglicans and English and Scottish Presbyterians. James had allowed a measure of religious freedom to the Presbyterians, and granted privileges known

OLD ENGLISH SETTLERS

Those who had settled in Ireland before the Reformation, and were closely identified with the native Irish. Those who settled in Ireland during the seventeenth century were distinguished by an English or Scottish identity, and a Protestant form of worship.

as the 'Graces' to the Catholics, which allowed them freedom to worship according to their faith. These rights were withdrawn by Charles, and both Catholic and Presbyterian groups were persecuted under Wentworth's regime in the 1630s.

In 1637 the religious tensions exploded when Charles attempted to force the Scots to accept a revised English Prayer Book, which led ultimately to the outbreak of war in three kingdoms. Both Scots and Irish contributed to the outbreak of war in England, and the English Civil War drew both groups into renewed fighting after 1642. Recent investigations of the Civil Wars have placed new emphasis on the effect of ruling 'multiple kingdoms' and the interaction of English, Scottish and Irish affairs in bringing the outbreak of war. Conrad Russell argues that the Scottish Covenanters were in close touch with the English opposition to Charles, and that their influence was a significant factor in the failure to find a compromise over the Church in 1641. He suggests that a Scottish 'Imperial vision' led them to put pressure on Pym and the Parliamentarian opposition to introduce Presbyterian reforms in the Church, which ultimately divided Parliament and created support for the King.

> The events referred to in this paragraph have already been explained in Chapters 3 and 4.

While there is debate as to the precise importance of Scottish intervention, certain facts are indisputable. The first is that it was the Scottish rebellion that enabled English opposition to confront Charles in the Long Parliament, and the second is that the Scottish Parliament and some of the nobility pursued a consistent purpose throughout the 1640s, to secure the purity and independence of the Presbyterian Kirk. It was this policy that led to the Solemn League and Covenant of 1643, to the support given by the Covenanters under David Leslie to the Parliamentarian forces, and to the later Engagement with Charles I and support for Charles II. Essentially the Scots supported whichever English party seemed most likely to ensure the safety of the Kirk. In 1640 this appeared to be the Puritan opposition to Charles, but by 1647–8 the situation had changed. Not only did Charles promise to introduce Presbyterian reforms in England, but the Scots now also regarded the English radicals and their allies in the army as a greater threat than the King.

> This analysis inevitably glosses over some of the complexities involved in the activities and relationships between different Scottish and Irish interests. Whilst it is unavoidable in a general survey of this kind, readers may well wish to investigate further. A good starting point is the *Oxford Illustrated History of Tudor and Stuart Britain* (see Further Reading) containing relevant chapters and a useful bibliography indicating further avenues for research.

The alliance with Charles in 1648 also brought the Covenanters into line with their Highland and Irish neighbours, who had always supported the King. When Ireland erupted in rebellion in 1641, the aim of the rebels was to oppose the direction of parliamentary policy in England, not to attack the King. Their leaders claimed to have the King's commission, helping to increase suspicions that he was a secret Catholic. Charles was not involved in the outbreak of rebellion in 1641, but in 1643 he negotiated with the Irish rebels and signed a Cessation, which promised toleration for Catholics and greater self-government for Ireland. His intention was to release Irish forces for

ISSUE
How did the Civil Wars affect the status of the three kingdoms?

MAKING THE UNITED KINGDOM

1603	Accession of James VI of Scotland as James I of England
1604 –6	James's efforts to create Anglo-Scottish Union defeated in English Parliament
1607	Flight of Irish Earls to Spain initiates Anglo-Scottish settlements in Ulster
1637	Scottish Rebellion provoked by Charles's attempt to impose a Prayer Book on the Scottish Kirk
1639 –40	Bishops' Wars
1641	Outbreak of Irish Rebellion
1643 –4	Solemn League and Covenant between Scots and English Parliament Cessation in Ireland creates Irish/Royalist alliance
1647 –8	Charles's Engagement with the Scots opens a second Civil War
1649 –51	Third Civil War – Cromwell conquers Ireland and Scotland
1654	Ireland and Scotland incorporated into the English Protectorate

the war in Britain. This helped to drive the Scottish Covenanters and the Ulster Scots into alliance with the English Parliament and made the struggle in both Ireland and Scotland an integral part of the war between King and Parliament. The Old English settlers and the Irish aligned themselves with the Royalists in 1643, and fought against Parliament's allies in both England and Scotland. While the Highland Scots under Montrose conducted a successful campaign for the King in north-east Scotland, Irish forces led by Alasdair Macolla invaded the Western Isles, giving the Royalists control from Aberdeen to Glasgow and beyond for much of 1645–6.

In every sense, therefore, the 'English Civil War' was a war of three kingdoms. It might more properly be called the 'British Civil War'. While religious divisions originally cut across the national and cultural loyalties of all three kingdoms, the political changes arising from the search for a settlement in 1646–9 led to a realignment, in which the English Parliament was faced with Royalist hostility from Ireland and Scotland. The internal history of these kingdoms reveals that they were far from united, but from the English viewpoint their hostility placed them in the Royalist camp. English rulers had always been aware of the strategic importance of the Celtic kingdoms, but the Rump and the leaders of the New Model Army were faced by a direct and immediate threat. The safety of their political settlement now required that it be imposed across the British Isles.

The result was the Third Civil War of 1649–51, which, from the English point of view, could more accurately be called the conquest of Britain. In 1649 the Irish settler Michael Jones, who had changed sides in the aftermath of the Cessation of 1643, achieved a major victory against the Royalist Ormonde at Rathmines, near Dublin. This allowed Cromwell and his forces to land unopposed, and in a quick and brutal campaign (see page 145), to secure control of Ireland. The conquest was completed by Henry Ireton, while Cromwell moved on to face the threat of the Royalists in Scotland. His 'providential' victory at Dunbar and the 'crowning mercy' of Worcester (see page 146) completed the military phase, while the incorporation of Scots and Irish MPs into the English Parliament under the Protectorate gave the conquest a political framework.

Despite the reversal of this settlement in the Restoration of 1660, these events proved decisive in the developing relationship between the three British kingdoms. Between 1651 and 1660, the Scots and Irish were governed largely by English officials and controlled by English armies of occupation. To pay for these forces, the Irish were robbed of more of their land, extending a process of deprivation that had been operating since the reign of Elizabeth. While the Scots were treated less severely, they were equally tightly controlled. Nor did the Restoration bring relief. Charles II restored the Scottish Parliament, but ensured that it was dominated by the ruling nobility and the Lords of the Articles, who acted largely as English agents. The Kirk was brought under English control by bishops appointed by the King and by the 1669 Act of Supremacy. When Covenanter rebellions broke out in 1667 and 1677, they were brutally suppressed, and those who fought on became outlaws known as Whiggamores (Whigs). In Ireland, which was governed by a Viceroy chosen by the King, the Cromwellian land settlement was largely upheld, the Anglican Church was restored, and both Catholics and Protestant dissenters were persecuted.

c) The Union of Britain, 1688–1714

In 1688–90, therefore, the imposition of the new settlement on Scotland and Ireland was entirely consistent with events since 1649, which had shown the Civil Wars to be decisive in determining the relationship between the three kingdoms. Whatever sense of national identity existed among the Scots and Irish, there were factions among them who shared particular political and religious aims with the rival parties in England. The most important effect of this was to provide allies for the English who could be used to maintain English control. From 1660 to 1688 the King governed Scotland and Ireland by backing the Anglican/Royalist nobility against their internal enemies. The Scots nobility and the Irish landowners used the power of England to secure their wealth and power, and paid their dues in loyalty to an essentially English King. In 1689 the Irish Protestants who held Derry against the Catholic forces of James II and supported William at the Boyne were reacting in much the same way. The Protestant Ascendancy established by William was a system in which the Protestant minority controlled the Catholic population on behalf of England, to secure their own safety and privilege.

A similar process created and maintained the Anglo-Scottish Act of Union in 1707. In 1690 the threat of Jacobite resistance forced William to grant a measure of independence to the Scots in order to ensure the support of the Covenanters. Significantly, and consistently, they concentrated on the freedom of the Kirk and of the Parliament, leaving Scottish merchants at a disadvantage against English competition. Not only were they excluded from trade with the colonies, but Scottish goods were also subject to import duties in England. Simmering resentment increased in 1701 when the Act of Settlement ignored the Scottish Stuarts and imposed a remote German cousin of the Queen as the successor to the throne of Scotland. In 1702 a Scottish colony and trading post established at Darien in Panama failed, and its collapse was blamed on English competition. In 1703 the Scottish Parliament passed a series of

1660	Scottish and Irish kingdoms restored, both dominated by ruling nobility on behalf of English Crown. Scottish and Irish merchants excluded from English Colonial trade
1667 –70	Covenanter Rebellion in Scotland led to the 'Clanking Act' which prescribed the death penalty for preaching at a conventicle
1669	Act of Supremacy placed Scottish Kirk under English control
1677	Scottish landowners given the power to enforce religious uniformity in their tenants
1677 –80	Covenanter Rebellion, leading to the murder of Archbishop Sharp (1679) and harsh repression by James, Duke of York, known as the 'killing times' (1680)
1689	Scottish Convention Parliament demanded repeal of 1669 Act of Supremacy, abolition of bishops and of the Lords of Articles; Irish 'Patriot' Parliament passes anti-English legislation demanding independence; Jacobite rebels in Scotland win victory at Killiekrankie in July; defeated by Presbyterian 'covenanter' forces in August
1690	William rewards Scots Presbyterians by accepting their demands; William defeats James in Ireland at the Battle of the Boyne, in July

1690 –2	Legislation of the Patriot Parliament repealed
1695	Penal Laws against Catholics to secure the Protestant Ascendancy prevented Catholics owning land, entering the professions or even possessing a horse worth more than £5
1701 –2	Failure of Scottish trading settlement in Panama blamed on English merchants; resentment in Scotland of English privileges increased by Act of Settlement
1703	Scottish Parliament passes a series of anti-English laws, including the Security Act which allows for ending of joint monarchy on death of Anne; real threat of Stuart restoration in Scotland encourages English to press for Union. This would confer trading rights and equality on the Scots and protect Presbyterian lowlands against Catholic threat
1707	Act of Union between England and Scotland

anti-English laws, including a Security Act, which permitted the dissolution of the joint monarchy.

Faced with a possible Stuart restoration in Scotland, the English Parliament acted. Contacts were established with the lowland Protestants, for whom such a restoration would create a Highland/Catholic threat, and terms were negotiated for a complete union of the two kingdoms. Scottish merchants would gain access to English trade, both in England and in the growing overseas empire, the independence of the Kirk would be respected, and the threat of the Catholic Stuarts averted. In 1707 the Act of Union was passed by both English and Scottish parliaments, confirming a political alliance between the lowland Scots and their English neighbours that secured the pre-eminence of the lowland culture in Scotland and the English in Britain. The Jacobite rebellions of 1715 and 1745 were not so much a nationalist backlash against foreign domination, as an attempt by the defeated Highlanders to reverse the process, which is why many of the lowlanders fought with the English to ensure that they failed. The development of the United Kingdom was speeded up by the events of 1688–9, but its underlying logic arose from the power of England, allied to the religious and cultural divisions that operated across national borders throughout the century and reached a decisive point in the course of the British Civil Wars of 1637–51.

ACTIVITY

Section 1, including the keydates will help you to define the main stages in the making of the United Kingdom. Use the information to decide what part was played in the process by:
▼ religion;
▼ economic advantages;
▼ strategic needs.

Did the events of 1640–60 create irreversible changes that made eventual union inevitable?

ISSUE

How did the British economy change in the seventeenth century?

2 The Expansion of the Economy, 1603–1714

In 1603 English governments were in the minor league of European states, with limited resources and an inadequate economic base, as well as an outdated financial system. Although trade had expanded in the sixteenth century, its growth was erratic. Exports were reliant on the single trade in woollen cloth, and England possessed no overseas colonies. London was the only large city, and her merchants were greatly resented among provincial traders for their control and restriction of trade elsewhere. By 1714, Britain was a world power, controlling a significant overseas empire, protected by a large and effective navy. The domestic economy saw an agricultural revolution and produced a wide range of goods for export to Europe and the colonies, while imported colonial products were also processed and refined in Britain for re-export. The huge profits produced by these trades, and by British control of the slave trade between west Africa and the Caribbean, provided capital for investment in Britain and encouraged the development of financial institutions that made London the centre of world banking and investment.

A number of factors contributed to this economic transformation. Its origins lay in the pattern of population change during the sixteenth and seventeenth centuries (see Chapter 1, page 16). The rapid rise in population between 1500 and 1650 first stimulated growth by raising prices and expanding the market. After 1650, however, the rate of growth slowed and the population stagnated. This led to a reduction in the price of food, allowing wages to catch up with prices and providing many families with a small surplus to spend on consumer goods. What requires explanation is why such goods became available at this time, and how population changes, developments in domestic and foreign trade, and political events, combined and interacted to transform the working of the British economy

a) Population and the Domestic Economy

The rise in the population led to pressure on resources and price rises. Rising prices stimulated both agricultural and industrial production, laying the foundation for an agricultural revolution in the later seventeenth and the eighteenth centuries. Since this required capital investment, it encouraged the development of financial institutions such as investment banks. As agriculture became more efficient it also developed greater specialisation for the market. The production of cash crops for industrial use, such as hemp and flax for cloth manufacture, encouraged rural industry to develop and offered new employment opportunities. Increased industrial production provided more goods for both internal and external trade, encouraging the development of a consumer society at home and more diverse trades abroad.

ISSUE
How did population changes affect the development of the economy?

The Agricultural Revolution

The term Agricultural Revolution refers to the widespread adoption of new farming methods, which allowed a rising population in the eighteenth century to be fed by a reduced agricultural labour force, releasing surplus population for employment in industry. By 1750 this process had laid the foundations of an industrial revolution. The key changes in agriculture involved the use of crop rotations that replenished the soil, increased yield, and provided winter feed for animals. There were also some improvements in tools and equipment, and the selective breeding of animals to improve the quality of stock. These experiments required the enclosure of open fields, waste and commons, to keep animals and crops separate and to allow individual farmers to use the methods they wanted to rather than having to fit in with what their neighbours did. All this tended to involve considerable investment of money (capital) in the early stages. This was difficult for small farmers and even the minor gentry, and it was the greater landlords who gained most.

Some historians have suggested that it is misleading to use the term 'revolution' to describe changes that had been ongoing before 1640, and methods that had long been known. In 1523 John Fitzherbert had published a *Book of Husbandry*, which described crop rotations, mixed farming and the use of specialist crops, but its circulation was probably very limited. The influence of Protestant ideas, the spread of education and ensuing growth of literacy ensured a very different reception for Sir Richard Weston's *Discourse on Husbandrie used in Brabant and Flanders* (1645) and John Worlidge's *Systema Agriculturae* (1669). The widespread adoption of new methods after 1660 was probably a result of time and better literacy enabling knowledge to spread, combined with falling agricultural prices that made more efficient methods essential to maintain profits.

ISSUE
How did the domestic economy develop?

Growth began before the Civil Wars, but a number of factors made it inconsistent at first. The mainstay of English trade and industry in the sixteenth century was the cloth trade, organised on a rural basis whereby master clothiers delivered the fleeces and raw fibres to family units and collected the cloth for finishing and sale. By the early seventeenth century lighter cloths known as the 'new draperies' were replacing the older trade in raw wool and woollen cloths. Based initially in East Anglia, the new draperies proved highly successful and spread to the north and west as the century progressed.

The cloth trades suffered from problems in their European markets – the infamous **Cokayne Project** and the effects of the Thirty Years' War – but the religious upheavals in Europe brought a steady flow of Protestant refugees, many of them skilled workers. The new draperies of Norwich and Colchester gained from some 4,000 Dutch craftsmen in the early seventeenth century, as did lace-making and stocking-knitting in Nottingham, while silk production in Spitalfields, London, was helped by French Protestants (Huguenots). A further boost came later in the century, when Louis XIV revoked the

Edict of Nantes in 1685, driving out thousands of Huguenot workers. The development of the cloth trade did much to stimulate other industries as well as agriculture. The new draperies encouraged specialist farming of flax and hemp, for example, to provide new fibres, and the development of support industries such as the production of alum for fixing dyes. A further example was the development of English pin-making, originally an offshoot of the cloth trade. Using new Dutch techniques it became successfully established in East Anglia, and later spread to areas such as the Forest of Dean.

By 1660, however, the population rise had been replaced by stagnation and even a slight decline. The reasons for this are unclear. Overpopulation and economic difficulties tended to lead to later marriage, reducing the number of births, while emigration to the growing number of overseas colonies would also help to remove some surplus. The arrival of new diseases such as malaria and smallpox increased death rates, as did migration to towns, where conditions were less healthy and disease more able to spread than in the rural areas. What is important, however, is that the reduction in the rate of population growth did not cause a slowing of the economy. Because agricultural improvements were already taking place, falling prices simply encouraged greater efficiency and specialisation. Because rural industries were already developing they competed with agriculture for a shrinking labour force, and helped to drive up wages. The combined effect was to improve real wages (the amount of goods that wages can buy) and increase spending power, allowing ordinary people to spend money on 'consumer' goods such as pots, pans and glassware, and to emulate their betters in buying the tea, sugar and tobacco that was coming in from the colonies. The resultant higher standards of living encouraged further aspirations and stimulated demand.

Another effect of the changes in population was to increase the number and size of urban centres. While London remained by far the biggest, other towns also attracted migrants in search of work and opportunity. It has been estimated that overall, the urban population rose from 255,000 (5.8 per cent of population) in 1600, to 718,000 in 1700. This was 13.3 per cent of the population – and 11.5 per cent of these were in London. In turn, the growth of towns encouraged agricultural production for the market and improved methods of transport to bring the food to the people. The activity overleaf illustrates the nature of urban development in this period, while its effects on the overall development of the economy are demonstrated below from the greatest example of all – the growth of London.

THE COKAYNE PROJECT

The ill-fated Cokayne Project involved an attempt to develop cloth-finishing in England, and replace the export of unfinished cloth with finished cloths instead. James I supported the project in an attempt to encourage industry, and to line his own pocket. In fact English finishing was of poor quality, and the merchants of the Low Countries simply closed the Antwerp markets to all English cloth. The project was abandoned and the cloth monopoly returned to the Merchant Adventurers, but cloth exports did not fully recover until the 1640s.

ISSUE
What changes took place in towns?

ACTIVITY

Questions on the Sources

1. List the range of goods that could be purchased from James Leach in 1668.
2. How do you know that these goods were not produced locally?
3. What inferences can you draw from these sources about trade, transport, and the lives of ordinary people in this period?

Urban Development and a Consumer Society

Evidence of economic change and the social changes that resulted from it can be seen in the growth of the number of shops (as opposed to workshops where craftsmen sold goods that they had made) in provincial towns. Consider the examples below, and answer the questions that follow.

We may tell how diversified its goods were by the detailed list of the goods of James Leach, of Bury in Lancashire, who ran an Aladdin's cave of a general shop in 1668. He had a wide variety of textiles and all the thimbles, pins, hooks and eyes, needles and threads a customer would need for making them up, and cheap lace, tape and ribbon for decorating the finished products as well as soap and starch for washing them. He had knitted stockings at different prices for men, women and children. He also had groceries. Tea from India was there, and so was sugar from the Americas, both white and brown. Cheap tobacco from the Americas was there too, and so were the pipes to smoke it in. If you wanted to drink spirits instead of beer, you could buy them from James Leach. If you felt more intellectual, you could buy white paper from him for writing on and books to read, and ready-made candles for reading by. If you suffered from eye strain as a result, you could even purchase a pair of spectacles at 2d apiece to help. Most of the goods necessary to clothe and feed the body and even to entertain the mind could in fact be found in James Leach's provincial general shop in 1668. He was not at all unusual. What was unusual was the appearance, in a few shops in Kent at the end of the seventeenth century, of ready-made complete suits of clothes. There indeed, was a foretaste of things to come, but even James Leach in Bury stocked items that would have been an outrageous luxury to most of the population a century earlier.

Source A From *The Making of Britain: The Age of Expansion*, ed. Lesley M. Smith (Macmillan 1986), pp 119–20.

Year	London	Norwich	Towns with a population over 10,000
1500	50,000	10,000	London, Norwich.
1600	200,000	15–20,000	London, Norwich, Bristol (12,000)
1650	400,000	30,000	
1665	500,000	30,000	
1700	575,000	32,000	London, Norwich, Bristol (21,000), Newcastle, York, Yarmouth, Colchester, Exeter.

Towns with a population between 5,000 and 10,000 in 1700 were: Nottingham, Coventry, Leicester, Worcester, Bury St Edmunds, Leeds, Bradford, Manchester and Sunderland

Source B Patterns of urban growth. In 1600 the three largest towns in England were London, Norwich and Bristol. Patterns of growth were all well above the overall national rate of population increase.

b) The Growth of London and its Effects

Before 1640 most provincial towns remained small, with only Norwich and Bristol rising to a population of more than 10,000. London, however, had increased from around 60,000 to approximately 200,000 by 1600, and continued to grow thereafter. The effect was to create a market economy for agriculture in the Home Counties, leading to agricultural specialisation, an improved road and transport network and the stimulation of rural industries. In 1581 John Houghton recorded that London and its needs provided work for farmers and shopkeepers for thirty miles around, and even as far as eighty miles away. In specific areas, the city could stimulate demand on a wide scale, through its port and coastal trade – for example the import of coal from Newcastle to provide for domestic fuel. In addition, London was the centre of overseas trade and the home of the Merchant Adventurers who held the cloth monopoly. The wealth of the greater London merchants was such that they

ISSUES
Why did London grow so spectacularly? How did this influence the development of the economy?

TAX FARMERS

In the absence of an effective system of tax collection, the Crown relied on tax 'farmers' to turn parliamentary grants of taxation into real money. Merchants and financiers who held significant quantities of capital bid for the right to collect the taxes: estimating the likely yield and subtracting collection costs, then offering the king a capital sum. The king received his money quickly and without worrying about collecting it; the farmers, if they got their sums right, could make a tidy profit.

How might the growth of London influence and shape the way of life in the city; the development of the economy; social life and attitudes in the seventeenth century?

became **tax farmers** and bankers to the Crown. In these arrangements, the rudimentary beginnings of a banking system, capable of providing money for high-cost capital projects, were taking shape.

As the population of the city, and especially of its suburbs, continued to rise, its impact on the economy extended beyond the Home Counties to achieve a national effect. By the 1650s the dominance of the London market had already created standard national prices for textiles, coal, grain, cheese, cattle and hosiery, based on the London market. By 1700 there were 575,000 inhabitants, and their needs for food, clothing, fuel and other necessities had created a national market. London shops were supplied from all parts of the country. To make this possible there had been improvements in transport and communications, with the Thames and other rivers in the Midlands and north made more navigable by removing obstructions and replacing fords with bridges. A start was made on road improvements with the establishment of the first turnpike trusts after 1660, usually financed by the local businessmen and landowners that benefited from the expanding market. As the market became more national, farming was able to become more specialised, with the cool uplands of the north and west focusing on dairy products and the 'champion' lands of the south and east on arable farming. Such specialisation was efficient, but only possible once the national market and communications made self-sufficiency unnecessary. The growth of London was the single most important factor in this process. Moreover, where London led, other towns would eventually follow.

URBAN GROWTH AND THE CITY OF LONDON

Why London? It was the national capital and seat of government. The greatest nobility and gentry had houses there. It was the greatest port in the land – its merchants were the wealthiest, its tradesmen the most numerous. Such a place was a magnet for the ambitious, whether they were gentlemen aspiring to a political career, lawyers, clerks, tradesmen and apprentices, domestic servants or criminals and vagrants. For all such people London offered the best opportunities and the richest pickings.

> Within these forty years [Spitalfields] had on both sides fair hedgerows of elm trees, with bridges and easy stiles to pass over into the pleasant fields ... which is now, within a few years made continual building throughout, of garden-houses and small cottages ...
>
> **Source C** From John Stow, *Survey of London*, 1603.

The habit of most gentlemen and noblemen is to house themselves in the suburbs [when they visit] the city of London, because most commonly the places are healthy and we have as little to fear from diseases as in the Country.

Source D From *Civil and Uncivil Life*, 1579.

It is well known that at this time there are in London some merchants worth £100,000, and he is not accounted rich that cannot reach to £50,000 or near it.

Source E From Sir Thomas Wilson, *The State of England*, 1600.

London, not only the city, but also Westminster, Southwark and the suburbs was the thief's Mecca, because it was unique and had unique opportunities for the criminal ... The rise in its population was due to large-scale immigration ... dispossessed cottagers, the rural unemployed, apprentices and unattached people ... Temporary residents swelled the numbers – the nobility, gentry and their entourages visited London regularly.

The London palaces and lodging houses were rich in pickings ... [and] the size and mobility of the population made it impossible to isolate or control London's criminals.

Source F From J. Briggs et al., *Crime and Punishment in England* (UCL Press 1996), pp. 21–2.

The parish church of St. Giles, Cripplegate was incapable of serving its population of 30,000. No ecclesiastical courts held sway in the teeming alley-ways. Its shopkeepers and artisans went 'gadding' to whichever sermons they liked. There John Milton, the great Puritan poet, wrote *Paradise Lost* (which the ecclesiastical censor wanted banned). The parish harboured several Nonconformist meeting-houses or 'conventicles', as well as communities of Huguenots, Irish catholics and Jews (whom Cromwell had allowed to resettle). The parish was an early epitome of modern cultural pluralism.

Source G From Mark Goldie, 'The Search for Religious Liberty' in *The Oxford Illustrated History of Tudor and Stuart Britain*, ed. J. Morrill, pp. 293–4.

Source H London in 1710.
Although Wren had been able to reconstruct the cathedral of St Paul's and other churches after the fire of 1666, his plan to change the layout of the city was ignored. Hence the maze of streets and alleyways, riddled with disease and crime, reappeared.

c) The Expansion of Overseas Trade, 1600–1714

i) Trade and Colonies before 1650

The growth of London and the development of a consumer society were accompanied and supported by a huge expansion and diversification of overseas trade. English trade in the early seventeenth century was dominated by European markets and by one main export – the sale of woollen cloth. It has been estimated that in the 1640s some 63 per cent of trade was with northern Europe and 31 per cent with southern Europe and the Mediterranean. The mid-sixteenth century had seen attempts to move into new markets, with the foundation of **Joint Stock Companies**, but it was difficult to make headway. The Spanish monopoly in South America and the Caribbean was difficult to break, while the Portuguese and Dutch dominated trade in the east. England lacked the naval power to protect her merchants against competition, and continued to depend on trade in Europe. She was at the mercy of markets in the Low Countries, as the disastrous Cokayne Project demonstrated, and suffered serious trade depressions because of European conditions.

Early attempts to establish overseas colonies faced similar obstacles. In 1583 Sir Humphrey Gilbert set up a colony of 200 settlers in Newfoundland, but the scheme collapsed when the ships were wrecked and Gilbert drowned. Attempts by Sir Walter Raleigh to colonise Virginia in 1584 and 1587 failed because of hostility towards local Indians and difficulty in maintaining supplies. In 1607, however, an expedition in search of gold established a settlement at Jamestown, Virginia, to which 900 new settlers came in 1610. Despite hardship, disease and Indian attacks, the colony grew because of a steady supply of new settlers, and began to produce tobacco as a cash crop. In 1632 Charles I granted lands nearby to Lord Baltimore, as a refuge for Catholics, which became established as the colony of Maryland. In the meantime a group of Puritan refugees had landed further north in Massachusetts, to become the first of the New England colonies.

The success of these settlements encouraged others, and by the 1630s there was a steady flow of emigrants to the colonies. This may have played some part in reducing and reversing the population rise, and it certainly offered economic opportunity to those who settled. From the 1650s the colonial population was swelled by the transportation of convicts and political exiles, many of whom were able to contribute to the growing colonial economy. Others settled further south, on isolated West Indian islands that the Spanish were unable to control. Bermuda was settled in 1612, St Kitts in 1624, and from there, settlers occupied the neighbouring islands of Barbados, Nevis and Monserrat. Cromwell's capture of Jamaica in 1655 provided a

ISSUES
Was there a 'commercial revolution'? How did overseas trade influence the domestic economy?

JOINT STOCK COMPANIES

Groups of merchants who joined together to set up a company in which the stock was shared and jointly owned, in order to share the risks involved. They were particularly suitable for long-distance trading, where both the risks and profits were high. In 1555 a group of London merchants were granted a royal charter to form the Muscovy Company, to trade with Russia and the Baltic, while merchants from Bristol, Newcastle and Hull had begun to trade in West Africa and Scandinavia.

strategic naval base, and proved more valuable than first thought. Although the first settlers began by producing tobacco, they soon adopted the Dutch practice of growing sugar cane, producing a highly profitable crop that created and sustained a growing demand in Europe.

Moves had also been made to establish trading bases and secure profitable markets in the east, in Java, Sumatra, the Moluccas and in India itself. In 1600 242 London merchants formed a joint stock company, with a royal charter naming it as the East India Company. Early success in establishing bases at Surat in India, in spite of Portuguese claims to the area, and in Java and Sumatra, was followed by the establishment of a base at Madras. However, rivalry soon developed with the Dutch, who controlled the area from Amboyna in the Moluccas, and the English were eventually driven from the islands. This encouraged the company to concentrate on the Indian mainland, and they were helped by the marriage of Charles II to the Portuguese princess, Catherine of Braganza, who brought Bombay as part of her dowry.

By 1650, therefore, colonial development had begun to make some headway, but the full benefits were only felt in Britain after the passing of a series of protectionist Navigation Acts. In its early stages, colonial development owed little to any political events in Britain. The motives of inventors and settlers were economic opportunity, ambition, and sometimes a desire for political or religious freedom, but they were only faintly and indirectly linked to political developments. The passing of the Navigation Acts, however, marked a new phase of government intervention, and a policy of promoting trade and colonial development to which historians have given the name of **mercantilism**. The value of colonies to a domestic economy lies in the provision of new markets and new sources of raw materials, but neither will have much effect if the colonists are free to sell their products to the highest bidder, as they were until 1650. By closing the colonial markets to foreign competition, the Navigation Acts brought the full benefit to England. The northern settlements in America provided an expanding market for English goods, while those in the south and the West Indies were a source of raw materials like tobacco and sugar. Their demand for slave labour allowed English merchants to break into the lucrative slave trade with West Africa, while control of the carrying trade increased both the numbers and profitability of English ships.

ii) Mercantilism and the Changing Role of Government

The Navigation Acts of 1650 and after, and the commercial wars against Spain, France and Holland that followed, have sometimes been presented as evidence of a change in the attitude of English

MERCANTILISM
An economic theory that places emphasis on achieving a positive balance of trade by exporting more than is imported, and building up supplies of bullion by being paid the balance in gold. Basically a protectionist theory, encouraging high duties and regulation to protect domestic industry, combined with aggressive expansion of foreign markets by denying access to competitors.

governments, attributable to the political revolution of 1640–49 and the growing power of the merchant interest in parliament. It is certainly true that the new legislation was initiated by the Rump Parliament, and that its members consciously sought to promote trade. It is also true that Cromwell pursued an active foreign and colonial policy, the effects of which are described by John Reeve below:

> The Commonwealth readily established its authority over the colonies, where many royalists had gone into exile. The civil wars apparently did no enduring damage to Britain's world trade and a Council of Trade was established in 1650. The Navigation Act of 1651 constituted the beginning of a system of regulated imperial commerce. Under Cromwell a treaty of 1654 gave access to the Portuguese Empire (balancing Dutch power in Asia), the East India Company was re-chartered in 1657, and trade with China was begun. But it was in the Americas that British interest and activity were increasing by 1650. English West Indian plantations began concentrating on sugar cultivation, exploiting the horrors of the African slave trade. Cromwell instigated a policy of aggressive annexation, taking possession of Jamaica (1655) and using force against French and Dutch colonists in North America. In rivalling other European powers in the American hemisphere and giving momentum to imperial expansion, his policy pointed the way to the future.

Source I From John Reeve, 'Britain and the World under the Stuarts' in *The Oxford Illustrated History of Tudor and Stuart Britain*, ed. J. Morrill, pp. 418, 426.

However, the link between political changes and the new economic policy should not be oversimplified. Mercantilist policies were adopted in many states in this period, including Catholic, absolutist France as well as Protestant, republican Holland. Nor was the approach entirely new. Tudor governments had sought to protect trade and the economy in order to maintain social stability, with mixed results. The Poor Laws, for example, restricted the mobility of the labour force, but also encouraged efforts to promote rural industries. Both James I and Charles sought to encourage trade, if only to increase their own revenue, but the sale of monopolies restricted growth and was only justified in the case of long-distance ventures like the East India Company. Although Charles used the proceeds of Ship Money to expand the navy, there were bitter complaints that piracy raged unchecked in the North Sea and elsewhere. The evidence would suggest that governments of all kinds attempted to improve the economy, but that their motives and understanding of the likely results were not always well judged.

The Civil War, however, encouraged further naval expansion, especially after a Royalist rebellion in the West Indies that followed the execution of Charles I. It was put down by a naval expedition under Sir George Ayscue, but it highlighted the need to control the colonies and protect trade. The first Navigation Act, which followed in 1650, probably benefited from the influence and expertise of merchants and the London companies in the Rump Parliament, as did the determined management of the Dutch War that followed. By the Treaty of Westminster in 1654, the Dutch agreed to respect the Navigation Acts, which restricted trade between England and the colonies to English ships and allowed imports into England only in English ships or ships of the country in which the goods had been produced. What is implied by these events is not necessarily a new policy, but certainly a more informed and effective one.

Cromwell followed this up by the seizure of Jamaica from Spain and the provision of military support for settlers in both North America and the West Indies. While his motives included traditional hostility towards Catholic Spain, he also showed an awareness of the needs of commerce and willingness to back commercial effort with military power. Equally importantly, he had the military power to act. The naval policies of Charles I, combined with the experience of civil war had strengthened English forces on both land and sea. It may well be that the new effectiveness of English commercial policy reflects greater knowledge and better resources as much as a change in motives and priorities.

Whatever the reasons, it was from this time that English commercial, colonial and naval expansion gathered pace. It was not a record of unbroken achievement. In the commercial wars after 1660 the Dutch and French were often successful, both in pitched battles and as privateers. The Dutch destroyed an English fleet at Chatham in 1666, and sailed virtually into London with impunity. In 1693 French privateers captured 200 out of 400 ships being convoyed to Turkey, and the Admiralty estimated that over 4,000 merchant ships were lost between 1689 and 1697. On balance, however, successes outweighed failures. The Navigation Acts sparked off a huge increase in shipbuilding and shipping capacity, which allowed the navy to draw on reserves of strength and expertise.

In turn, the value of colonial trade expanded, providing revenue for naval expansion and commercial wars. Even relatively unsuccessful wars produced some benefits. In 1664 the Dutch settlement of New Amsterdam was captured and renamed New York, providing a vital strategic link between the colonies of New England and the southern settlements of Virginia, and later Georgia and the Carolinas. With time and experience naval techniques improved. A Council of Trade was established in 1696 to coordinate a convoy system to protect merchant shipping, and in 1708 a Convoys and Cruisers Act provided a permanent reserve of 43 ships to act as convoy escorts. The French war of 1702–13 saw the capture of Gibral-

GROWTH OF NAVAL POWER

1635–7 Charles I uses Ship Money to expand the navy;
1642–9 navy fights for Parliament;
1650 navy sent to put down Colonial (Royalist) Rebellion;
1651–4 Navigation Acts and Dutch War
1655 seizure of Jamaica provides naval base in West Indies;
1666–90 serious losses in wars against the Dutch and French, but Navigation Acts encourage development of shipbuilding;
1696 Council of Trade initiates convoy system;
1708 Convoys and Cruisers Act establishes permanent naval reserve.

tar and Minorca as naval bases in the Mediterranean. By the Treaty of Utrecht in 1713 Britain also took over French possessions in eastern Canada and control of the 'triangular trade' in slaves for the American and West Indian colonies. As a bonus, her Dutch allies had been exhausted by the struggle against Louis XIV – in naval and colonial terms, Britain had become a great power.

iii) The Expansion of Trade, 1660–1714

The resulting expansion of trade could be considered a commercial revolution, since it involved a significant change in the structure as well as the size of Britain's overseas trade. In 1640, 94 per cent of England's trade was with Europe and the Mediterranean; by 1700 this had dropped to 67 per cent. Textiles remained a major export, with the fustians, worsteds and cotton mixes of the 'new draperies' selling well in colonial markets, but a growing proportion of exports were re-exports, based on imported colonial crops. In the 1640s England imported goods worth £2.7 million, of which £0.5 million were re-exported, while domestic exports totalled £2.3 million. By the 1660s domestic exports were worth £3 million, while imports had reached £4 million, of which £0.9 were re-exported. By 1700 the totals were £4.4 million in domestic exports, £5.8 million imports and £2 million re-exports. These developments also stimulated new industries based on refining and processing the colonial products before re-export.

A further change in the structure of trade came with the highly profitable 'triangular trade' in slaves. Goods were taken to West Africa and there exchanged for slaves. These were taken across the Atlantic to the southern colonies of America and the West Indies, and sold. Part of the profit was then used to purchase sugar, tobacco and indigo, which was brought back to Britain for processing, consumption and re-export. There were profits for England at every point in the triangle. In the east, the East India company had much greater costs, including military struggles against native rulers, but the value of their imports of tea, coffee, silks, calicoes and spices was rising steadily. Although these goods were purchased by a decidedly un-mercantilist export of bullion, the profit margins were high enough to make it worthwhile.

The profits of overseas trade also played a part in another revolutionary aspect of economic development – the establishment of effective systems of banking and insurance. Again, London played a major role. Within the domestic economy the huge London market and the transport of goods and people to and from the capital had encouraged the development of credit facilities. Bonds of exchange were developed by which the supplier charged a higher price because he had to wait for payment, developing a form of interest. A similar method was used to insure or underwrite ships and their cargoes in the more long-distance trades, often with several insurers joining together to share the risk.

The wealth of the greater London merchants facilitated these arrangements, as did the profits of overseas trade. Gradually the bills of exchange came to have a value as currency, and those who issued them began to keep accounts for their customers, on which they could draw for credit, set up overdrafts, buy and sell stocks and shares, and use for insurance. By the late seventeenth century these arrangements had effectively created commercial and personal banks. In 1694 one group of bankers were given a government charter to issue shares as the Bank of England in return for managing government credit. The efficiency of the system and the backing of government established London as the major financial centre on world trade.

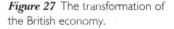

Figure 27 The transformation of the British economy.

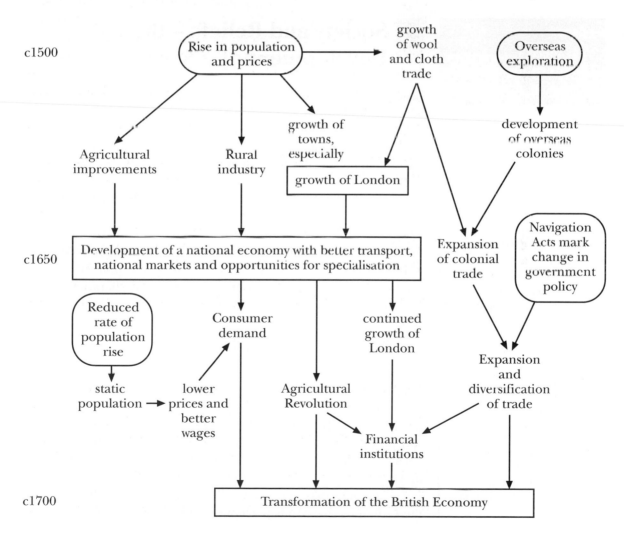

ACTIVITY

The Transformation of the British Economy

Figure 27 summarises the growth of the economy and the role of different factors in the process. Use this and the information in Section 2 of the chapter to answer the following questions:

1. How did each of the following factors contribute to the expansion of the economy between 1603 and 1714 (a) the rise in population; (b) the growth of London; (c) the expansion of trade and colonies; (d) changes in government policy?

2. Explain how these factors combined and interacted to achieve an overall transformation.

3. Did the 1650s constitute a turning point in the process of change?

ISSUE
Was there a seventeenth-century revolution in ideas?

STATE, SOCIETY AND INDIVIDUAL

The term State refers to a unit of authority that exercises power in government. It refers to the complex structure of institutions and individuals who run the government at any given time. The term individual does not mean a particular person, but all particular people, whatever their views and circumstances. The term secular means non-religious, and a secular State is one that concerns itself with people's non-religious affairs.

3 Society and Beliefs – the Development of a Secular State

Economic changes and the growth of trade helped to bring changes in society and in the lives of ordinary people. With a greater variety of goods to purchase and the growth of new industries and agricultural methods, a more complex social structure began to emerge. At the same time, equally great, or greater changes were taking place in the attitudes and beliefs of many people about the world that they lived in and their place in it. Historians have defined these changes in various ways, and some have argued that the most revolutionary effect of the mid-century conflicts was a revolution in ideas that redefined the nature of the **State** and its relationship to the **individuals** who lived under it. Derek Hirst, for example, has pointed out that the intense religious enthusiasm and debate that characterised the 1640s and 1650s led to a reaction against religious enthusiasm itself, and that the result of the Puritan attempt to reform Church and State was to bring about their separation, to create a new secular State and **society**.

Charles I was the ruler of a confessional State, in which uniformity of 'confession' (belief) was essential. Not only did he and his predecessors claim to rule by divine right, they also believed that the State had a divine purpose and that one of his primary duties was to care and provide for the wellbeing of his subjects' souls. This view had been strengthened in England by Henry VIII's seizure of the church in the 1530s.

For the most part, those who opposed Charles in the years before the Civil Wars shared his perceptions of the nature and role of the

State – what they objected to was his version of it. The vast majority of Puritans sought to reform the national Church and purify it of all traces of Catholicism. Their aim was to strengthen it, not to destroy its power and place in society. Nevertheless, by challenging its power over their own consciences, they opened the way to other ideas and influences that were already operating before 1640 to create a much more fundamental challenge to the confessional State and the place of religion within it.

a) Challenges to the Confessional State, 1500–1640

i) The Influence of the Renaissance

The late fifteenth and early sixteenth centuries saw the spread of a renewed interest in the classical world of ancient Greece and Rome, which came to be known as the Renaissance (rebirth). Interest in the classical world was not new – medieval scholarship had been dominated by admiration for the late (Christian) Roman Empire and the authority of its writers and thinkers. Increasing contact with the eastern civilisations, especially the Byzantine Empire where classical scholarship had survived the fall of Rome and the empire in the west, only deepened their admiration. New and better translations of classical works were made available, and scholars and artists studied and copied the ancient techniques of observation and experiment. Gradually, however, this revealed errors. In the mid-sixteenth century Copernicus proved that the earth and the planets revolved around the Sun, discrediting Greek and Egyptian ideas, while Vesalius demonstrated that Galen's theories about human anatomy, which had dominated medieval medicine were also incorrect. It appeared possible that there was more to be discovered, and that modern men could extend knowledge beyond that of the ancient authorities. The spread of printing, the discovery of new lands, and even the Protestant challenge to the authority of the Church, encouraged this sense of new possibilities. The concepts of progress and improvement began to take shape.

It was this idea above all, that human societies could improve their ways and conditions by the application of scientific thought and rational thinking, that inspired further development and opened up new possibilities. The scientific methods of experiment and observation, the demand that traditional beliefs be justified on a rational basis, and the willingness to challenge authority created a climate of intellectual exploration that affected political and religious assumptions as well as more obviously practical applications. The new approach was summed up by Sir Francis Bacon, whose essay, *The Advancement of Learning*, was published in 1605. Although his ideas were not widely influential until after 1640, Bacon encouraged schol-

ISSUES
What was the Renaissance? How did it influence ideas about religion?

ROYAL SOCIETY

There is still considerable debate among historians about the nature and extent of the seventeenth-century 'scientific revolution' and the part played in it by the Royal Society 'for the promotion of physico-mathematical experimental learning', which was founded after the Restoration and patronised by Charles II himself. On the one hand it reflects genuine scientific experiment, modelled on Bacon's ideas, and leading to major discoveries. Newton discoved the laws of gravity, Napier the slide-rule and logarithms. Robert Boyle's experiment on atmospheric pressure and a revolutionary analysis of the laws of physics was published in Robert Hooke's *Micrographia* (1664). At the same time, many of its debates were pointless and sterile, and 'scientists' like Newton and Napier applied their talents to such matters as the alchemist's dream of turning lead into gold, or the use of mathematical laws to interpret the Book of Revelations in order to discover when God would return to earth in person. Such contradictions are best understood by seeing the Royal Society as part of a much wider development, reflecting the gradual evolution of scientific study. This did not preclude religious belief – indeed, many of the early scientists such as Boyle and Newton were motivated by a desire to gain a better understanding of God's handiwork.

ars to subject all aspects of society to rational examination. He stimulated a response among an influential minority that eventually led to the foundation of the **Royal Society** after 1660. While it is important not to exaggerate the influence of the new learning in the years before the Civil War, it did inspire a number of influential men to challenge the religious and intellectual restrictions imposed by the confessional State.

ii) The Development of Rational Theology

While Bacon and others who became associated with 'science' applied rational analysis to the natural world, some were more interested in the implications for society and religion. Among them was Lucius Carey, Lord Falkland, who made his house at Great Tew in the Cotswolds a centre for learning, and welcomed friends and acquaintances from the University of Oxford nearby. Encouraged by the study of classical texts, which formed a significant part of the university curriculum at the time, they engaged in intellectual debates that were far removed from the practical problems of the Church. They were therefore able to explore uncharted waters. The result was an approach to religious debate that emphasised rational logic and the need for intellectual freedom.

Among those who benefited from the patronage of Falkland was William Chillingworth, who published a tract entitled *The Religion of Protestants a Safe Way to Salvation* in 1638. Chillingworth began with the conventional Protestant belief that the truth about God was to be found in the Bible. Applying a rational approach, he pointed out that there were many books in, and versions of, the Bible, and that much of it was contradictory and required interpretation. Therefore, he concluded, errors were unavoidable, and beliefs would inevitably vary. If God allowed this to happen then such variation must be acceptable to him. By implication, only a few, broadly accepted beliefs, were essential for salvation.

The ideas of men like Chillingworth were not intended to challenge authority or encourage social revolution. The members of the circle were largely Royalist in the Civil War and included Edward Hyde, later Lord Clarendon. They did, however, represent a more flexible and tolerant Anglicanism than that enforced by Charles and Laud. Falkland accused the Laudian bishops of keeping the people in darkness 'so that they might sow more tares (weeds) in the night' to enhance their own power. The rational theologians insisted that variety of opinion was inevitable, and that error must be accepted as part of the search for truth just as experiments were part of science.

The same approach influenced some Parliamentarian supporters, such as Robert Greville, Lord Brooke, who published a plea for religious toleration in 1641 entitled *A discourse opening the nature of that*

Episcopacy which is exercised in England. Brooke argued that religion was first and foremost a search for 'truth', by which he meant more accurate knowledge of God. Freedom to pursue this search should be extended to all. If there were mistakes, rational argument and debate would deal with them. Brooke declared:

> The ways of God's Spirit are free and not tied to a university man or to any man, to any bishop, or magistrate or church. The light shines where it will among men, no matter how humble or ignorant, moves them to utterance, to inquiry and discussion, to ceaseless search for more light, until truth in its entirety shall become known to all, and men have once more become one with God.

Unlike the Tew circle, Brooke and his supporters were arguing for the right of all individuals, regardless of education or class, to search for God in their own way and in whatever company they chose. Their vision was not a single broad Church, but many churches, and if it came to fruition, it would destroy the confessional State.

iii) Popular Culture – Education, Literacy and Protestant Influence

This was made more likely by the spread of literacy that had taken place since the early sixteenth century. It is difficult to estimate what proportion of the population could read, but it is likely that the wealthy and 'middling sort' (at least in towns) were almost universally literate, and that some of the poor were also able to read to some degree. It has been estimated that, by the end of Elizabeth's reign, about 38 per cent of the male population were able to read, rising to around 78 per cent in London, which tended to attract literate migrants in search of opportunity and was also well-endowed with schools. In 1660 the Royalist Earl of Newcastle warned Charles II that 'The Bible in English under every weaver's and chambermaid's arms hath done us much hurt' and that 'the abundance of grammar schools and Inns of Court' had sown the seeds of rebellion. 'When most was unlettered' he concluded, 'it was a much better world both for peace and war.'

There were a number of reasons for the spread of literacy in this period. The Christian humanists of the Renaissance, such as John Colet who refounded St Paul's Grammar School in London in 1509, believed in the power of education to reform and improve society and encouraged the endowment of schools and colleges. There were also many economic advantages in being able to read, for example, property records, apprentices' indentures and contracts. Career opportunities were enhanced in a variety of trades and professions. Social mobility was encouraged, and helped to spread awareness of the benefits of education. At the higher levels of society, the acquisi-

RATIONAL THEOLOGY

The term rational means based on the use of logic and reason. Theology is the study of religious belief. Hence the rational theologians were intellectuals who applied the test of logic and reason to religious beliefs in order to define what should be accepted and/or enforced. This does not mean that they challenged belief in God, but that they studied the evidence about Him in the Bible and tried to distinguish between important beliefs and the stories and myths in which they were sometimes presented.

ISSUES
Why was literacy increasing?
What factors encouraged wider education?

tion of a suitable education was an essential step in moving from the merchant or yeoman class into the ranks of the gentry. At every level of society, education was increasingly seen as a useful, if not a necessary, part of preparing the young for life.

In many ways, however, it was religious belief, and Protestant influence in particular, which was most responsible for the spread of literacy, especially among the middling and lower orders; and it was this aspect of educational development which would prove most immediately dangerous to the authority of the confessional State. The core of Protestant theology was that salvation for the soul was obtained as a gift of free grace from God. To receive this gift, the individual need only believe in the gospel of Christ and His sacrifice of atonement for the sins of humanity. Belief, however, came from knowledge of the Word of God as presented in the Bible, which contained all that was needed for the individual soul to understand Christ's message and for churches to plan and organise the practice of Christianity. The role of the minister was therefore to teach and preach, to guide the individual in their personal search and to shed light on the more obscure aspects. While the early reformers undoubtedly saw this as a major role, and expected that the laity would need and accept the guidance of an educated ministry, the logic of Protestant beliefs also placed great emphasis on private prayer, private reading and study of the Bible, and individual understanding of its message.

ISSUES
What were the implications of these beliefs?
How did they challenge the confessional State?

These beliefs not only encouraged literacy, but also greater independence of thought. Individuals needed to be able to read in order to study the Bible. Given the difficulty of some texts, it was useful for ministers to hold Bible meetings, at which the meaning of more obscure passages could be discussed and debated. Such meetings were attended by the more intensely religious parishioners, and tended to distinguish them from the average sinner, encouraging the Calvinist distinction between the predestined 'saints' and the unregenerate multitude who would be damned. Debate and discussion tended to blur the line between the minister and the more educated or gifted laymen, allowing greater confidence and willingness to challenge the views and interpretations put forward by existing authority. The logic of the Protestant faith was to involve the individual in his own salvation, to extend his responsibility for his own soul, and to provide him with the tools to make his own judgements.

For the vast majority of individuals, this was as far as it went, even among the 'hotter sort' of Protestants who came to be called Puritans. Bible reading within the home and discussion of sermons which had been heard and noted down was widely practised, without ever causing the Church or the ministry to be seriously challenged. For a few, however, the enthusiasm generated by a fiery preacher and the mystical obscurities of the Bible itself produced different results. Told that they were among those predestined to salvation, that true equality was spiritual equality, and that it was the duty of God's chosen saints to exercise their talents, it was hardly surprising that some should feel able and willing to follow their own ideas and their own path. Encouraged to believe that the Bible was the infallible Word of God, it was not surprising that some placed greater faith in what they perceived the Bible to be saying than in the words of men, however well-educated. And if the Church, for whatever reason, was unable or unwilling to go with them on the road to salvation, it is hardly surprising that they should choose to go without it. For this minority, the logic of Protestant ideas led to separatism, and the development of independent churches to challenge the confessional State.

iv) The Origins of Separatism

Separatist movements are difficult to trace because they were illegal, and therefore secret, but some sense of their development can be acquired by analysing the careers of specific individuals through the scattered references that appear in records of persecution, and through their own writings. What this reveals is a pattern of initial separation because of a desire to join with like-minded individuals, which became more radical with time. While specific beliefs were not necessarily unorthodox at the point of separation, they tended to become more eccentric as they were debated and explored in isolation from the mainstream and in the company of other enthusiasts. The effects of this are illustrated in the Profile, which analyses the careers of two early separatist leaders, John Robinson and John Smyth. The numbers of separatists increased in the 1630s as Laud's pursuit of uniformity drove more Puritans out of the Church, but until 1640 they remained few in number. They also tended to be geographically scattered, although there was, as might be expected, some concentration in London.

BAPTISTS AND CONGREGATIONALISTS: THE DEVELOPMENT OF PURITAN SEPARATISM

-*Profile*-

The evolution of separatism can be most effectively demonstrated by considering some of the more important examples, such as the careers of John Smyth and John Robinson. Both were originally Lincolnshire men, educated at Cambridge and ordained to the ministry. In 1602 Smyth was preaching in Lincoln and Robinson at Norwich. In that year, Smyth lost his post, presumably because of his Puritan views, and little is known of him until he is recorded as leading a separatist group in Gainsborough in 1606. Shortly after, Robinson appears to have left Norwich in order to preach to a similar group at Scrooby, near Gainsborough; whether this was linked to Smyth's group or not is hard to say, but there seems to have been a measure of cooperation between the two. By 1608, both had been forced into exile in Holland, to avoid persecution, where they settled in Leyden. There they were joined by a number of separatists from Sandwich, led by a woolcomber named Richard Masterson.

In Holland the paths of the two groups diverged. Robinson's congregation prospered until they tired of living in a foreign land and set out to find a new home in America in 1621. As the Pilgrim Fathers they settled in Massachusetts, New England, and established the first of many Puritan colonies in the area. In the 1630s their numbers were swelled by a steady stream of immigrants, driven out of England by the policies and persecutions of Laud.

Smyth's group remained in Holland, where contact with continental reformers inspired him to re-baptise them as a sign of their conscious, adult choice in becoming members of the church. This implied a rejection of the Anglican practice of infant baptism as a relic of popery. His adoption of adult baptism as the sign of entry into Church membership established the first English Baptist congregation.

The congregation seem to have accepted Smyth's advice on this matter, but when he went further and began to challenge the doctrine of predestination, many of them left him. Smyth argued that God would not sacrifice his Son to save humanity, and then deny that salvation to all but a few, an argument which was very close to that put forward at much the same time by Arminius and adopted by that enemy of all separatists, William Laud. In this period of religious debate and exploration, the challenge to rigid Calvinism, like the challenge to the confessional State, was not limited to one part of the religious spectrum.

While Smyth's claim that God offered salvation to all men who were willing to accept the message of Christ divided his congregation, it also led to important developments in religious separatism. His congregation split and some returned to England. By 1626 there were Baptist churches in London, Canterbury, Salisbury and Tiverton in Devon. Most of these held on to their Calvinist beliefs, and adopted the name of Particular Baptists – exclusive gatherings of 'saints' believing in predestination. Although it is difficult to trace their development in the years of persecution, they clearly prospered; in 1641, there were seven Particular Baptist Churches in London alone, and in 1643 they issued a joint Confession of Faith in order to distinguish themselves from the emerging Independent congregations. More importantly in the long run, some of his followers accepted Smyth's views and established a General Baptist movement, which encouraged ideas of spiritual equality and freedom of choice. In 1616 Thomas Helwys established the first General Baptist congregation in Spitalfields in London; little is known of them, but their emphasis on human choice and reason laid the basis for arguments in favour of religious toleration, and for the emergence of Leveller ideas.

b) The Effects of Civil War

Until 1641, separatist development was inevitably fragmentary and uncertain, but the rapid emergence of separatist groups in that year is evidence of their prior existence. With the calling of the Long Parliament and the attack on the authority of the Church, they were now able to expand and flourish. The collapse of press censorship permitted a flood of pamphlets and publications, lay preachers and 'tub-thumpers' such as Thomas Lambe and Samuel Oates were active in London, and all kinds of ideas were advocated and debated. According to Clarendon:

> The license of preaching and printing increased to that degree that all pulpits were freely delivered to the schismatical [separatist] and silenced preachers who till then had lurked in corners or lived in New England: and the presses were at liberty for the publishing the most invective, seditious and scurrilous pamphlets that their wit and malice could invent.

Within a year, the outbreak of Civil War would provide even greater opportunities for the exploration of radical ideas. It was impossible to reimpose censorship, and Parliament's own justifications of rebellion encouraged an exploration of new religious and political concepts (see pages 117–20). The Puritan preachers who called for volunteers to save Parliament depicted their cause as a godly crusade, and identified this war between King and Parliament with the last great struggle between good and evil promised in the biblical Book of Revelations.

It was no coincidence that these activities emerged first in London. As the profile on pages 228–9 illustrates, the combination of a mobile, young, and relatively articulate population (many of them earning a precarious living as tradesmen and apprentices) with a Puritan tradition and in close proximity to the centre of religious and political affairs was always likely to be explosive. When the breakdown of censorship in 1641 was added to the existing weakness of the mechanisms of social control in the city, the scene was set for the emergence of radicalism.

In this heady atmosphere, and freedom for open debate, ideas became more radical. In 1644 five of the ministers who had been called to debate reform of the Church in the Westminster assembly made a plea for 'liberty for tender consciences'. It was a cautious, restrained request for the right of orthodox Protestants to set up their own, voluntary churches alongside the national establishment. Once the debate had been opened, more radical thinkers like Roger Williams, the founder of the religiously tolerant colony of Rhode

ISSUES
How did the Civil War influence the development of separatist groups? How important were wartime conditions in the emergence of religious and political radicalism?

This plea was published as an 'Apologetical Narration' in 1644. It was the first open claim to religious freedom and limited though it was, it sparked off a public debate and a far more extensive campaign.

Island, and the later Levellers, William Walwyn and Richard Overton, quickly widened this concept into a call for complete religious toleration. Attempts to restrict the debate provoked the Puritan John Milton to extend the argument and demand freedom of speech and of the press in *Areopagitica* (1644), echoing Chillingworth and Brooke in his defence of a free search for truth. By 1645 the influence of the New Model Army and sympathetic officers like Cromwell was encouraging the spread of separatist groups throughout the country. They never attracted more than a small minority of the population, but even this minority was enough to terrify conservatives and threaten their cherished vision of a reformed confessional State.

The origin of many of these claims lay in the ideas of John Smyth, and his rejection of the idea of predestination. Like the Arminians and many other Anglicans, Smyth ridiculed the argument that God would sacrifice his Son to atone for the sins of humanity, and then deny the gift of salvation to all but a predestined minority. Unlike the Arminians, Smyth expressed this idea in terms of an inner spirit, the Spirit of God in man. 'Christ lives in all' he declared, 'but all know it not.' What determined salvation, therefore, was the ability to recognise and accept the gift of Christ within. This argument had significant implications for human freedom, equality and rights. If Christ existed in all, then all were equal. If humans were all capable of making decisions about their salvation, then they were certainly capable of making decisions about which Church they attended, or how they should be governed. The Leveller leaders, who were closely associated with Smyth's General Baptists, turned his ideas into a coherent political programme, but their original inspiration was religious. Others focused more specifically on religious issues, but many of them defined belief in terms that carried political implications and threatened the political and social hierarchy as well as the confessional State. As early as 1647 Joseph Salmon was arguing that God, the devil, heaven and hell all had their existence in the human mind, while others, influenced by scientific study and natural philosophy, suggested that since God had created the natural world He existed within it. The Diggers argued that God had created the earth as a resource to be shared by all, the Ranters that nothing was sinful if it was natural. Groups and individuals who have been labelled 'seekers' came to the conclusion that God did not exist in any of the churches or the Bible, and that they must seek until He chose to reveal Himself. In 1652 George Fox united many of these seekers in the Quaker movement, whose central message was that God exists within the human spirit and speaks directly in the human heart.

The common feature among these later radicals was the repudiation of all external authority in religion, in favour of the inner spirit.

Unlike the Puritan separatists, many of whom were shocked by these later developments, they did not issue formal declarations of faith or lists of members. Nor did they accept the Bible as the Word of God. They regarded it as a useful guide, containing the story of Christ and much more, but only if interpreted and enlightened by the individual spirit. The expression of these concepts was often eccentric and short-lived, but in the ideas of George Fox this view found a coherent and lasting expression. If the key features of religious radicalism are defined as an individual search for truth, an emphasis on the free expression of ideas derived from this search, and the right of all to find God in their own way, then Quaker ideas might be said to embody religious radicalism in its most complete form. It is perhaps no coincidence that so many radicals – Salmon, Winstanley, Lilburne himself – ended their lives as Quakers.

c) Reaction and Revenge – the Restoration of the Confessional State

ISSUE
How far was the confessional State re-established?

The fears engendered by such radical ideas and the steps taken to suppress radical groups have been outlined in Chapters 5 and 6. By 1650 the Levellers had been broken, the Diggers driven from their communes, and the Ranters imprisoned. Nevertheless, throughout the 1650s the more orthodox religious radicals enjoyed a measure of freedom, and even the Quakers found pockets of sympathy and understanding. Above all, the regimes of the 1650s sought to establish a broad and flexible Church and to allow a continued search for truth. It was in 1660, with the return of the Royalists and the Anglican Church that this attitude began to change. Despite efforts by King Charles II to soften the effects of persecution, the years that followed the Restoration saw Puritans first driven from the Church, and then subjected to persecuting laws designed to destroy them. The events associated with the Clarendon Code and the attempt to destroy nonconformity have been described above in Chapter 7. The focus of this section is therefore not to describe persecution, but to explain how dissent and nonconformity were able to survive it. The two terms are largely interchangeable, describing those who disagreed with (dissented from) the rules of the Church, and were therefore unable to conform to the demands made of its members.

i) The Survival of Dissent, 1662–89

Religious uniformity was restored in theory, but never in practice – the Clarendon Code caused great suffering to dissenters, but it never succeeded in enforcing obedience. The incidence of persecution varied. At its worst it could be inhuman. The Quakers bore the brunt in many areas, because they were unpopular, vulnerable and refused

ACTIVITY

Questions on the Sources

1. Interpret Sources J to M in the context of the chapter so far, and explain:
(a) How does the demand for religious toleration widen and develop in these sources? **[5 marks]**
(b) How did ideas about spiritual equality turn into a demand for civil and political rights? **[5 marks]**
(Analysis, cross-reference and synthesis)

2. What similarities and differences are there in the two explanations of how God exists offered by Winstanley and Fox? **[4 marks]** (analysis, cross-reference)

3. What do these ideas imply about the role of government and the State in religion? **[4 marks]** (inference)

The Evolution of Radicalism: A Case Study

The most significant characteristic of religious and political radicalism was the way in which it evolved, first from within the ranks of Puritan reformers, and then in a complex variety of forms during the heady excitement of Civil War and regicide. An enormous variety of ideas were put forward. There was a movement towards ever-greater personal freedom. The religious debate gradually raised implications and ideas relating to political rights and freedoms. There was an increasing tendency to portray God as a Spirit that existed within human hearts and minds, rather than as a separate Being existing somewhere in the universe. The sources below illustrate this process, and the questions are intended to help you to analyse the main developments.

> We could not ... but judge it a safe and allowed way to retain the government of our several congregations for matters of discipline within themselves, to be exercised by their own elders ... yet not claiming to ourselves an independent power ... to give account or be subject to none other; but only a full and entire power complete within ourselves, until we should be challenged to err grossly.
>
> **Source J** From the *Apologetical Narration* (1644) issued by five members of the Assembly of Divines.

> There are two things contended for in this liberty of conscience: first to instate every Christian in his right of free, yet modest, judging and accepting what he holds; secondly, to [seek] the truth, and this is the main end and respect of this liberty. I contend not for variety of opinions; I know there is but one truth. But this truth cannot easily be brought forth without this liberty; and a general restraint, though intended but for errors ... may fall upon the truth. And better errors of some kind suffered than one useful truth be obstructed or destroyed.
>
> **Source K** From *The Ancient Bounds*, an anonymous pamphlet, 1645.

> It is the will and command of God that ... a permission of ... consciences and worships be granted to all men in all nations and countries ... God requireth not an uniformity of religion to be enacted and enforced in any civil state; which enforced uniformity, sooner or later, is the greatest occasion of civil war, ravishing of conscience, persecution of Christ Jesus his servants, and of hypocrisy and destruction of millions of souls.
>
> **Source L** From Roger Williams, *The Bloody Tenent of Persecution*, 1644.

The General Baptists regarded their doctrine [of general redemption] as the foundation of their faith. To all Baptists, the foundation of Puritan reformation was the guarantee of liberty of worship for the saints, and in defence of this liberty they made a substantial contribution to the cause of toleration. They argued that the true Church was the creation of divine grace, not of man. Since it was not of this world, it must necessarily be completely separate from the state.

This provided the elements of a radical reform programme [such as that formulated by the Levellers] ... If [as Smyth claimed] all mankind had God in them and were potentially to be saved, there could be no distinction between the civil rights of saints and of citizens. To guarantee the liberties of the saints, it was necessary to seek rights and freedoms for all.

Source M From J.F. McGregor, 'The Baptists – Fount of all Heresy' in McGregor and Reay (eds) *Radical Religion in the English Revolution* (OUP 1984), pp. 23–6.

In the beginning of time the great Creator, Reason, made the earth to be a common treasury, to preserve beasts, birds, fishes, and man, the lord that was to govern this creation. For man had domination given to him over the beasts, birds and fishes. But not one word was spoken in the beginning, that one branch of mankind should rule over another.

And the reason is this. Every single man, male and female, is a perfect creature of himself. And the same Spirit that made the globe dwells in man to govern the globe; so that the flesh of man, being subject to Reason, his maker, hath him to be his teacher and ruler within himself, therefore need not run abroad after any teacher and ruler without him[self].

Source N From Gerrard Winstanley, *The True Levellers Standard Advanced*, 1649.

We found this light to be a sufficient teacher, to lead us to Christ, from whence this light came ... to dwell in us ... And so we ceased from the teachings of men and their words and their worships and their temples ... that we might become truly wise, and by this light of Christ in us we were led out of false ways and false preachings and false ministers; and we met together often and waited upon the Lord.

Source O From George Fox, *The great Mystery of the Great whore Unfolded*, 1659.

4. Neither the Diggers nor the Quakers had a coherent political programme. Why do you think they were regarded by conservatives as no less a threat to government than the Levellers? **[7 marks]** (inference, cross-reference, interpretation in context)

5. Using the sources and the information in the chapter, how far do you think that the development of these ideas depended on conditions and events related to the Civil War? **[25 marks]** (causation essay).

to hide. Not only did they insist on meeting openly, it was easy to bring them into court on some trumped-up charge and then imprison them under the Quaker Act for refusing to swear an oath in court. By 1666 when George Fox was released from imprisonment in Scarborough Castle, most of the early Quaker leaders were dead, and the movement near collapse. Nevertheless, by tireless travelling from 1666–69, Fox was able to visit most areas and establish a new organisational structure that ensured the survival of a Quaker Church. If it was more disciplined and less idealistic than in earlier years most felt this to be a price worth paying. By the early 1670s the Quakers had a national organisation capable of supporting members and even of bringing prosecutions against those who abused the law in pursuing them. In addition, missionary work overseas had succeeded in establishing Quaker meetings in America and elsewhere – far from destroying the movement, the fires of persecution had hardened it into an international Church.

The Quakers were the most extreme example of resistance and success, but other dissenters had also suffered and survived. Persecution was at its worst in the 1660s, when political bitterness was at its height, but even then some places were relatively safe. In Hull, for example, there were complaints that dissenters operated unhindered, and that Puritan ministers were even invited to preach in Holy Trinity Church. In 1666 there were angry scenes when the Mayor, John Tripp, allowed Joseph Wilson, who had been ejected from Beverley in 1662, to preach in Holy Trinity at the end of morning service. When local Royalists objected and tried to interrupt, the remaining congregation drove them out. Hull housed two regular conventicles (meetings), one Presbyterian and one Independent, throughout the period of persecution. When the governor, the Earl of Plymouth, ordered the corporation to enforce the law against them in 1682, he was plainly told by one Alderman, Mr Humphrey Duncalf, that he would rather resign than apply such unjust laws against peaceable neighbours.

ISSUE
Why was dissent able to survive?

These incidents offer some clues as to why Protestant dissent was able to survive the onslaught of persecution. Popular support for persecution in the 1660s was to some extent a reaction to fears that, in the preceding decade, the radicals had brought society to the point of collapse. As well as a simple desire for revenge among those who had suffered, there was an overwhelming desire for peace, order and security. Puritans of all shades provided a convenient target for blame and a symbol of all that threatened those characteristics. Thus the party of revenge in Church and State had a particular opportunity to impose their views on more neutral or indifferent elements. However, by defining the Anglican Church so narrowly as to exclude Presbyterians like Baxter, they had swelled the numbers of potential dissenters and excluded many whose views were known to be moderate. Had they established a broadly comprehensive Church in 1662, only those who held determinedly separatist views would have chosen to remain outside, and lacking both numbers and social connections, they might well have dwindled further. As it was, the dissenters had friends and allies in many quarters who were able to protect them until the desire for revenge had begun to die away.

This help came in many forms, but the three main sources were Puritan gentry, occasional conformists and Latitudinarians (see Chapter 7 page 199). These were not necessarily distinct categories – some individuals could come within all three, but each offered a different way in which those who were sympathetic to dissenters might be able to avoid persecution themselves, and offer support to others who were vulnerable to it. There is abundant evidence that gentry of Puritan views offered places to ejected ministers as chaplains and tutors, allowing them to earn a living and often to preach to groups of supporters. These contacts provided the main source of aid outside the larger towns and boroughs. A second source of allies was provided by the practice of occasional conformity, in which many moderate Puritans found themselves able to attend their parish church sufficiently often to fulfil the requirements of the law, while also maintaining links among the dissenters and even attending conventicles at times. This was particularly prevalent in corporate boroughs like Hull, and explains why the corporation there was notoriously sympathetic to dissent (although not to the Quakers). Similar contacts existed in most boroughs and the larger towns.

Thirdly, and perhaps most significantly, help came from within the Church itself, in the form of a Latitudinarian party, made up of men who interpreted the rules of the Church to emphasise its breadth and capacity to embrace a variety of views. As the heirs of Chillingworth and Falkland, they were concerned above all to establish religious peace. They represented a brand of Christianity that emphasised forgiveness and brotherhood and sought to minimise dispute. Some drew on scientific principles, arguing that belief must be supported by reason, that what was not demonstrable was not sufficient cause for harshness and persecution. At its best, the Latitudinarian spirit portrayed Christ as a loving saviour, at its worst it could undermine faith itself. Either way it emphasised the virtues of tolerance and dismissed persecution as illogical and unworkable. Moreover, it was shared to a considerable extent by the King himself.

The role of Charles II in the survival of dissent is in some ways contradictory. On the one hand, his Declaration of Indulgence in 1672–3 provided a vital breathing space and allowed dissenters to organise effectively. At the same time, he was probably motivated by a desire to ease the conditions of Catholics, and was responsible for the renewal of harsh persecution in 1682–5, in the aftermath of the Exclusion Crisis. The most likely explanation is that while Charles was genuinely opposed to persecution as irrational and unnecessary, he was, above all, a politician, and his concern was to use the weapons available to control the State. Unlike his father he had few religious convictions beyond a general preference for Catholic practices, and regarded political loyalty as a separate issue. In that sense, as in much else, he embodied the interests and values of the more secular society that was now emerging in the aftermath of civil war and regicide. One legacy of the upheaval was a revulsion against the intense spirituality and the concern with other men's souls that had marked the disputes of those years.

This outlook was reinforced by the emphasis on rational argument and practical observation that accompanied the scientific revolution. While theoretical science remained of interest mainly to an intellectual minority, the emphasis on rational thinking and learning by observation and experience was more widely influential, and this also helped the dissenters. It was perfectly clear to many that the dissenters of the 1670s and 1680s were not the dangerous radicals of the past. They were respectable, hard-working neighbours, often craftsmen and businessmen, who played a useful part in the community. Apart from their religious eccentricity, which should be largely their own business, the dissenters were perfectly normal citizens who should be left in peace.

Ironically, what finally drove the Anglican authorities into alliance with dissent was the re-emergence of an older enemy – fear of Catholicism. When James II challenged the power of the Church on behalf of Catholics, Anglicans and dissenters closed ranks against him. In return for their loyalty to the Protestant cause, the dissenters expected and obtained religious toleration. The Toleration Act of 1689 did not mean the end of religion as a political issue. The issue had the power to raise passions and prejudices – for example in the Sacheverell riots of 1710 and the Schism Bill of 1711, and even in the Gordon Riots of the 1780s – and the issue of the validity of a State Church remains today. What the Toleration Act did signify, however, was the end of the confessional State.

Despite the failure of the radical schemes that emerged in the years between 1640 and 1660, the Civil Wars do, therefore, mark a turning point in political thought and in the attitudes and beliefs of society. The failure of the 'godly revolution' in all its forms was followed by the failure of the attempt to persecute it out of existence. The whole experience revealed that it was impossible to enforce religious uniformity, and that political stability required the attempt to

ISSUE

Did the end of the confessional State mark a revolution in ideas?

Figure 28 The development of the secular State.

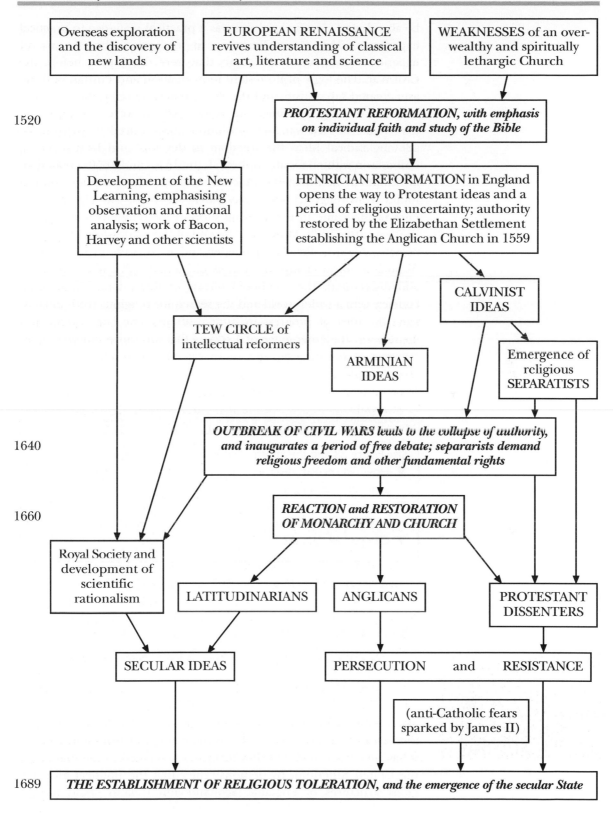

1520

Overseas exploration and the discovery of new lands

EUROPEAN RENAISSANCE revives understanding of classical art, literature and science

WEAKNESSES of an over-wealthy and spiritually lethargic Church

PROTESTANT REFORMATION, with emphasis on individual faith and study of the Bible

Development of the New Learning, emphasising observation and rational analysis; work of Bacon, Harvey and other scientists

HENRICIAN REFORMATION in England opens the way to Protestant ideas and a period of religious uncertainty; authority restored by the Elizabethan Settlement establishing the Anglican Church in 1559

CALVINIST IDEAS

TEW CIRCLE of intellectual reformers

ARMINIAN IDEAS

Emergence of religious SEPARATISTS

1640

OUTBREAK OF CIVIL WARS leads to the collapse of authority, and inaugurates a period of free debate; separarists demand religious freedom and other fundamental rights

1660

REACTION and RESTORATION OF MONARCHY AND CHURCH

Royal Society and development of scientific rationalism

LATITUDINARIANS

ANGLICANS

PROTESTANT DISSENTERS

SECULAR IDEAS

PERSECUTION   and   RESISTANCE

(anti-Catholic fears sparked by James II)

1689

THE ESTABLISHMENT OF RELIGIOUS TOLERATION, and the emergence of the secular State be abandoned. At one level this was a practical response to practical experience, but the willingness to recognise the lessons of experience owed much to factors that were developing before the Civil War. The logic of Protestant individualism and Puritan enthusiasm created separatism, and the development of scientific logic and rational theology justified it. Above all, however, it was the experience of civil war and revolution that ensured its survival. By allowing radical ideas the freedom to develop, and by associating enthusiasm with chaos and upheaval, the 1640s and 1650s created an environment in which the rational solution, of separating political loyalty from religious belief, was widely accepted. The clearest evidence of this came in the growing support for religious toleration in the years after 1672. Moreover, the end of the confessional State represents only one facet of a deeper and more widespread change. Although radical claims to a variety of human rights were dismissed and discredited, the combined effects of Renaissance humanism, contacts with a wider world and the search for religious truth encouraged the idea of progress in human affairs. The late seventeenth century saw the emergence of a society that was more rational, more sceptical of enthusiasm, and more capable of development in all aspects of life.

ACTIVITY

Use Figure 28 and the information in Section 3 to explain:
▼ How did secular ideas and religious freedom evolve from the sixteenth century Renaissance and Reformation?
▼ How important was the impact of the Civil Wars in this process, as compared with the gradual evolution of ideas and attitudes?
▼ Can you explain the interaction between them?

---

4 Conclusion – Was there an English Revolution in the Mid-Seventeenth Century?

The events of the period between 1640 and 1660 have now been assessed in a variety of contexts. In the context of Britain as a whole it has been suggested that they formed a watershed in the making of the United Kingdom. By demonstrating that the political and religious structures of England, Scotland and Ireland could not be settled in isolation, and by giving England the military capacity to impose its solutions on the Celtic kingdoms, the Civil War period ensured that some kind of union would take place at some point in the near future. In the context of economic development, it has been demonstrated that while long-term developments relating to population and the development of trade and colonies were essential factors in causing growth, the changes in government policy during the 1650s did much to accelerate development.

In the context of ideas and beliefs the 1640s created a revolution that could not be reversed. Although changing attitudes before 1640 created the potential for radicalism to emerge, the experience of civil war was crucial in ensuring that separatist ideas became established and initiated an intellectual revolution. While this was largely unintended by the Parliamentarians of 1642, the impact of war unleashed forces and energies that destroyed their schemes for the Church and transformed its place in the State. While the revolutionaries were unable to establish their new order, they survived in sufficient strength to prevent the restoration of the old one.

Perhaps most significantly, these separate developments did not occur in isolation. The impact of radical beliefs helped to divide Scottish and English reformers and contributed to the shaping of the United Kingdom. The development of English trade was a major incentive for Scottish merchants to support the idea of union. Increased knowledge of the wider world helped to encourage scientific ideas and the decline of superstition. It can therefore be suggested that the three accounts of development provided in this chapter had a cumulative effect in transforming British society. However difficult it may be to define, it can be argued that the political, economic and intellectual changes that took place between 1640 and 1660 constituted an irreversible change of sufficient breadth and importance to merit the name of revolution. Moreover, while significant events occurred throughout Britain, the crucial core of political, economic and intellectual changes were largely English. Their combined effect was to transform Britain into an imperial state in which, for better or worse, the English predominated.

Further Reading

Books in the Access to History Series

Various volumes of the Access to History series provide a sensible second stage of reading if you wish to further explore the issues addressed in this chapter. Nigel Heard's *Stuart Economy and Society* is extremely helpful on the economic developments outlined above, and he includes some useful ideas on social changes and the so-called scientific revolution. Nicholas Fellowes considers the competing aims and claims of Anglicans and dissenters in Chapter 4 of his *Charles II and James II*, while Angela Anderson looks at radicalism and its impact in Chapter 6 of *The Civil Wars, 1640–49*. Michael Lynch considers the nature of radicalism in the 1650s and assesses the effects of foreign and commercial policies in the same period in *The Interregnum*.

General

The range of books that address all or part of this chapter is vast, and much depends on how deeply the student wishes to explore particular aspects. Most of them are addressed in the *Oxford Illustrated History of Tudor and Stuart Britain*, edited by John Morrill. (OUP 1996) This is an excellent and varied general work, to which many historians have contributed. It also contains an extensive glossary, chronological lists and a useful bibliography. Similarly, the issues are all addressed in *Years of Turmoil*, ed. R. Wilkinson, in greater depth than is possible here. Barry Coward's *Stuart England* is also helpful, and its format allows students to identify and explore particular issues. Students who wish to explore various aspects of radicalism more thoroughly could begin with F.H. Dow, *Radicalism in the English Revolution, 1640–60* which provides a clear and manageable survey. J.F. McGregor and B. Reay have edited an excellent volume of essays as *Radical Religion in the English Revolution*. Studies of different radical groups are included in the source book published for the Cambridge History Project by Stanley Thornes in 1994 and entitled *People, Power and Politics: a study in depth* (Modules 3 and 4).

GLOSSARY